Legal Education

Reflections and Recommendations

A.W. Heringa

Legal Education

Reflections and Recommendations

intersentia

METRO

Ius Commune Europaeum

A.W. Heringa

Legal Education
Reflections and Recommendations

Intersentia Ltd
Trinity House | Cambridge Business Park | Cowley Road
Cambridge | CB4 0WZ | United Kingdom
Tel.: +44 1223 393 753 | Email: mail@intersentia.co.uk

ISBN 978-1-78068-166-5
D/2013/7849/87
NUR 823

PROLOGUE

This book has been inspired by many. A multitude of academic contacts and talks about teaching and legal education have, for many years, fed my thoughts. Maastricht University and the Faculty of Law have been fertile grounds for initiatives and forward thinking, as well as experiments, in the domain of legal education. I am also grateful for the contacts within the International Association of Law Schools (IALS) as well as with the Dutch law deans in the context of the Association of Dutch law deans.

In writing, or composing, this book I was struck by the many initiatives that take place in legal education but also by the inclination to stick to tradition: lawyers are certainly not among the greatest innovators! I was also struck that, when and where those innovations have taken place, legal academics have not taken the opportunity to record and test the achievements and benefits. There is, in other words, not very much evidence-based research about 'best' legal education practices, to say the least. Legal educators, being less sensitive to empirical sciences, have not shown themselves to test the teaching practices empirically and to set up relevant benchmarks. This is also one of the omissions in this book. I have tried to collect data but very soon I neglected that ambition because the scarcity of data is overwhelming, and no comparisons can be made, because the data that does exist is not really comparable (between universities/law schools, let alone between countries).[1] This book is a description of things that I have noted, and which have struck me as particularly interesting, as a legal educator. This book is therefore to a large extent a personal story: a journal of my observations and experiences. Based upon

1 In a Communication (COM(2011) 567 final, 20-9-2011 (supporting growth and jobs, an agenda for the modernization of Europe's higher education systems), the European Commission has indicated to improve data on European higher education learning mobility and employment outcomes, and work towards a European Tertiary Education Register.
And when data do exist and empirical research is undertaken, it seems only to circulate among the (social) scientists doing that kind of research, and does not reach (and does not seem to be written for) law schools nor law school teachers; a few examples: Haaral-Muhonen 2010; Nadolski, Kirchner, & Merriënboer 2006; Nievelstein 2009.

these observations and experiences, I have undertaken to share them with you and to make them available to others and for discussions and the comparisons with others' experiences and findings.

There are many lessons that I have learnt and which I have described in this book and present to you as conclusions. At the basis of all these conclusions is however that we as law schools set up a research agenda for legal education; that we seek ways to import lessons from other disciplines and their teaching approaches into legal education; that we seek objective parameters and try to test them to discover the best ways to combine skills and academic knowledge, to choose selection mechanisms, to make combinations of E-learning and traditional teaching; to provide good modes of delivery and teaching and educational materials.

The first step is to get the message across that legal educators and their stakeholders must be open to discussion and be transparent in what they do and why: within countries, across borders, regionally and globally. I hope this book will contribute to that endeavour.

I thank all those who have lent me their ears and who have inspired me in writing this book; I hope that I have been as generous with my comments and ideas to you as you have been to me. I wish that the legal educational community will be inspired by this book, or at least by some of its messages, and by the need to maintain and improve the quality of legal education. We owe it to society and to our students that the legal education we provide is the best, according to our convictions but also to be, as much as possible, evidence based and/or considered to be the best in thorough and open discussions.

Maastricht, February 2013

TABLE OF CONTENTS

PART A

GENERAL

Chapter 1

INTRODUCTION

This book has been inspired by many and is the result of a long career in teaching law in two universities: Leiden and Maastricht, both located in the Netherlands. Furthermore I have also taught and guest lectured abroad and participated in evaluations and assessment exercises. Those exercises, combined with my deaning between 2003 and 2011 of the Law Faculty of Maastricht University, have made me realize how scarce is the, much needed, literature on teaching law and on legal education. Exchange of opinions and perspectives; reflection upon skills, upon didactical methods, or coherent design of a curriculum are not widely present. I had the chance on a few occasions to be in a position to devise a curriculum: first in 1991 a master program (*Magister Iuris Communis* – master of European, international and comparative law) and later in 1995 a bachelor program (European Law School LLB), as well as in 2005 the bachelor program European Law School, English Language Track (the first fully English-taught bachelor in law in a non-native country).[1] I have also been involved in the design and operation of the China EU School of Law in Beijing, as a representative of one of the partners, as a member of the Managerial Board and in the first half of 2013 as a co-dean. These experiences have taught me many lessons, which I hope to convey to you, not as lessons to follow uncritically but as experiences to be shared so that we can discuss legal education and can improve it, learning from experiences of others.

I have decided to write the book in English. I am fully aware of the many differences that exist between the models of (legal) education in the world. I am also fully aware that my thoughts and perceptions about legal education are influenced by having grown up, been educated and having taught in Dutch and in The Netherlands, in Dutch law schools.

1 As well as many LLM programs which had to be developed and devised as part of the introduction of the bachelor-master Bologna structure, I have further benefited from participating in the design and running of the China-EU School of Law in Beijing and the work on the improvement of the law curriculum offered by Udayana University Law School in Denpassar, Bali, Indonesia.

However, I believe there are also many similarities and commonalities[2] to allow for a general analysis of legal education. This conviction was strengthened by the large number of international/European moot court competitions that enable students from different legal and cultural backgrounds to compete. Witnessing these competitions has made me realize how common the values are in assessing the quality of a memorandum, skilful knowledge of the law or an oral plea.

In my opinion, law schools specifically are at a strategic juncture and so are universities in general. Law schools however have been able to hide behind their assumed protective cloak of having a monopoly in raising new lawyers. In bonds with bars and professional organizations, law schools felt they were shielded against rough weather. I believe that a lot is changing here for law schools, which poses a variety of reasons to reflect on legal education: growing competition between schools and between countries and programs; IT technologies; outsourcing; the costs of legal education and the costs of legal services; the entrance on the market of cheaper E-learning, combined with globalization and Europeanization trends. Law schools have endeavoured to offer as many courses as possible to their students and to enable their professors to combine research with teaching. What might certainly happen however is that students, wanting value for money, will choose online popular mainstream courses, with automated testing and marking. Lectures by top academics can be put online and made available for many. How will universities and law schools (have to) respond to these and similar developments? Do they all want to be comparable (and imitate the best schools, knowing that they do not have the resources to copy what they are doing), or do they have to charter out their own different courses? How can law schools contribute to access and the low price of legal education and to the trend that legal costs for society cannot keep going up and that stakeholders will always seek ways to avoid legal costs? Education is an expensive commodity for the public sector and/or for private individuals. The public sector will try to keep the costs of education as low as possible; if education is privatized, the students will be looking for the best deal. In both contexts it is inevitable that legal education will have to seek ways to improve productivity, or to decrease costs and seek ways to carve out business models which benefit from IT technologies and the benefits of economies of scale.

Educating lawyers is the business of law schools and law faculties. We train students to become skilled academics, who are capable to work with the law, to assist clients and advise their companies or ministers, to litigate, and to do so professionally, according to the standards of the profession and with the advancement of fair play and the rule of law in their mind. We generally do not ask our graduates to swear an oath as physicians tend to do with the Hippocratic Oath. It is

2 And this is not to detract from the also major differences. Despite these differences it is worthwhile to learn from legal education practices and especially reforms and improvements abroad, such as the legal education reform of Harvard law School, which to the extent possible, in the US context, introduced problem-solving courses and international or comparative law. See Minow 2010. See also <http://www.law.harvard.edu/news/spotlight/classroom/related/legal-education-past-present-and-future1.pdf> and Washburn 2010.

not even common in many law schools to teach courses such as professional ethics (let alone as a compulsory course for all students), which I submit we should.

Educating students to become lawyers implies that a variety of skills/knowledge/competences/know-how must be conveyed, which they must make their own and must master and apply in their day-to-day life as a qualified lawyer:

- knowledge of the applicable laws, case law and basic concepts
- (legal) reasoning and drafting
- oral and writing skills
- running a business/law firm
- advising clients, negotiation skills, acting as a policy adviser, client counselling
- professional ethics/rules of conduct
- dispute resolution
- an academic approach with regard to reflecting upon the quality of the law, inventing solutions and drafting creative proposals.

Many of this is self-evident, but it is easier said than done. How these aspects are realized also depends on the pre-law school history of law school students. It also depends on whether a law school is allowed to select its intake. In addition, it relates to the length of the curriculum and to the eventuality of a post-law school professional training for attorneys, judges or public prosecutors. That is to say, the academic legal curriculum sits in a context of prior and post education and training and must be adapted to fit the needs of the incoming students and of the labour market/postgraduate training. The entry level of the students and the demands of what comes after law school determine, with the length of the (in many cases mandated by law or the profession) curriculum, what it is that law schools can do in a curriculum. Even then, in some cases even the content is prescribed by law or by the professional organizations, so that a school has very little to say about how to set up the curriculum, how to update it to modern needs, or to academic insights and developments. I submit here that this is not a good phenomenon. Having respect and regard for the professional wisdom and expertise of law professors mandates that they must have professional scope within which they can design curricula and courses. Trust the educators, trust the teachers!

The scope for manoeuvring in a law curriculum is sometimes also impacted by existing situations such as that some disciplines or professors may have vested interests in a specific set-up of the curriculum. In short, in many instances, change or independent judgment about a law school's curriculum is indeed not easy. This fact can hinder or prevent hasty and unwise changes, but it can also prevent necessary changes and adaptations. Changes in law schools come about through a variety of reasons. What is necessary, however, is that a discussion takes place in law schools (and also with the stakeholders around it), constantly and without end, about the curriculum, about improvements, about new skills and new programs. With that purpose in mind I have written this book.

Introduction

This book about legal education must address issues about teaching law and above all about raising our present day students for a career in our *future* societies. We have to define the future needs and demands of society and of legal society. We have to be forward looking and we have to identify what lawyers need and will need in order to be able to function as good lawyers the next 40 or 50 years! And if changes occur as fast in the next decades as they did in the past, there is a lot to be done, also considering that the amount of academic learning and areas of the law has soared. This means that law schools must not be hesitant and must look to other disciplines and how they rewrote and updated their curricula and they must reflect on the impact of the changes in the law and in society on what we teach and how we teach.

Talking and writing about legal education in general is complicated by the fact that the intake and output, the stage of development of society, and the relationship to professional life differ from country to country. Access to the bar is different; there are differences between professional training (preparation for the bar or the judiciary) and academic training, as well as that the employment perspectives of law graduates differ greatly between countries and continents. However, I still believe that it is possible to make many common general comments and reflect upon commonalities in legal education. The precise implementation and the extent to which these commonalities could and should be implemented might differ between countries but also between schools, even if they sit in one and the same country and legal system and culture. I hope to generate a debate on legal education, in order to promote the much desired quality of the education and the quality of the lawyers.

Also I will focus a great deal on diversity in legal education. The labour markets, local/regional/global circumstances differ greatly and no law school will be able to cater for all needs or meet all circumstances. Diversity and competition as well as diversity and collaboration will be my message. Another trend in that respect will be the growth of online courses or law schools. Business models of online courses are being developed: MOOCS: Massive Open Online Courses. Specifically for domains such as international law, international trade, European law, comparative law courses, IP law, international commercial law and others. One could imagine that students might look for these online alternatives, which could be cheaper or taught by top professors and have these courses acknowledged by their own law school.

I wrote in the introduction that we have to concern ourselves with reflecting on the education of our future generations of lawyers, who will be equipped to work in, and meet the needs of, future societies. What will be those needs and how do we have to prepare for them? These questions will be central in this book, but allow me to make some preliminary and general remarks here.

First of all I am convinced, and that conviction will be central in this book, that the continuing trend of globalization, international collaboration, exchanges and cross-border work will continue and is here to stay and to intensify. Preparation of lawyers with linguistic, comparative and international skills is therefore increasingly necessary.

Second, there will be a more diversified world of lawyers, in what they do (routine work versus top notch legal consultancy bordering on full scale consultancy mixing legal skills and knowledge with other expertise). As the labour market diversifies, so will legal education be diversifying and it will have to do so.

Third, legal reality, laws, will keep on changing and changing rapidly. New problems will have to be countered and regulated; new legal solutions will have to be invented; and new legal institutions will be set up. Think for instance of the rapid changes and developments in economic and financial rules in many countries, globally and in the European Union. We have to train students in how to keep up-to-date with knowledge of the law (in a specific domain). There will always be a place for top specialists who know everything of one specific area of the law and, through the Internet and other networks, they will feed other lawyers with the knowledge they need when they have to tackle that specific area of law. And, in turn, those specialists will be fed by other specialists. But we will also need more generalist lawyers, who do not specialize very much in one domain but have a 'front-office' knowledge about the most common problems; who know when to consult a specialist and who are fed through a variety of sources (the Internet, journals, newsletters, lectures, post-graduate training) about specialist developments which are relevant to them. This implies lifelong learning developments, to which law schools must also cater and maybe even remodel their programs and curricula.

Fourth, society will require a category of lawyers with creativity and powers of innovation; lawyers who are lawyers but are also much more, who can combine law with society and economics and business and technologies and trade and who are prepared for changes and who can think pro-actively and are forward looking.

Fifth, I submit that, considering the complexity of societies, domains of the law and regulations and the abundance thereof, corporations, individuals and groups/organizations need to rely increasingly upon compliance consultants, such as compliance (legal) officers that advise on policy steps, strategies, marketing, mergers, branch organizations, product liability, environmental standards, corporate social responsibility, employment and labour conditions etcetera. Here, lawyers will perform an important role, if and when they will also have (broad) knowledge of the corporate world, economics and business, and the manufactured products.

Sixth, I submit that legal dispute and conflict resolution will change even further from official courts and arbitration towards being domain or sector oriented, regional, or general, Internet based, or offered otherwise in a flexible manner by dispute resolution offices or consultancies. Quick and expert resolution of disputes may also even take place by lawyers in other countries when the files are in English.

Seventh, I foresee that legal consultancies in specific domains will be established, offering their specialized (online?) services to the world. We already see this occurring frequently in public procurement and intellectual property and damages in tort cases. However, the question arises, and the development might be similar here as in health care, why not have more small, flexible, firms offering specialized, quick and quality advice in specific domains? This could operate similar to eye clinics specialized in cataract, or orthopaedic clinics specialized in knee surgery. For law, this would work with a major difference: lawyers do not need a big office to provide those services. They do not even have to work in the same country; they can work with a specialized, part-time work force with specialists at hand. They can work Internet-based in the same way we see working for robot surgery, which can take place over the globe, so too can lawyers offer their services and interact globally.

These are added reasons why I endeavoured to write this book. I feel the sense of urgency to adapt legal education to these challenges and I do not perceive a similar urgency in the world of legal education itself. I might be wrong here, for some specific schools which work on being innovative, but, because of the predominantly domestic nature of law schools and their students, the discussions (if any) that do take place, take place within schools and within a specific jurisdiction. This does not allow enough possibility for global discussions and lessons to be learned from each other. Furthermore, research of legal education is also very limited, which I blame, at first sight, on many lawyers' dislike, or maybe better unease, with empirical research. There is not much empirical research, unfortunately.

The seven aspects which I mentioned add to the existing qualifications of lawyers, who know (of) the law and are skilful in writing and pleading and resolving and preventing problems but can also work in a different (legal) environment and in different legal settings, and ask lawyers to work in different manners than present day lawyers.

How many law schools are there in the world? This is extremely difficult to assess because of the different names (faculty, college, school) and programs and legal regulations in many countries. In Europe I have counted approximately 350; in Africa: 55; in the Middle East 20; in the Caribbean: 15; in Central America 20; in South America: 165; in Asia 925 (with 623 in China alone accounting for approximately 400,000 students!); in Oceania: 35; and in the US and Canada: 200 and 21 respectively. This makes a total of approximately 1,800 law schools[3] (and knowing that new law schools are being set up in South America and Asia, as we read and speak, the numbers may be growing).[4] These law schools offer different programs, serve different purposes, are different in size ranging from anything between 20,000 students (the law school of Buenos Aires University to 189 students in 2010/2011 in the law school of the Netherlands Antilles (UNA)). US, Canadian, European, Australian and New Zealand law schools make up for 30% of the law schools worldwide; they however do dominate the global rankings as we will see later in

3 For this survey I relied upon: <http://www.hg.org/schools.html>; the ABA website: <http://www.americanbar.org/groups/legal_education/resources/aba_approved_law_schools.html> and on <http://stu.findlaw.com/schools/foreignschools/index.html>.

4 And on October 1st, 2011, 8,824 universities worldwide in 203 countries: <http://univ.cc/>.

this book. The increase in the number of law schools in China has been particularly spectacular, in the sense that now 30% of the law schools in the world are in China.

Many of the issues in this book are very new variations on an old theme. The old theme is how to provide the best legal education in the present context. This issue relates to the question posed in an essay by Tamar Frankel, What Makes a Great Law School?[5] Her answer is that the main distinguishing feature is that great law schools serve and produce segments of the country's leadership. This is, in my opinion, a very limited definition of 'great', because it might tempt readers to equal great to good, and there are many more good law schools than great law schools. Greatness is indeed linked to a high quality of the intake and therefore a high level of teaching of not only the law but also theory and intellectual thought. Such a definition of great law schools is much less prevalent in Europe than in the USA. Grooming the elite is in many European countries the business of many law schools. However, it is an interesting approach to construct a system of legal education which consists of great schools and not so great schools. This could be the by-product or outcome of an increasing diversity between law schools.

The new variations are certainly the increased globalization and, for Europe, Europeanization; the increased mobility of students; the development of the Bologna system; the mobility of faculties; the growing number of books, papers and articles in English about international, European and comparative law; the increased impact of European law and the development of a common law of Europe; the many possibilities for exchange and E-learning; the growing diversity in employment for legal graduates, apart from the regular straight-forward jobs as lawyers, prosecutors and judges, etcetera. In addition, the economic crisis and financial issues (in Europe and abroad) will also have an impact upon students' choices and abilities and upon job markets. These changes are evident from a 1988 book entitled Legal Education: 2000, containing the papers and proceedings of an international conference in 1988.[6] When we now consider the state of affairs in 1988 and the authors' predictions, and we compare them to the perspectives and present day challenges, thorough reflections and discussions on legal education are long due. Or, in other words, many of the present day changes of rapidinternationalization/globalization and IT, simply were absent in 1988, as were the growth in student and staff exchanges and the use of comparative law and English as a common legal language.[7]

I will not describe the history of legal education, nor will I try to give surveys of systems of legal education across the globe.[8] I will use my experiences and insights to provide examples of legal education and of various experiences and utilize various literature (to a large extent US and UK literature) written about the subject, but, above all, this book is inspired by having run a law school for many years,

[5] Frankel 2001.
[6] Grant, Jagtenberg & Nijkerk 1988.
[7] Kornet 2012.
[8] See e.g. Economides 2001.

having set up and coordinated many curricula and programs, having participated in international collaborative projects, and having taught and attended conferences and met and talked with colleagues. I have noted that, with the due exceptions, legal education is not hindered by scholarly studies, extensive analysis and thorough visions about what and how we teach.[9] This is certainly different in other disciplines.[10] In medicine I have noted in my own country that there is a lot of thought given to the curriculum, assessment and teaching standards and from American literature I deduce similar findings that this is also the case in the US.[11] My purpose with this book is to bring together a variety of experiences and findings and relate them to legal education and to reflect on legal education as well as to formulate tools and recommendations for the future. I hope to contribute to the reflection on legal education and its proper place in our systems of professional and academic education and to do so in the light of pedagogical values, the globalization of law and of the needs and developments in the legal profession, and the requirements of the legal professions in the coming decades.

The difficulty of writing this book is found in trying to accommodate as many legal educational systems as possible. Legal systems differ and legal educational systems differ. There are no one–size-fits-all solutions or one overall model; however, I hope that many will benefit from achievements elsewhere, from looking into the mirror and looking through the window to the outside world and across borders, with a purpose, in order to improve legal education and to have not only a domestic, but also a regional and trans-border/international debate about legal education. What this improvement entails, what it should and should not do, and how new insights and experiences can be beneficial for all those engaged in legal education, for the (future) students and law professionals and academics and societies as a whole are questions which must be addressed.

I am aware that the many issues and chapters that I have chosen to deal with in this book do warrant separate and full in-depth studies, with country specific research and comparative and regional analyses and the collection of data. This book is therefore also a call for more research and study into legal education and a call for law schools and associations of law schools to reflect more on what legal education entails and what it is about. Researchers tend to ask for further research and further studies. I do indeed call upon the many scholars who work in legal

9 This is not to say there is no research about (aspects of) teaching law; however what is available does not seem to reach the law teachers and stays to a large extent with educational specialists. Do they talk to lawyers and vice versa and exchange information?

10 One might argue that these other disciplines are less linked (or not at all linked) to a domestic culture or language. However I do believe that despite distinctions between legal systems and legal cultures and legal languages, many of the underlying didactical concepts will be similar and can therefore be researched in one legal system and be relevant also in others.

11 For instance, an ample reference can be found in Stuckey *et al.* 2007, about assessment practices in medical schools as an example for law schools (p. 250-253); and Heringa & Akkermans 2011, p. 193: '...medical education has been receptive to pedagogical and curricular change to advance the goals of a more seamless integration of theory, practice, and professional responsibility'.

education also to reflect and share their thoughts on legal education. I do hope that law schools and associations of law schools will collect data about students, study behaviour, skills, contact hours, knowledge, employability, input and output in such a way that this information will be accessible and can be compared. I also call upon law schools to report on innovative projects and law school curriculum data, (new) selection mechanisms, exam practices, and approaches as to how to best learn the law. When this book will stimulate these researches and collections of data and also the discussion about legal education and the exchanges of ideas and experiences, I will be happy to have written it and to have stimulated thinking, albeit that opinions will be encountered that are contrary to the ideas I have put forward in this book. These researches and availability of comparable data can also assist us to work on the drafting of standards and good/best practices. Let us start a thorough discussion and exchanges of ideas that will set the stage for research of innovations and practices and lead to the improvement of legal education.

Chapter 2

FOR WHICH EMPLOYMENT DO WE TRAIN LAW STUDENTS?

In many (civil law) jurisdictions the labour market for law graduates is very diverse. Law graduates will work as lawyers (as in law firms), as members of the judiciary, but probably even to a greater extent as civil servants, in consultancies, as policy advisers and in a variety of jobs in the corporate world and in non-governmental organizations. The substance of their tasks varies from very and strictly legal, through legal and policy, to non-legal.

It might seem a bit odd, to start a book about legal education with the goal of legal training, but I feel that an analysis and description of what we want our graduates to be capable of is the best starting point and the first thing to be discussed in the following chapters, because it leads to an answer to the question what it is we want to teach law students and how and what best to train them in. Training people and students for successful careers means to reflect upon the goals to be achieved. And the goal is to educate students who are well prepared for professional life for 40 years. Education has many other purposes as well: legal education must also academically form students and prepare them for life as responsible and valuable citizens. Education also serves the purpose to get the best out of people and develop their potential to the full. These aspects will indeed have an impact upon the shape and substance of legal education. In this chapter I will however focus upon the demands of the legal professions as one of the determinant factors of good legal education.

To allow a goal to determine the contents of the training and to search for the impact of the goal upon the substance of a training is evident in sports. To devise the best tactics and training methods is related to the goals of the game: in sports it is important to know how to score the points and to relate the coaching and training to those goals; in legal education the goal is to educate students to become valuable academically trained lawyers who will be greatly appreciated in the labour market and as citizens in our societies. These issues will be the subject of the chapters to follow; in this chapter I will focus on employability and the jobs we train and educate our students for. The demands from employers and from the labour market as a whole is certainly a relevant factor for any education but certainly also for an education which is so closely related to the legal professions and the qualities needed to work as a lawyer, judge or prosecutor. Professions are not simple jobs but relate to the rule of law, the due process of law and the regular functioning of a stable and just legal order. These professions therefore must require special characteristics and influence legal education. Since these professions are connected to the rule of law, it appears relevant that these aspects are an important part of legal education. The fact that there is also the importance of a stable, functioning legal order for economic growth and the well-being and legal certainty of the people also remains. Legal education has to bear that aspect, its societal role for the prosperity of (legal) society, in mind and give it a proper place in education.

For many countries the answer to the question, for which professions and jobs do law schools educate law students, is more diverse than for others. In the US the large majority of law graduates enter the labour market to do the bar exam and subsequently to become a lawyer.

In the US figures differ as to the number of lawyers: from roughly 760,000 (according to the Bureau of labour Statistics) to 1,100,000 according to the American Bar Association.[1] In 2005 there were roughly 44,000 graduates of accredited law schools. In a paper by Harvard Law School's Program on the legal profession, containing an analysis of the Legal Profession and Law Firms,[2] the figures state that 74% of law graduates works in a law firm (big, small, solo-practice); 16% for the government (federal, state and local); 8% for business and 2% in education.

These figures seem to imply that, also considering the control of the ABA of the accreditation process of law schools in the USA, the primordial focus of US law schools can and must be on preparing their students for the bar exam and for the bar. This is more so the case since bar exam success and failure rates are important for the ranking and standing of law schools.[3]

Recently employment for lawyers in the US has been in decline with increasing difficulties for law students to find jobs.[4]

For many other countries the labour market perspectives of law graduates are completely different: for the Netherlands the statistics are less clear but do confirm the European trend that law schools do train lawyers but not for the bar (alone). On average 5,000 first year law students enter law schools every year (in 2010: 4,975);[5] on average 1,000 graduates join the bar every year; in 2009: 999; in 2010: 961; and in

1 Morgan 2010. He reports also that law schools produce 40,000 or more new lawyers each year.

2 <http://www.law.harvard.edu/programs/plp/print.php> (14-9-2011).

3 Consult, for example, the statistics on the website of the National Conference of Bar Examiners: <http://www.ncbex.org/bar-admissions/stats/>.

4 Morgan 2010. He argues that the nation's demand for new lawyers most closely tracks the rate of increase in the nation's gross domestic product. This creates a lawyer surplus every time the economy slows, but law schools keep churning out the same number of new lawyers. Welch Wegner 2010, reports a decline of almost 10% in legal jobs between November 2008 and November 2009. She quotes future projections which show a growth in legal jobs, however! This growth was expected to be specifically in the employment of paralegals and legal assistants. See footnote 5, p. 2 of the paper.

5 <http://statline.cbs.nl>.

2011, 1001.[6] The assumption that only 20% of law graduates therefore joins the bar needs to be corrected, however, since output of Dutch law schools (though figures are difficult to obtain) seems to be around 60/70% of intake. It seems likely to roughly estimate access to the bar at approximately 30% of the graduates.

For England and Wales, in 2007 75% of the graduates entered private practice; commerce and industry were second with 9% of the graduates and 4% went to the local government.[7]

For the European Union as a whole, the CCBE collects data about lawyers in Europe:[8]

Austria	5,496
Belgium OVB	9,057
Belgium OBFG	7,008
Bulgaria	
Cyprus	2,056
Czech Republic	10,049
Denmark	5,562
Estonia	695
Finland	1,893
France	50,314
Germany	15,3251
Greece	41,000
Hungary	11,784
Iceland	820
Ireland	9,346
Italy	
Latvia	1,297
Liechtenstein	170
Lithuania	1,680
Luxembourg	1,771
Malta	
The Netherlands[9]	15,542
Norway	7,150
Poland	
Portugal	27,188
Romania	
Slovak Republic	4,964

6 *Jaarverslagen Orde van Advocaten*: <http://www.advocatenorde.nl/consumenten/documenten> (Annual Reports Dutch Bar Association).

7 Boon & Whyte 2010, p. 190.

8 <http://www.ccbe.eu/fileadmin/user_upload/NTCdocument/2010_Table_of_Lawyer1_1313141496.pdf>.

9 On 31/12/2011 there were 16,808 lawyers, with an average annual increase of approximately 3%.

Slovenia	1,330
Spain	161,988
Sweden	4,601
Switzerland	8,423
UK	12,241
Northern Ireland	2,444
Scotland	10,380

How do this data relate to the number of graduates? The answer to this question has not been easy to determine, but a selection of data for some countries does indeed suggest a confirmation of the findings for the Netherlands that many law graduates do find other professions after graduation. In Germany the latest figure for the total number of law students was 89,331 for 2009. The figures show a decrease in law students compared to the last decade of the previous century when the number of law students was more than 100,000.[10]

When we can safely assume that many law graduates have a diverse range of jobs to choose from and go into legal practice, business,[11] government and other employment, without a significant share choosing for one of the different options in particular, it implies that law schools must take this variety into account when teaching law. To give some examples, in many law schools legal clinics have been set up or participation in moot courts is promoted, or skills related to client counselling, mooting and representing clients are an important part of the curriculum. However, when it can be assumed that many graduates will not practice law as an attorney, why do we not train students (also) in other skills, such as negotiation in the public domain (about a treaty, EU directive) or about drafting policy advice for the minister? In private legal practice a great emphasis is put upon private and corporate law related issues, because those are the money-making domains in large law firms, which are inclined to hire young graduates. However, when we take into account that a significant number of law school graduates will enter the public domain, we could teach more public law, or public administration or social sciences.[12]

The employment opportunities for law graduates is amazingly diverse and varied; apart from the approximately 30% in Europe entering into legal practice, the remaining 70% will find jobs in consultancies, in companies, in sector organizations,

10 http://www.destatis.de/jetspeed/portal/cms/Sites/destatis/Internet/EN/Content/Statistics/TimeSeries/LongTermSeries/Education/Content100/lrbil03a,templateId=renderPrint.psml>.

11 'The power of in-house lawyers has grown hugely in the past ten years. (...) The main reason is that the legal thicket has grown thicker.' (Schumpeter 2012, p. 62). This trend implies that lawyers must work closely with and acquire knowledge of the business, finances, marketing and other tools of the specific trade, in order to be a well valued counsel.

12 Later in this chapter I will show some figures about the high proportion of US lawyers in corporate law practice. In (continental) Europe this figure is much lower because many European law graduates find work in the civil service and related employment.

in government and the public sector in general, as policy advisors; and the work they do in these sectors is as diverse as their employers. Some jobs entail a strong focus on strictly legal work; other jobs focus on academic skills and on support for the business or government minister; and we find employment in which the lawyer has specialized in a specific sector (telecommunications, business, food etc.) in which (s)he delivers integrated services combining expertise in law with a specialized knowledge of that sector.

Now that I have tried to indicate that many law schools actually train students for an abundance of jobs, we might try to generate a list of skills they will need in possible and probable future employment. I also include among these skills knowledge of the law (though we still have to determine how much knowledge of the law and what it means exactly when we talk about legal knowledge; see Chapter 4). I make this comment because for many professions, such as policy advisor, knowledge of the law is not per se an indispensable requirement, but in those cases knowledge of the law stands for an academic qualification and the ability to do all those things qualified academics are supposed to be able to do.[13]

What, apart from sufficient knowledge of the law, do we have to expect from our law graduates and do we therefore have to teach our students?

1. Analytical and critical thinking, reading and listening and reflection;
2. Creative thinking and solution-oriented thinking;
3. Clear writing;
4. Oral skills and skills of persuasion, lobbying and networking;
5. Research capabilities;
6. Life-long learning skills;
7. Negotiation and conflict resolution skills;
8. Advising clients, CEO's, ministers, etcetera;
9. Client counselling skills;
10. Political and policy sensitivity;
11. Social communication skills;
12. International communication skills;
13. ICT skills;
14. Sensitivity to other (legal) cultures and knowledge of more languages;

13 In a report on Trends and developments of the Dutch legal labour market, the interim company Yacht has analysed that in the first three months of 2012 there were 24% less vacancies than in the same period of 2011. However, compared to the whole of 2011 it appeared that the decline in vacancies was halted. In the same report the conclusion was reached that employers were looking for 'quick start' lawyers (lawyers with appropriate training and experience) who could be productive immediately without further training and coaching. That in itself led the authors of the report to argue in favour of a permanent general continued education: <http://www.yacht.nl/content/corporate/nieuws/2012/03/20120328_kwartaalbericht_legal.xml?cfv=&cfb=&cfk=&cp=1>.

15. Basic understanding of other disciplines such as ((social) sciences and economics);
16. Pro-activity;
17. Curiosity and precision;
18. Entrepreneurial skills (to set up one's own business);
19. Understanding of the law in its context;
20. Professional ethics; and
21. Collaborative skills.

In this list I have tried to be as exhaustive and explicit as possible. I do fully realize that some are more important in a specific job than others; some might already be very much present in our student intake body, others might need more attention and focus. However, my argument is that these skills, which graduates will further develop during their professional lives, will be and will remain essential and will give them the tools to be what we call good lawyers or good professionals or good academics. Twining has encapsulated the necessary skills in a shorter list:[14] rule-handling, fact analysis, skills of questioning, reading and interpretation; conceptual analysis; articulating assumptions of propositions and questions, of criticizing and re-posing questions and of constructing and criticizing arguments. He considered reasoning and analysis to be central to the discipline of law. And the best way and place to teach them is by direct learning as a central component of every stage of legal education and training.[15]

Some of the skills I have listed partially overlap, certainly. Some of them might be self-evident, others are less so, and do deserve an explanation.

The first four skills I have identified are skills that have been taught in many law schools for many years. For that purpose schools have set up legal writing programs, have introduced law and literature courses, made essays and papers a compulsory part as well as presentations and mooting. I have added here under number 2 'Creative thinking and solution-oriented thinking' to make it explicit that lawyers are not trained solely in detecting the barriers but also in seeking solutions. Lawyers must be strict when it comes to obedience of the law but also creative in assisting their clients, seeking solutions and resolving disputes. That ought also to be an explicit part of legal training, as is the case in business training when young professionals are taught to always to come to their boss with two solutions to a problem. This approach shows the young professional's creativity and gives the boss a freedom of choice with regard to the solution. Bosses/clients and society at large need and prefer solutions to problems and not new problems. Solutions, and this is an aspect to be aware of, need not necessarily be purely legal but must be effective. Options can be designed through which an issue is resolved and made to disappear or made much less urgent. Lawyers and legal issues are relevant and

14 Twining 1997, p. 190-191.
15 Twining 1997, p. 181.

important, but sometimes solutions other than the purely legal kind maybe of more value for the client.

We must train our students to research questions thoroughly and quickly, also in those domains where they have no prior knowledge. How to do it, what are the tricks of the trade, what are reliable sources, as well as trying to be as updated with developments and changes in the law are questions to be addressed. This implies training students that the law is in flux and that we teach them in a law school to know what they do not know!

Negotiation skills, advising clients and client counselling are another category. They relate to the fact that lawyers work for others and therefore have to defend the client's interests and have to be able to read the client's mind. It is important to understand the minister's wishes and to assess his relationship with his political party and with parliament; to understand the company's strategy and its policy; to understand a client's problem and to be able to communicate properly with the client and to be able to negotiate and to get the best deal for the client/company/government, within the legal boundaries and with due respect for the other party. This implies, in many contexts, a sound political sensitivity and sense of political conditions.

The communication skills mentioned in the list are also present and inherent in many of the other skills but need to be included separately. They do seem self-evident, though I have included international communication skills, as well as sensitivity to other (legal) cultures and knowledge of (another) language(s) as separate criteria. I have done so to make it abundantly clear that a law curriculum in the modern day's world cannot do without these aspects. Globalization, and in Europe, Europeanization with and within the European Union, show the importance of these aspects. Law firms set up international desks, international branches, work closely with foreign firms and do trans-boundary work. Civil servants from the capitals in Europe can be seconded to the Commission or travel regularly or occasionally to Brussels to negotiate with their EU partners. These aspects require international and linguistic communication skills.

Basic ICT skills hopefully speak for themselves, which is probably not so for other sciences. This is a complicated skill because of its possible vast and indeterminate scope. I do not mean to educate lawyers as (social) scientists, but I do see the need for lawyers to have an understanding of other disciplines, such as economics (because of the obvious links with corporate law, EU law, WTO law, financial regulation, competition law and with law and economics), psychology, sociology and criminology (behavioural aspects of the law, forensic psychology), and other relevant sciences (such as for criminal lawyers: DNA, accountancy). Lawyers must be able to understand these sciences in order to read psychology reports about the state of mind of a defendant, or to be able to access statistical analysis,[16] or to understand banking and stock market regulation. Also, for many lawyers (legal) philoso-

16 See for example, Finkelstein & Levin 2001; in 2011-2012 Columbia law School offers a course 'L6248 Statistics for Lawyers' (Michael O. Finkelstein & Nathan A. Schachtman).

phy, political science or international relations will enhance their perspectives. For practical reasons, I do not think that lawyers in law schools can be trained in those disciplines, but it ought to be feasible to include, for example, basic social sciences in a curriculum in order to give students a basic grasp of terminology, concepts and methodology.

Pro-activity, curiosity and precision are self-evident: pro-activity in the sense that a professional also seeks the question behind the question; probes into what the client might want and needs; and is interested and shows an interest in his domain and in his clients. Precision is the tool of the lawyers' trade.

Entrepreneurial skills, entrepreneurship, are a neglected subject in many law schools, although the number of self-employed lawyers is on the rise. Lawyers setting up their own shop; lawyers working for interim consultancies, with a high degree of flexibility, are an increasing phenomenon. Don't we have to train them how and what it is to be your own boss: how to liaise with clients? How to access the market? How to set up a proper administration and do your own taxes?[17]

I have added the law in context as a general caption as we must be aware that law is not an isolated issue, nor the central issue in society: it comes jointly with other issues. Law is certainly not the absolute truth: the real world is more than law. Clients might have a legal problem, but it will be linked with social or other issues. Some issues might be better resolved through, or in conjunction with, other experts. Also, we tend to teach law in law schools in doctrinal areas of the law: constitutional law, contract, criminal procedure etcetera. But issues in real life do not neatly follow the distinctions between those areas of the law. Sometimes it might be better to bring many domains together as defining a problem or an issue (and they then might lead to a new area of the law): migration law, environmental law, educational law, consumer law. Or perhaps the solution is to train students (as happens in real life) in researching and resolving an issue which has tentacles in various legal domains as well has been impacted by other sciences. (Im)migration issues link to demography, climate, insight into what constitutes immigration and what are effective instruments, European law, human rights, politics, military conflicts, policies of other countries etcetera. This is also the context within which problems land on a lawyer's desk. If that is the case, why do we not train the students in law school how to entangle these issues, where to seek assistance, how to define the issue at hand, how to research them, whom to involve and how to coordinate efforts and people to come up with proper approaches and solutions?

Professional ethics, although not a very prominent course in many legal curricula, ought to be an integral part of legal education also. We expect lawyers to be pro-active, creative, resourceful, client-oriented and offering assistance, but/and at the same time we want them to behave ethically and according to the law and their proper codes of conduct. Lawyers do not generally, after leaving law school, swear an oath to uphold the law, though they sometimes do so when being admitted to

17 An example: the Entrepreneurial Law Clinic of the University of Colorado Law School (<www. Colorado.edu/law/clinics/entre/>).

certain professions (such as the bar or the judiciary), but we can certainly expect them to behave and act according to the rules and ethics of the trade. Therefore, we must teach law students professional ethics and inject ethics in the curriculum.

Finally, my 21st skill in the list relates to collaboration. Many of the examples I gave before show that many lawyers do not operate in an isolated setting. Collaboration is a key word: expertise is so specific that many issues require teams to work on them; work improves generally when people sit together and comment and contribute, but such collaboration requires certain rules and certain skills and do's and don'ts. One way or another, students must be stimulated to become capable in this respect.

These skills do not require separate courses; my argument here is not that we must now set up 21 courses devoted to these skills. At this stage I argue that these skills (taking into account intake and output) must have a relevant and substantial place in the curriculum. Law schools must breathe these skills into their teaching and educational design. Combining skills and teaching, exercising collaboration and resolution of cases and disputes, analysing texts and exercising arguments and exchange of views, presuppose a didactical design adapted to train students in skills and integrated knowledge.

I reserve for later chapters the questions as to how much, in what shape and form (separate and/or integrated) and when these skills could be integrated into teaching and educational design.

These skills, taking into account what students can already be expected to master when they enter law school, I submit, must be an integral part of a law school curriculum. I underline these aspects, not because I believe that a law school is purely a professional school, training good lawyers for the (legal) professions but because I believe that a law school is two things: an academic education as well as a preparation for professional life. In Chapter 10 I will elaborate further on the academic aspect of legal education.

The intensity of making these skills an integral part of a law school curriculum not only depends on the intake but also on what follows afterwards. In some countries, some professions, such as bar associations, for example, or traineeships in governments or major companies, have set up continued professional training for law graduates who enter this profession after law school. These professional training programs also pay attention to (some of) the skills I mentioned. Thereby such training programs will probably make it less urgent for law schools to focus fully on those aspects.

It is therefore important to take into account how a law school's curriculum is situated in the domestic educational system. We will discuss the intake of students in the next chapter, but, in this chapter, it is indeed important to consider what occurs in the labour market after graduation. In some countries, for example, professional organizations and public entities or corporations or sectors have established a system of traineeships or apprenticeships for new graduates. The extent to which this has taken place must certainly be relevant for law schools.

In this sense, we have to make sure that we know what might follow, in order to tailor our curricula and make them fit precisely between intake (expectations) and output requirements.

The precise balance cannot be prescribed for all law schools, however, I argue here that law schools must give them the right attention and make them explicit for the students. We also have a duty to make the students aware of what we want them to acquire, in knowledge as well as in skills, as we also want our staff to be aware of what skills to incorporate in the curriculum and in the course offerings.

There is however a caveat here. In 2008 Richard Susskind wrote a book entitled 'The End of Lawyers? Rethinking the Nature of Legal Services'.[18] He described a new market for lawyers, a buyer's market as well as a market with many emerging legal technologies. In 2011, The Economist described one of them.[19] It noted that clients are switching to unconventional law firms. They do not have an office but work from home and are connected through a technology platform. Clients also have access to this platform. They offer cost estimates for each phase of the legal job.

It also describes a firm which takes on chunks of legal work, for a flat fee. The lawyers doing the work were, as The Economist described it, stashed in cheap places such as Houston and Hyderabad. Indeed, why not outsource routine legal work (contracts,[20] discovery) to lawyers elsewhere? Why not outsource the drafting of bulk decisions by governments, or provide dispute resolution through the Internet: clients can choose the lawyer; they send in the files and papers and briefs; and they will have a quick resolution. Quick, cheap and quality assured, because that will be the basis of the success.[21]

Another example is a social networking site which would have lawyers answer short questions from clients, who then can choose them as their lawyer. Legal Zoom[22] is another example of one of the new services made possible by Internet, through which a variety of legal services are being provided to clients (contract drafting, divorce documents, real estate deed transfer etcetera).

Thomas L. Friedman and Michael Mandelbaum describe similar far-reaching perspectives for the lawyering business caused by the Flat World: the globalization and IT developments.[23] Their argument is that the merger of globalization and the IT revolution is changing everything - every job and every service. And this merger has raised the level of skills a person needs to obtain and retain any good job and

18 Oxford 2008.

19 August 13th, 2011, p. 52: 'Alternative law firms: Bargain briefs'.

20 See also The Economist, 'A contract lawyer or radiologist is vulnerable to offshoring; a divorce lawyer or family doctor isn't', 24 September 2011, p. 24.

21 See also Susskind 2008, p. 217 *et seq*. about Online dispute resolution.

22 <www.legalzoom.com>.

23 Friedman & Mandelbaum 2011; especially in chapters 4 and 5. See also: McCrimmon 2010: he concluded (1) that advances in information technology and globalization will continue to influence domestic law; (2) our connected planet provides opportunities for consistency of regulation at a national, regional and global level; (p. 93) principle-based regulation will play an increasingly important role in achieving internationally compatible regulatory regimes; (4) a pervasive factor in the formulation of legislated outcomes is the allocation of risk (p. 67).

increases the global competition for those jobs. Add to that the fact that with Internet connectivity, smart phones, I-pads, laptops, anyone can find anyone (s)he needs for contact or information and any information about everything. They then distinguish four typologies of jobs which are in different levels vulnerable to global competition or being replacing by computers. The first group are the creative creators (people who do non-routine work in a distinctively non-routine way (and in that category the best lawyers are specifically mentioned)); the second are routine creators (who do their non-routine work in a routine way - average lawyers); the third are the creative servers (non-routine low-skilled workers who do their jobs in inspired ways - an excellent baker or nurse); and finally the routine servers (routine serving work in a routine way, offering nothing extra). Their argument is that all these jobs are not safe considering globalization or IT developments. However, they argue that routine work and doing work in a routine way makes people and jobs vulnerable.

These developments also affect the lawyering business. They describe[24] the example of discovery: lawyers examining thousands or millions of documents in civil cases in the US. 'Now thanks to advances in artificial intelligence, 'e-discovery' software can analyse documents in a fraction of the time for a fraction of the cost.' This illustrates the case that routine work is vulnerable and that the focus is on non-routine work and non-routine workers. Therefore for more innovation and education serving that need it is essential to educate as many creative creators and creative servers. Their story continues with an example of an American law firm[25] which argues for critical thinking and the ability to innovate. And, I may add, it illustrates the need for education to educate the law students in these new realities which ask for their creativity, forces of innovation, legal skills and technical skills to work with being connected to information, clients and colleagues.

These characteristics define the creativity of the lawyers and what kind of lawyer they will be and therefore how they can compete in the domains of globalization and IT. Lawyers have to be pro-active, specialize in niches and areas where they have an added value. The question in this respect is whether the future is indeed for large law firms or for (virtual and flexible) networks of experts and expertise, which can adapt themselves to changing demands and with less costs for running the firm and with lawyers who can work anywhere and have access to clients and information and to their knowledge networks from anywhere.

I would not at all be surprised if these new modes of working will also (have to) affect the law schools themselves.[26] I will argue in a later chapter in this book

24 Friedman & Mandelbaum 2011, p. 79.

25 Friedman & Mandelbaum 2011, p. 85-87.

26 In the same vein Boon & Whyte 2010, p. 222: 'Despite the traditional appeal of law as a subject, these trends may presage a slackening of demand for legal careers and for the familiar undergraduate and vocational courses. At the same time, increasing diversification of legal careers, and the potential for their assimilation into existing structures (e.g. the Law society offering routes into the solicitors' profession for paralegals), suggests potential for the diversification and proliferation of law and law-related courses. Both of these strands of change →

that law schools will not only have to train their students for the Flat World, but also will find working methods to introduce the impact of the Flat(ter) World in their curricula and programs and delivery of teaching and imparting of skills.

Law schools will have to prepare their students for these new working environments and job competition features. But law schools must also practice what they teach. That is, they must introduce, in the substance of teaching and in the modes of delivery, these new future-oriented trends: more training in ICT techniques; more online learning experiences and teaching. Or law schools could set up trainings or courses in business models or entrepreneurship, which can then focus on the ICT developments and their consequences for jobs and employment.

For this book the stories by Friedman and Mandelbaum illustrate the prospects foreseen by Susskind, in the sense that real legal work might be (and already is!) computerized and secondly that legal work has different aspects and that some of these aspects might be open to globalization and global competition and for computerization.

I have not taken it upon myself to go into the field and to analyse the changes in the legal labour market, but it is indeed fair to assume that important changes are taking place. This must in itself be a reason for law schools to prepare their students for these new businesses and new approaches to legal jobs. Preparing them for an old fashioned career in a law firm only might not be the right thing, considering that our present day students will work far into the second half of the 21st century and they will have to compete with, or witness, paralegals or legal executives, to do routine work. Also, they have to work in a world that is also becoming flatter in the legal domain for international legal issues and for more routine legal work.

Larry E. Ribstein,[27] in a 2011 article, has analysed a variety of the consequences of these developments for American legal education. His conclusion is also that the changing environment is creating markets for skills and that globalization of law practice is changing the market for legal education. He argues that big law firms are in danger because of the increasing competition with clients' in-house counsel, small niche firms (he calls them boutique law firms) with lower costs, big firms in other countries, low cost legal outsourcers and technical advances. He argues as well that there is an increasing social demand for cheaper legal services. And he focuses on the need to adapt legal education: to train students to design legal products (contracts, complaints, legal information); to train students for multidisciplinary collaborations in teams rendering integral advice to clients. These arguments lead him to conclude that law schools must train lawyers as collaborators (accountants, finance economists and lawyers, are an example); manufacturers (designing products for markets); as lawmakers (designing laws as products and standard setting for legal systems); and also for global legal competition. He con-

may ensure that an increasing number of law schools may need to adapt and change or grapple with the challenge of a more diverse student body.'

27 Ribstein 2011.

cludes that uniformity in legal education must be abandoned, allowing law schools to seek their approaches to the education of lawyers for (segments of) the markets.

Although aspects of Ribstein's analysis specifically relate to American legal education, his forward and market looking perspectives are highly interesting and underline the need for law schools to investigate trends in the monopoly of lawyers, in legal costs and demands for cheaper legal services and the availability of legal services for the middle class,[28] the developments of Internet services and outsourcing, as well as global competition, the growth of boutique law firms, and finally the need for lawyers to develop into collaborators who can do more than pure legal analysis, but can work in teams for the resolution of varieties of issues.

A few years earlier Thomas D. Morgan also extensively showed the changes for legal education due to the future legal profession(s).[29] He described eight trends in the world of clients for legal services that will impact legal education. Clients will face an increasing degree of competitive pressure; clients will increasingly have to think globally; clients are likely to become more impatient with what they see as the complexity and inflexibility of legal rules; clients are likely to expect lawyers to understand their business or personal affairs and not just their apparent legal issues: future clients want their lawyers to resemble multidisciplinary consultants rather than legal technicians (lawyers might be retained among a mix of advisors);[30] many business-clients bring more work in-house; clients see legal services rather as 'commodities' than as unique and worthy of a premium fee (this development is impacted by information technology and for instance by commercial firms delivering legal services over the Internet); clients will be less loyal to their lawyers; many clients will not be able to afford a lawyer. These developments, combined with the large number of lawyers and the many students in training in law schools, will lead to changes in the legal profession. Morgan predicted that the days of lawyers as talented generalists are likely over. The provision of commodity legal services will become common (standardized products sold primarily on the basis of price) and lawyers will have to learn to compete for the opportunity to provide them. Lawyers will distinguish themselves by being the best at delivering unique, tailored legal services. Globalization has impacted and made the reality of today's law practice more complex and made it less possible to be a generalist. Second, the days of

28 These trends towards cheaper legal services applies to individuals but also increasingly to companies. Clients will seek flexible legal deals which suit their needs, are cheap and are not necessarily tied to one big firm.

29 Morgan 2006;. Morgan 2010.

30 Securities lawyer: economics and finances' trade lawyer: cultures and languages; patent lawyers: sciences; corporate merger lawyers: accounting, finances. Morgan points out that non-lawyer providers will compete and make it a point to learn enough about the law relevant to their own activity that lawyers will not be able simply to bluff them into submission by asserting an exclusive right to explain legal issues (2009, p. 12). 'The lawyers who prosper will be those who can make themselves the best available go-to person in combined law-and-substantive field... Morgan predicts that the future lawyers in greatest demand are likely to be those who have specific, recognizable skills and who can work well with a team of lawyers and complementary professionals to meet a client's needs.' (p. 13).

lawyers specialized in law alone may be ending (combinations with management expertise or financial expertise). He elaborated on this point in his 2009 paper by stating that the interaction of law with increasingly complex economic and social issues will make distinctively legal questions less common and make many of the skills that we stress in law schools less relevant: the world will require legally-trained persons to be more fully integrated into the substantive challenges tomorrow's clients face. In this paper he concluded that there is a need for 'Multi-service practice organizations'.[31] This conclusion links to my argument above that clients will increasingly go for multidisciplinary consultants and advice.

In the context of a merger between two hospitals I was involved in, we had to seek the advice of competition lawyers, accountants, consultants with expertise in merging different organizations, IT specialists, labour law experts/HRM people, communication advisers and mediators for the talks between the doctors of the two hospitals who in the future had to agree upon divisions of labour and the reconciliation of procedures and processes. For each and every activity we had to hire different outside expertise. This led one of my colleagues to reflect upon the desirability that one might look for 'merger' specialists who can deliver a variety of services which are generally sought for in cases of a merger. This direction of thinking is reflected in accountants with legal qualifications (allowing them to give accountancy and legal advice to the client) and in law firms specializing in societal or issue-related sectors (telecommunications, IT, food, cure/care).

Third foreign language facility will be central as well as local knowledge of culture. Fourth, law firms will change from supermarkets (and large entities) into shopping centers, diversifying their service offerings. Fifth, legal suppliers will emerge helping clients to help themselves; the services (investment, finances, estate planning) may be offered standardized and delivered through the Internet. Thomas D. Morgan added in his 2009 paper, from the perspective of (prospective) clients, much of the information lawyers have traditionally sold is now freely available on the Internet. He also showed figures indicating that 64% of the lawyers are corporate lawyers, while lawyers for individuals have fallen to a mere 29% (from 40% in 1975). This means that there will be fewer opportunities (in the US) for lawyers who do not want to do corporate work.

What has also occurred is the rising power of in-house counsel. Furthermore, he notes the declining significance of having an American law license, as well as corporations now using non-lawyers to help deliver the total package of services they need done.

In his paper Thomas D. Morgan furthermore stressed globalization as an important factor, putting American lawyers in competition with legal service providers all over the world.

These developments envisaged by Morgan led him to argue in favour of changes in legal education. He offered five propositions in that respect.

31 Morgan 2010, p. 17.

1. No in-depth study in all domains but a good theoretical background in the area of one's specialty, with clinical and externship experiences.
2. End the law school homogeneity; in the future most law schools will be unable to do everything well. 'The diversity of student interests and the range of potential uses of a legal education are so great that, ultimately, the demands of law students and a recognition of schools' self-interest are likely to require law schools to concentrate their efforts in subject matter areas where they can quickly be seen as among the very best.'[32]
3. The cost of legal education for most students must come down; law schools must find more efficient ways to deliver a legal education. The cost and breadth of law study can be reduced by distance learning, in specific programs or as a supplement to live teaching in upper class courses.
4. Law schools should move beyond teaching law to recognizing that education about non-legal matters will be increasingly important to lawyers.
5. Law schools will have to make continuing legal education a larger part of their program.

His final conclusion is that the shape of today's law schools must be determined by the shape of the world the next generation of lawyers will face. Lawyers need to know the following four broad categories:[33] (1) analyse legal issues and think like a lawyer; (2) enough substantive law to be able to place new knowledge into context; (3) concrete skills for helping to improve a client's situation; (4) enough non-legal understanding to see a client's problem from the client's point of view.

Judith Welch Wegner addressed similar issues with similar conclusions in a 2010 paper.[34] Access to legal services will be less dependent on geographical location; requiring a likelihood of specialization, globalization and technological delivery systems and diversity among legal providers. The reduction in recent years in the American legal job market and the costs of legal education in the US (with high debts for graduating students) make it imperative to reflect upon legal education. She is less specific than Morgan about the consequences for the substance of legal education in the US but still formulated proposals about the design of law schools, suggesting a part I bar exam after the end of the first year. As well as reshaping the second and third year, she emphasized content knowledge, professional enhancement, professional skill enhancement, professional values and integration of knowledge/skills/values at a higher level of expertise.

Matasar pointed out similar and other developments in and for the labour market for lawyers:[35]

> 'State and federal government regulation (and deregulation) of the legal profession may profoundly affect the need for a vast supply of highly paid new lawyers. Tort

32 Morgan 2010, p. 15.
33 Morgan 2010, p. 22.
34 Wegner 2010.
35 Matasar 2005, p. 495-496.

> reform is quite likely, with the effect of depressing returns for personal injury lawyers. The very complex tax system (and much of the work associated with estate planning) may be simplified. New forms of competition from online providers of legal advice to computerized forms to breaking the monopoly of lawyers to dispense advice may undercut the meat and potatoes of small firm practice. Legal work (like other services in the economy) can be outsourced to English speaking workers in other countries with lower wages than currently provided to American lawyers. The partnership track in firms will be constricted; lawyers may be members of corporations, with limited chances to share in profits and firm growth. Non-U.S. competition will siphon off international business from American firms.'[36],[37]

Matasar proposes that law schools impart knowledge to people who are not lawyers; law schools with multiple entry and exit points and students taking the whole program or parts of the program. He suggests that law schools will have to offer advanced trainings for professionals. Furthermore he argued in favour of co-operation between law schools: sharing resources and using combinations of in-person teaching (experts being responsible for a course at two locations and delivering the core materials). He also suggested international consortia of law schools.

It emerges from the above that the labour market, and the different kinds of legal work and lawyers needed and requested, will diversify continuously and further. Susskind[38] identifies in that respect for the future five kinds of lawyers: (1) the expert trusted adviser (purveyor of bespoke legal service); (2) the enhanced practitioner (supporting the delivery of standardized, systematized, and packaged legal service); (3) legal knowledge engineer (highly skilled lawyers); (4) legal risk manager (proactive legal services; (5) legal hybrid (multi-disciplinary).

In the present state of affairs, whether his analysis will hold true or not, there is already a great diversity in law firms and in the legal work that is being performed. When we add the other jobs, other than real lawyering lawyers, which law graduates seek (consultant, policy advisor, in-house counsel, civil servant etc.), we witness a huge diversity, which leads to the question whether law schools can

36 Subsequently he also points to the growing numbers of graduating students, as well as to the education of lawyers from around the world in US LLM programs, who will have skills that will be used by non-US firms to compete for business. 'The legal profession is a worldwide market and non-U.S. firms can under-price the market because their lower salaries and lower educational costs. If so, business may shift to them at the expense of U.S. firms and their highly paid workers.' I believe this trend is strengthened by the international attractiveness of English and Australian legal education, the increase in English-taught legal programs in Europe, and the growing presence of Chinese legal education.

37 Regulation or deregulation of legal professions in one country may affect global competition between providers of legal services. For example, in Great Britain the law has recently been changed (2011), enabling a law firm to set up as an ABS: Alternative Business Structure. These can be set up as a firm with shares, or as a co-operative (co-op). The idea is to liberalize legal services, thereby making them cheaper, and promoting competition and innovation (more services online; off-the-shelf products). (The Economist, 'Legal Services, Psst, wanna buy a law firm?', 28 January 2012, p. 55).

38 Susskind 2008, p. 271 *et seq.*

and should cater for all of these jobs, or should specialize. Is the best way forward for a law school to offer a general legal education, opening the way to all legal jobs available, or do law schools have to set up specialist focused tracks leading to a specific cluster of jobs, or must they allow for and stimulate master programs and post-graduate professional training programs to be tailor-made for specific jobs? In other words: a reorientation for the old fashioned law school legal education which intends to educate for all legal jobs, or specialize and instead go for diversity between law schools and between programs.

This question is even more pertinent when we take into account the internationalization and Europeanization of the legal trade. As I have argued in another recent publication,[39] there is a need and demand for truly European lawyers: lawyers raised and educated in comparative, international and European law and with linguistic skills. Since not all lawyers in all areas of employment might need or seek such an education, I have proposed to work towards a system of selected and specialized European law schools. Specialization, therefore, is based upon the presumption that that is the best way to cater for the labour market. This creates a situation which is not so terribly different to that in the US, where local law schools cater for the state bar and are focused upon getting their students through the bar exam in the specific state.

The Europeanization issue underlines the possible argument for specialization. Some schools training routine legal-work lawyers; others train for what Susskind calls the legal hybrids[40] (multidisciplinary lawyers); again others train European lawyers who work trans-boundary and internationally. Whether this approach is the right approach, and if other approaches will be more likely or successful, or whether didactical perspectives will point in other directions, will be discussed in the final chapter.

In some countries one already speaks of a bifurcated system:[41] some (elite, top) law schools train students for law firms that cater for corporate clients - these clients are international, or have international links. Furthermore, there is the world of the private clients, serviced in smaller and more local law firms. The relevant law which is at stake is also different: competition, mergers, international financial transactions, stock market issues, intellectual property, international trade, securities; and on the other hand labour and social law/welfare law, family law and criminal law. How will this play out in the future for the legal curriculum?

A well-functioning legal system is important for a country, its economy and its prosperity, its legitimacy and fairness and equal access to goods and participation in the public domain. In that respect lawyers play an important role. There exists, for instance, a World Bank site ranking countries and their economies on their ease

39 Heringa & Akkermans 2011; also Heringa 2011b, p. 221-224 (added as chapter 17 this book).
40 Susskind 2008, p. 273.
41 Boon & Whyte 2010, p. 191.

of doing business.[42] Educating lawyers to contribute to the goal of building and maintaining a stable legal environment, where contracts can be enforced and investors enjoy proper protection is therefore highly important for the well-being of a country. The value for society to have a well-educated and well-functioning society of lawyers and legal professionals is of the highest importance.

Freedom House on its site[43] ranks states in three categories: Free, Partly Free, and Not Free. Cross-checking the 30 best performers on the World Bank ranking on the Ease of Doing Business, 21 out of the 30 are characterized by Freedom House as Free; 5 as Partly Free and 2 as Not Free. That is almost 70% as free, whereas in the overall Freedom House list not more than 45% is Free; Only 2 Not Free states made it into the top 30: Saudi Arabia and Bahrein. The 2 top positions are for 2 Partially Free states: Singapore and Hong Kong.

Cross checking the top 30 list of the World Bank with income levels we also find a correlation: 7 countries disappear; thus leaving 23 countries which are rich and Free (with the exception of Singapore, Hong Kong and Bahrein).

This is evidently no conclusive evidence for or against a specific constitutional or legal model; however, it does tell us something about the economic and business benefits of high quality legal systems, with legal stability and a constitutional model of the rule of law and lawyers have a role to play in that respect.

Twining very precisely described the ambitions university law schools should adopt: they should grow in the direction of being multifunctional institutions that regularly serve a wide variety of constituencies at a variety of levels: 'from legal literacy to judicial training; from different kinds of law for non-lawyers to advanced specialist studies for a variety of consumers; from primary academic and vocational studies to continuing education...'[44] And to do so one has to focus less on knowledge but on intellectual skills.

Law schools in the world are quite varied; the assumption that all law schools have the same mission is not realistic. A main distinction is between a law school as a professional school (servicing the profession) or as an academic (university) institution (advancement of learning). Clearly many variations do exist, such as the American post-graduate professional law school model; and the training institutions/colleges for judges or prosecutors.[45]

This book is very much concerned with the academic model (or the post graduate professional school model). It is my belief that studying law is and should be an academic endeavour, educating students to become reflexive academics who have become learned and who have specifically been trained in intellectual legal skills. Lawyering, law-making, rendering justice are tasks that do require these skills. In that sense the profession of the law graduate is more than simple legal mechanics. For 'mass' legal work (due diligence, contracts, 'bulk' work in some

42 <http://www.doingbusiness.org/rankings>.

43 <www.freedomhouse.org>.

44 Twining 1997, p. 293.

45 About the different models Twining 1997, p. 301-304.

administrative domains such as tax and administrative law) it is questionable whether this is really work for fully-fledged lawyers. In medicine we witness the emergence of nurse-practitioners; in eye-medicine the bulk work is done by optometrists, so why not expect the same in many domains of the law where bulk work and production (repetitive work) are at the forefront and easily outsourced to (cheaper) paralegals and legal assistants?

The developments I have indicated concern legal work that is fit for global competition and for IT coverage. In that respect the language in which lawyering is conducted is indicative for globalization. And as it so happens, legal work is in many instances in the language of the domestic legal order. I fully grasp the idea that bulk work (discovery, contracts, due diligence) in English in the domain of American and English law might be susceptible for global competition. The English language is a world language and the American and English legal systems have for many decades accommodated students from all over the world. In that respect the exchange and mobility of students does contribute to a spreading of legal knowledge and slowly to competition. The flattening world might certainly take place there, as well as in all domains and disputes that are governed by trans-border aspects or international law. But doesn't this leave unaffected those local legal issues, playing under purely domestic legal rules? It seems fair to assume here that global competition might be less of an issue there. Competition could be just as relevant, as could the IT impact, creating a national competition for services, since services could be rendered (apart from court appearance and visits to detainees e.g.) from anywhere. Competition will become more apparent due to lawyers who work through the Internet and make their services cheaply available through written advice, phone conversations, Skype calls, and exchanges of E-mails. This implies less need for big expensive offices and opens the possibility for clients to search for the best deals and lawyers for their questions. Global competition can of course not be fully excluded but seems less likely for 'smaller' languages, however. That does not exclude the possibility of law firms' mergers or take-overs, and the growth of conglomerates and networks of expertise and collaboration, in which knowledge is shared and spread, and access to any legal information and expertise is available and can be resorted to.

Increasingly, legal information is available, for those who seek it, on the web. Patients check the web before choosing a doctor and paying a visit and after the visit they check the diagnosis and treatment on the web and search whether the medication given to them is the best and the latest. They share experiences with and seek advice from fellow patients. Would it be too farfetched to assume that this also happens with legal information; or that entrepreneurial lawyers build expertise networks providing for legal answers to questions and legal advice for an agreed price for more complicated issues? Global competition will not replace local legal clinics, where local people can walk in with the papers (but let's bear in mind here that we cannot be sure for how many years they will receive letters! It is much more likely that the bill will be made available to a client on a website and that business is being done through the Internet, without 'paper' work; people who can do that can also forward those electronic files to a lawyer for advice!).

It seems also fair to assume that legal work will increasingly be clustered in issues, or conglomerates of issues: consumer issues, welfare, labour/social, corporate, and others where consultants assist the clients with ranges of problems and not only with the legal issue. This implies multidisciplinary advice with legal aspects being one part of the overall advice. These aspects raise the issue of the increasing importance of specialization or knowledge of sectors of industry, possibly more than specific specialized legal knowledge. Lawyers and legal counsels will have to become advisers, with knowledge of the relevant sector, of the intricacies of doing business in general and in that sector, and who can support the business client in a general way, and not purely limited to legal issues.

To conclude, one can say that the legal employment domain is in motion. IT and competition, and new modes of work, must have consequences for law schools. The organization of the labour market will change and will certainly diversify much more. The trend is for more graduates to work as independent lawyers. The trend is for more visibility and more connections through the Internet and for flexible work space in the office, or no office at all, and a trend for clustering issues. Law schools must educate their students for future labour markets; law schools must therefore reflect on the changes, and prepare the students for those changes. That also implies that law schools must adapt and integrate, in what they teach and how they teach it, these trends of how lawyers will perform their work. They will also influence how law schools are organized and how they organize the curriculum and the delivery of education.

Why would law schools need so many offices for faculty? Certainly they need space for their research, and we want faculty to be at a law school for interactions among faculty and with students. For those purposes, flexible work spaces might suffice, as well as faculty being present and visible on Internet platforms, where communication with students can also occur; where faculty can post papers and drafts and solicit for comments and where students can do the same. In many law schools there is a sharp distinction between students and faculty, and the presence of academics, in their offices, does not seem to really remedy this distinction. However, open communication could be a tool to remedy this divide. I suggest that law schools reflect upon their internal structure and the way they have organized housing and one-way communication with students. Specifically post-graduate students and PhD students might be involved in faculty activities and exchanges. We certainly witness that academics communicate increasingly through electronic journals and forums (such as SSRN) and share the writing of articles with electronic media. I argue here that with the labour market being in flux in this respect as well, that law schools bring these models within their walls.

Legal education has to operate in and for a changing labour market of lawyers, where global competition has increased; in which IT has flourished; where others than lawyers offer legal commodities as services; where information is more easily available; and in which legal service providers will operate in teams with other specialties. In this changing labour market where the global markets operate in English; and where English is taught globally and relevant legal education is increasingly offered in English, the dominance of American legal culture in business transactions will decrease. Chinese legal education makes great strides in benefiting from American and European legal expertise and will certainly influence the legal labour market.

A generally shared notion among authors is that legal education will have to diversify, in programs, specialties and focus on segments of the labour market. Students will have to be given the possibilities to specialize and to re-specialize (with continued legal education). Lawyers will have to be taught to operate in teams and in multidisciplinary settings and clients will seek integral advice from people who master a specific domain (for example for mergers: legal, accounting and business aspects).

Lawyers will have to compete with other legal service providers (paralegals, legal assistants, legal advisors) who provide a specific legal service commodity cheaper and quicker. This resembles the phenomenon in health care that more and more work is done by nurse-practitioners or general practitioners or, in the field of eye doctors, by optometrists. They can do the first check and perform regular eye checks and refer specialist cases to the medical specialists. This is cheaper and quicker.

Legal education has to adapt and to diversify. The propositions which have been advanced can be summarized as the following:

1. enable students to specialize and to re-specialize;
2. build other relevant sciences into legal education;
3. build a profile and a curriculum according to the profile;
4. enable students from other disciplines (medicine, economics, business, sciences, accounting) to acquire certificates in law so that they can work in patents (sciences); mergers; health care, corporate domain as in-house (legal) counsel, etcetera;
5. Introduce IT information technologies and their relevance for legal services in the curriculum;
6. Build consortia to strengthen the profile and the mission: with the regional labour market or in international consortia;
7. Use combinations of in-person teaching and distance learning;
8. Ensure that the costs of legal education and the returns for the students are in balance;
9. Offer languages and international exchanges and knowledge of the international aspects of modern day lawyering to the students;
10. Collaborate with other law schools (which have different missions) and with schools that offer economics, business, accounting, medicine, sciences, in order to offer students diverse specializations and tracks.

PART B

STUDENTS

Chapter 3

INTAKE OF STUDENTS

Students and their backgrounds are probably as diverse as the labour markets and the jobs they might qualify for after graduation. The diversity does exist within jurisdictions, but also for the law schools with an internationally diverse intake. Within domestic jurisdictions the diversity differs: it is less prevalent in highly selective systems and a uniform school system, and it is more the case when intake is non-selective and open and students with different backgrounds and qualifications and interests may be admitted or must be admitted. For law schools which are also open to international students, diversity increases, because of cultural backgrounds, the quality of the language, and the school system from which a student originates. Law schools must therefore be focused upon a diversity of labour perspectives (in many cases) and take into account a diversity of student intake, and a diversity of levels, streams, tracks and interests.

Motivation, study attitude and study capabilities and study discipline can differ to a great extent between students; and more so in those instances when the student intake is not very coherent. In my law school in Maastricht, after having developed English-taught programs, we noted a sharp rise in the intake of foreign students. These students came, bringing with them a strong motivation (choosing a foreign school and charting out a new course of study, previously uncommon and unknown) and a background of study discipline and eagerness to perform well. This has influenced the other (Dutch) students who suddenly had to compete with eager, hard-working and motivated foreign students. Overall it has benefited the quality of the programs, which in the end benefits all students.

A law school's curriculum should be focused first of all upon the labour market; for what do we prepare the students; how do we take into account the employability of our graduates? That was the subject of the previous chapter. Now it is time to turn to the beginning of a legal study and discuss the second issue which is how to define the capabilities of the students' at intake. That will determine the gaps between input and output and will help us assess what to do and how to prioritize the teaching and the set-up of the curriculum.

Here we could distinguish between the US (and South Korean) model on the one hand and the European (continental model) on the other hand. In the US law schools intake is of students who have successfully passed high school and college.

They therefore already possess a university degree. They are generally older, also because quite a few have worked after college. It is fair to say, they already received an academic training and acquired some maturity and made a conscious choice to go to law school and study law.

In continental Europe the average age of 1L's is very much lower; most countries admit students after having completed secondary school, albeit a secondary school characterized as pre-university education. This leads to an average entry age of 18 or 19 years old students entering university for a legal education.

Two early observations seem obvious. The first is that, because of the relatively low age, motivation and consciousness of choice might seem more problematic. The second is that academic maturity on average might be less.

These two observations are redressed in some European countries (Scandinavian countries, UK) by allowing the universities to select their students' intake on the basis of academic merit (grades obtained in secondary school, admission exam/ test). Apart from the link with labour market perspectives (limiting intake has an impact on output and therefore on the labour market and competition within the labour market and prices and fees of the legal profession, sometimes even protecting the labour market and the legal professions), this system also allows universities to select the best.

Selection of students certainly also takes place in the US, but, unlike in the US, in the aforementioned countries the maximum number of places for studying law in the country is limited. Not being selected for one of the Finnish law schools means it is impossible to study law (in Finland); not being selected in the US means that you have to adjust your preferences for a school and accept the admission in a lower-ranked school.

Many European countries admit all students who meet the requirements of having the proper secondary school degree, without selection and without a *numerus fixus* (Belgium and France for example). In Italy and Spain universities may and do apply entrance tests or set further admission criteria, without however in most cases seeming to drastically limit access to law schools. The systems of low or no selection in access lead to sometimes crowded law schools, to many students who find it hard to cope and who therefore study longer than the allotted time,[1] and to students who, after a short or long while, change study, after having discovered that the law is not the best choice for them.

An added aspect is that, because of the variety of jobs available for law graduates in European countries, studying law is considered as an academic study for a nice job after university and not necessarily a legal job. This shows a resemblance to the increasing popularity of the study of psychology in recent years. Or it resembles the motivation for students in other countries to study history as a general academic undergraduate degree.

1 Italian statistics for instance showed that in 2008 5,480 law students did not complete their exams within the legal time (with 5,068 new law students): <http://en.istat.it/>.

The younger first year students are, and the more diverse and challenging the legal education is, as I have described all skills and future career paths where many changes are about to occur, the more necessary it is to have a selection process before students enter law school. This must be a selection process which takes into account capabilities, competences, skills, motivation and stamina or study discipline. This means that I am not in favour of solely taking into account the grades in secondary school but also envisage testing other aspects.

In the US students are tested through the LSAT: Law School Admission Test.[2] From the website of the LSAT Council I have taken the following information about LSAT:

> The test consists of five 35-minute sections of multiple-choice questions. Four of the five sections contribute to the test taker's score. The unscored section, commonly referred to as the variable section, typically is used to pretest new test questions or to preequate new test forms. The placement of this section will vary. A 35-minute writing sample is administered at the end of the test. LSAC does not score the writing sample, but copies of the writing sample are sent to all law schools to which you apply.
>
> What the Test Measures
>
> The LSAT is designed to measure skills that are considered essential for success in law school: the reading and comprehension of complex texts with accuracy and insight; the organization and management of information and the ability to draw reasonable inferences from it; the ability to think critically; and the analysis and evaluation of the reasoning and arguments of others.
>
> The three multiple-choice question types in the LSAT are:
>
> - *Reading Comprehension Questions*
>   These questions measure the ability to read, with understanding and insight, examples of lengthy and complex materials similar to those commonly encountered in law school. The Reading Comprehension section contains four sets of reading questions, each consisting of a selection of reading material, followed by five to eight questions that test reading and reasoning abilities.
> - *Analytical Reasoning Questions*
>   These questions measure the ability to understand a structure of relationships and to draw logical conclusions about that structure. You are asked to reason deductively from a set of statements and rules or principles that describe relationships among persons, things, or events. Analytical Reasoning questions reflect the kinds of complex analyses that a law student performs in the course of legal problem solving.
> - *Logical Reasoning Questions*
>   These questions assess the ability to analyse, critically evaluate, and complete arguments as they occur in ordinary language. Each Logical Reasoning question requires the test taker to read and comprehend a short passage, then answer a question about it. The questions are designed to assess a wide range of skills involved in thinking critically, with an emphasis on skills that are central to legal

2 <http://www.lsac.org/#slide2>.

> reasoning. These skills include drawing well-supported conclusions, reasoning by analogy, determining how additional evidence affects an argument, applying principles or rules, and identifying argument flaws.[3]

In other fields such as for MBA Admission, schools have opted for GRE (Graduate Record Examinations) tests.[4] The GRE general test contains three sections: Verbal Reasoning, which assesses the ability to analyse and evaluate written material and synthesize information obtained from it; Quantitative Reasoning which tests basic mathematical skills; and Analytical Writing which tests critical thinking and analytical writing skills. I am not aware of law schools using GRE as one of the selection tools for admission policies, but it might seem that it has many relevant aspects with added value for law school admissions.

For LSAT and GRE it is important to bear in mind that they both are being set up and administered for admission for graduate programs. Since studying law in many (European) countries is an undergraduate bachelor, as well as a graduate (master) project, a simple reliance upon LSAT or GRE for admission in law schools is not possible. However, especially in the European context, it seems sensible to rely upon these testing methodologies for admission purposes. The introduction of and the development of testing tools related to the study of law will improve intake and therefore the quality of law students and graduates. It will also be an important message for prospective students to reflect upon their choice of study and what it entails seriously.

In Sweden selection takes place through a mixed system of grades in secondary school and the results in the SweSAT (Swedish Scholastic Aptitude Test).[5] The SweSAT tests Vocabulary, Quantitative reasoning, Reading comprehension, Interpretation of diagrams, tables and maps, General information, and English reading comprehension. Universities have autonomy to decide on the admission procedures and selection devices. Since the government fixes the number of places and the number of prospective students is substantially higher a selection is crucial. Practice shows that usually 60% of the study places are allocated on the basis of the average grades from secondary school and 40% on the basis of the test scores. On top of this, universities may set other requirements related to the specific field of study.

In many European countries, such as France, Germany, Italy and the Netherlands, access to education in law schools is open to all applicants with the proper secondary school degree but irrespective of grades. This has led to a high failure rate and low throughput. In recent years Dutch universities have been permitted to expel those students who show insufficient progress in the first year of study. Although the precise criteria differ, the average criterion employed by Dutch law schools is presently approximately 40 ects credits (out of the 60 ects for the first year). Those students who do not succeed in obtaining 40 credits will not be allowed to continue with their studies. Although precise data are not generally

3 Further information about LSAT and LSAC: Pashley, Thornton & Duffy 2005.

4 <www.ets.org/gre>.

5 Arts. 20-23 Higher Education Ordinance (1993:100).

available, my estimates are that approximately 30% of the first year intake will be expelled after one year of studying law. For that reason Maastricht University Faculty of Law started an experiment in 2011 with the introduction of a compulsory questionnaire. This questionnaire replaces the absence of a real selection instrument such as GRE for undergraduate studies. The questionnaire asks for grades in secondary school (specifically in some courses such as math, languages and history), motivation for studying law, and dedication to study (study discipline). According to the scores, each individual student will be ranked in three categories: green means that we expect that student to meet all qualifications to study law; orange indicates a 'pass': this prospective student is made aware of our concerns, but the concerns are not that serious that we feel they warrant a rejection; the category red finally implies that we have grave concerns as to the suitability of the student for the study of law and therefore invite the student for a compulsory interview (in person or through Skype) to share our concerns and where there is an insufficient response from the student, to inform him/her of our strong conviction that studying law is not the suitable option.

The follow up of this questionnaire approach is to monitor all first year students carefully on the basis of the questionnaire data and responses with the questions in mind: have we set the correct criteria for green, orange and red? How quickly do we perceive the need to give extra assistance and study guidance (or advice about other avenues of study) to the students? Specifically those who scored less (orange/red) on the questionnaire can be monitored adequately. For that purpose we have trained the tutors in the first year courses, who also have been allotted a role as mentors, to pay close attention and to set up meetings at an early stage with those students who appear to have problems in keeping up with the teaching pace and schedules. We have called this approach 'Matching and Binding': it is a selection process with a positive approach, namely to try to engage in a discussion with (those) students about their academic study plan where we have the impression that there appears to be a mismatch between their track record and motivation and our expectations of pre-requisites and qualifications. We intend to bring about a process of self-reflection in the students. This process cannot simply end with the questionnaire or interview; therefore our commitment is to continue following the students during the first courses in the first year, monitoring them and, if necessary, offering them study guidance and assistance, or guiding them to another study and career path. It is a soft pre-law school selection with advice, supervision, counseling and guidance, and with a creation of awareness with the students about what it means and entails to study law.

How, if we want to do it, is the best way to select students? I have already referred to LSAT, GRE and SweSAT: the latter two tests have as an important part in their tests Quantitative reasoning. This coincides with American literature about access to undergraduate education that 'highest level of math courses completed having the greatest weight' as an academic predictor of success, as Camara states.[6] He continues by saying that

> 'There is a substantial body of research demonstrating that using admissions test scores in combination with a measure of high-school grades (...) produces higher validity coefficients than using either measure alone (...). The combination of scores and prior grades yields more accurate predictions of college grades than does either alone. Additional predictors have substantially less impact on validity coefficients once high school performance and admission tests are employed. (...).'

The addition of three SATII subject tests adds only a little to the validity coefficient. That is also the case when non-cognitive predictors are used.[7]

This leaves two further questions to be addressed. One is why in many instances so much effort is put into research and attempts to add additional predictors to the existing tests. And the second question is, why is it not better to allow students to enter university without any selection process whatsoever, pretending that university in itself might be a better selection instrument and predictor than reliance upon objective tests. The first question is also posed by Camara: his response is the prospect that alternative predictors (such as personal qualities and experiences and characteristics) may increase diversity in university and in classes.

The second question has, to my knowledge, not been properly researched; is it indeed more cost-effective to first allow all students in and have them discover during the first year whether they are well equipped to successfully complete the program? Also, we have to take into account that the presence of less qualified students affects the quality and level of a program and might hamper overall progress and quality. Data in the Netherlands (with open access to most academic programs) seems to suggest that this practice leads to a low study completion rate and low study progress.[8] The figures indicate that only 47% of the intake in 2006 completed the four year university curriculum in four years. The intake in 2005 had a 46% completion rate in four years and 62% in five. The intake in 2004 had a 44% completion rate after four years; 60% after five and 70% after six years of study. The intake in 2001 had a completion rate of 80% after 9 years. There is also a slow trend that the completion rates creep up (with 1% per year or so), but the figures show my point about the efficiency and effectiveness of the Dutch university selection mechanisms. Then we also have to bear in mind that the figures are university-wide averages and that progress rates for law are the lowest in the country, compared to studies such as medicine and business (in those domains a mechanism exists to

6 Camara 2005, p. 82-83.

7 Camara 2005, p. 97-98.

8 I do realize that other factors also account for these conclusions: the study loan system, the state of the economy, the quality of secondary education. The data about university study progress and completion rates are to be found at: <http://statline.cbs.nl/StatWeb/publication/?VW=T&DM=SLNL&PA=71199ned&D1=0-7&D2=0&D3=a&D4=0&D5=0&D6=0&D7=a&HD=080328-1132&HDR=G5,G3,G1,G4,T&STB=G2,G6>.

control intake because of a *numerus fixus* and a selection partially based upon secondary school grades!).

Leah M. Christensen[9] concluded from research done that the grade for lawyering skills was the strongest predictor of law student success. Students who do well in the first year on Skills will be more successful during the remainder of law school. Her second finding was that students who did well in lawyering skills are mastery-goal oriented students (as opposed to performance-goal oriented students). Mastery-oriented learners in her definition are focused on learning as something valuable and meaningful in itself. These students work for their own progress. Performance-oriented learners are more interested in grades and exam scores: they pursue activities at which they are more likely to shine; mastery-oriented students love learning, as she puts it. Lawyering skills are related to law school success; and so is mastery-goal orientation correlated to lawyering skills grades. These findings lead Christensen to argue in favour of integrated skills classes in the first year of law school, and secondly to create Mastery-Oriented Classrooms in the law school curriculum, through collaborative learning, having students provide class introductions (use students as teachers) and asking students for their feedback on the course.

Her interesting research fits in with other findings about effective learning by students (learning by doing and teaching your peers); and it links with the need to train skills. New in her study was the correlation between the two learning strategies and skills and between skills and law school success. The latter aspect would indeed lead to intensive skills training in (the beginning of) the first year. Specifically this fits well when the first year is a selective tool, but also because skills assist in becoming better lawyers and in studying more effectively and more successfully in the consecutive years. Finally, the link between mastery-orientation (and skills) and effective study progress shows the need to design a first year in law school carefully and with the purpose in mind to set a mastery atmosphere, skills training and a safe but challenging academic climate (academic fit). Here we must also integrate questions about a student's study attitude in pre-law school questionnaires (admission tests or non-compulsory/ non-binding questionnaires).

Secondary school results and grades do predict study success in university: longitudinal research in the Netherlands by Annema & Ooijevaar found that better scores on the final secondary school exam did coincide with a better chance to graduate within eight years; and students with a better average did graduate quicker than others.[10] An additional factor is to also take into account whether a student had an uninterrupted school career without delays: for the Netherlands this implies graduating from secondary school at the age of 18 years. Recent research in

9 The Power of Skills Training: A Study of Lawyering Skills rates as the Strongest Predictor of Law School Success (Or in Other Words, It's Time for Legal Education to get Serious About Skills Training If we Care About How Our Students Learn), <http://ssrn.com/abstract=1235531>.

10 Annema & Ooijevaar 2011. They raise the question whether grades for Dutch, English and Math are important as being specifically important for predicting study success.

Leiden University found that indeed there was a correlation between secondary school final exam grades and the completion of the first year of law within one or two years (and consecutively completing legal studies and scoring better grades on average). However, the conclusion was also that, although the secondary school results can be used for selection purposes, in order to achieve a substantial effect on first year completion rates, a rather strict selection is necessary, which will however imply that many applicants have to be rejected even though they had the skills and competences.[11]

As I have indicated before, within secondary school results we might have to probe further as to the quality of prediction for some specific grades, such as for Math, and/or History and/or Language. Secondly, it would have been interesting to link the completion rates to the ages of the students and their (un)interrupted school histories. Finally, it leaves the question unanswered as to the fit between desirable completion rates, profile of the law school, the way the first year is set up in order (as I will indicate below) to create the best possible environment in that first year to ensure that completion rates go up and lead to a sufficient level. With the profile of the law school, I refer to how the school wants to establish its market share: as a large and open institution, which wants to accommodate as many students as possible? Or as a selective institution which aims for the best and for the best only and wants to select for that purpose. This certainly must be an important factor in determining selection policies and setting the accompanying criteria.

These considerations and aspects, as the question posed by Camara about the desires to promote diversity in classrooms and my plea in this book for a comparative approach in legal education and an accompanying international classroom, do indeed make it worthwhile to probe further into the issue of selection policies. When we trust selection tests as generally reliable predictors of academic success, why resort to other intake criteria which might dilute the predictive value but may lead to an international and diverse classroom? Does that not mean that we set aside an objective selection mechanism? Do we select for academic success only or do we also want to recreate the outside world in our academic programs and classes, and in particular in law, in order to have the world we teach in a comparative manner, represented in our classes?

First of all we have to remember that in a diverse world of law schools, law schools will never accept students who score below a specific threshold. The (absolute minimum) threshold is ultimately set by the law school itself and/or the domestic legislature or other stakeholder such as the bar. The setting of a selection (above the minimum) threshold does probably relate to the strategy of the school and is linked to the numbers of applicants and number of places. It ought however (as a minimum) to be foremost related to the prediction that all students with the minimum threshold can and do satisfactorily graduate and that students who do not meet the minimum threshold do not and cannot meet the requirements. That is,

11 De Gruijter, Yildiz & 't Hart 2006.

the minimum threshold is supposed to indicate a match between law school entry and output. Unfortunately, that seems not to be the case in those European countries with an open intake.

For many European law schools this constitutes a shift in paradigm: what they (have to) do is simply accept all applicants and adopt a size of teaching which fits all incoming students. Setting a strategy, laws permitting, of being a selective institution and decreasing the size (and therefore possibly also the scope of faculty) is an unnatural thing to do for them. However, I believe that diversification, some schools being more selective, other schools more international, some focusing upon the corporate world and others on the bar and /or the civil service, will be the key issues for the future. Such a diversification will imply selection and the choice of an appropriate size: big enough to be successful, small enough to offer quality.

When a law school (in those cases it is allowed to do so) has set up a selection process, it will have to find its niche in the market. Will there be more applicants than available spots? What will be a minimum threshold below which a school will not want to admit applicants (and this threshold can consist of test scores, GPA, in conjunction with other criteria, relating to personality and diversity of class and class composition). Setting these criteria will be a difficult exercise; in the USA a lot of data is available about the validity of LSAT and about matriculation and about the link between LSAT and employment skills. In Europe this data is scarce so law schools have to work with the US and Swedish experiences and work towards other selection processes and standards, adapted to the domestic system in force. Such as the 'selection' process which has recently been employed in Maastricht law school for the first time in 2011.

LSAC has undertaken projects to work out procedures to combine LSAT and GPA scores with goals of diversification of their intake and classes. These goals might be part of a strategy to have an international class room; or to reflect the population composition in a given country or area; or to offer a balanced future workforce for the labour market, or because one is of the opinion that a diverse student body is essential for university and for future employment. I will not go into detail here but refer to the article by Peter J. Pashley, Andrea E. Thornton and Jennifer R. Duffy, referred to *supra*.

Boon and Whyte[12] point at the large growth in HE (higher education) which has led to an heterogeneous student body with many first generation HE students. They refer to the findings in international studies that these students have more difficulty to cope and that dropout rates are constantly high. These dropout rates relate to the transition from secondary school and the reliance in university on self-responsibility and independent learning. They argue that the most significant variable, and sensitive indicator of disadvantage is, more than socio-economic status, their status as first generation HE students. This confirms my conclusion that it is important for retention and dropout rates for law schools to guide students in the very beginning of law school and assist them in how to study, in cultural aspects

12 Boon & Whyte 2010, p. 201.

of law schools and teach students about expectations from the faculty. Do not simply take for granted that new generations of HE students understand what going to university and studying law implies and requires. We have to accept that new generations of students, who have the minimum qualifications to enter law schools, might still need assistance and explanations.

I have explained before that in many European countries selection does not take place prior to law school admission but during the study of law. One of the presumptions in that respect is that a first year of study is also an important factor for academic success. In an empirical study by Beekhoven, De Jong and Van Hout,[13] one of the results shown was that a first year is important, allowing students to orient themselves, but also to increase self-selection and a high(er) perceived likelihood of success. They conclude that for academic success

> 'the amount of integration [in the program and with fellow students and staff] influences the perceived likelihood of graduating in that same period and that conversely the likelihood of graduation affects the amount of integration in the forthcoming period'.[14]

Expectations of the students as to the duration of studies and the acquisition of the first (propaedeutic) year, as well as their satisfaction during and with the study and the academic fit, are according to this research, variables with the largest influence on the academic progress of university students. Interesting in this research are the findings that the students' own expectations do matter and that satisfaction and academic fit have an impact on success rate.

This implies that law schools with relatively high dropout rates must invest in these aspects of students' engagement and motivation. Motivation is not just a factor which is present for a first year intake and subsequently is there to stay, but is also related to study success and academic fit/engagement with the study.

These findings might lead law schools to undertake the following actions:

1. engage with prospective students about their expectations and study patterns and behavior (mastery-orientation); this input could be made a part of the Matching & Binding questionnaire, of admissions papers or of an interview, if such an interview is part of the admissions procedure;
2. ensure that students are being quizzed on their satisfaction with the program and the courses and follow up on the outcomes in individual cases as well as organization wise;
3. facilitate tutors, teachers, mentors and counselors to focus also on the students' expectations, and on their satisfaction and academic fit as well as study progress in the first year and the students' successfully obtaining the first year credits. Success in the first year, and the academic satisfaction in that same

13 Beekhoven, De Jong & Van Hout 2002.

14 Beekhoven, De Jong & Van Hout 2002, p. 597; Sousa 2011, p. 89-90, also underlines the importance of what he calls the Learning and Classroom Climate.

year of study, will influence the students' expectations for the next years and this will lead to better results in those subsequent years;
4. ensure a cohesive academic environment already in the first year with activities and events which promote satisfaction and specifically the integration and academic fit: introduction camps; active study associations, extra-curricular activities and social events; tutorial groups that have a fixed composition for at least one semester, stimulate group work and joint projects as from day one, or maybe even the whole first year, fostering social contacts and a sentiment of belonging.

Even when a law school does not have the legal possibilities or tools to select students before intake, many possibilities exist for them to engage with first year students and to influence their choices and to improve upon the quality of the intake. One means is to create awareness among the students about the substance of studying law and the exigencies of this academic study. I believe that a law school, which actively relates to the (prospective) students and promotes its values and requirements, will achieve results. Students and faculty will be sensitive for clear messages and transparent practices accordingly.

When a legal system allows for selection of students it is important to define the best selection parameters, which will also assist the law school to implement its strategy. To quote Christensen and Eyring: 'The most successful schools make careful choices about the types of students they serve.'[15] Strategy, and related tools to implement the strategy, as well as the selection which fits with this strategy, must be aligned. Selection is a tool to achieve certain goals; and selection, if used, must be established in such manner that there is a clear fit with these goals. For selecting only the intellectually best students, grades and exams are the best mechanism. However, if the composition of class, or diversity, or catering for the regional needs, are also to play a role, it is important to identify these aspects and to specify how they will play a role in the selection criteria and selection process.

15 Christensen & Eyring 2011, p. 348.

Chapter 4

KNOWLEDGE OF THE LAW

Lawyers must be knowledgeable. But what does that mean? Must they be able to recite codes and statutes? What makes a good and knowledgeable lawyer? One of the first things which comes to mind is a wise person, with diplomatic and oral debating skills, who masters the facts and the factual nuances and the relevant legal intricacies.

In the previous chapter I argued that law schools must train skills and must ensure that the students will become skilful lawyers. In the next chapter I will delve further into how to do that and what devices and courses are available to achieve that purpose. In this chapter, I intend to give some perspective on the substantive contents of studying law. What precisely is, or ought to be, the subject of study? How should details and structure and skills and analysis be taught, and how should skills of analysis, reflection and writing and debating, be balanced with knowledge of the legal system(s) as such, as a system/or as systems, with the necessary proportion of specific cases, details and sub items?

I will comment upon the length of the curriculum in Chapter 7 and argue that the substance, breadth and depth of a curriculum are linked to the intake, to the expectations and requirements of the labour market, as well as to the length of the curriculum and the rigor with which study discipline is enforced. The more space that is available and the more effectively students study, the better all requirements can be met for more of the students. A short curriculum, with high demands on the substance and the students, is facilitated by the fact that the intake is connected to a strict selection process so that those students who can manage the high pressure in a short time-frame can be selected. The faculty may also enforce students' study loads and monitors study hours in order to fully use all available time.

As a preliminary comment let us first define the concept 'knowledge of the law'. Of course, graduates must have knowledge about and of the law and be able to work with it. But what does that mean precisely? Does it mean that all students must have had courses on every aspect of the law with specialized courses on every imaginable subject? And, if we are able to define which domains a student must master, what does that mean: that the student must know all the ins and outs and recent case law? This may be more so the case when we come to the core of the curriculum, which probably is also less open for constant changes because it concerns the main domains of the law, where details might and do change but the basics remain unaltered, more or less.

I do not think there is much disagreement among lawyers as to what constitute the basic fundamental legal subjects in a curriculum. The absolute musts (leaving aside how they must be taught and to what skills they must lead) are: private law (contracts, property, tort); procedural law; constitutional and administrative law; criminal law and criminal procedure; company and business law; European law (institutions and substantive); international law (human rights, trade). These are also subjects which have a prime place in any European law school in the undergraduate (Bologna first cycle phase) programs; for schools outside Europe one might simply delete European law and have a survey of hard core legal subjects.

For the UK a joint Announcement (of the Bar and the Law Society) sets out the requirements for the so-called 'qualifying degrees'. The main requirement is (apart from skills) the inclusion of seven subject areas. These are: Public law (including Constitutional Law, Administrative Law and Human Rights); Law of the European Union; Criminal Law; Obligations, including Contract, Restitution and Tort; Property Law; and Equity and the Law of Trust.[1]

In Australia the Law Admissions Consultative Committee (LACC; also called the Priestley Committee), has recommended that for admission to the legal profession a student must undertake a study of at least three years and must complete the following 11 (Priestley 11) subjects: Criminal Law and Procedure; Torts, Contracts, Property, Equity (including Trusts), Company Law, Administrative Law, Federal and State Constitutional Law, Civil Procedure, Evidence, Ethics and Professional Responsibility.[2]

Next to this core I distinguish a second category of courses that are widely available in many law schools but are not generally mandatory: private international law, competition law, environmental law, labour law, family law, tax law, comparative law, commercial law, financial law. Courses such as philosophy of law, sociology and legal/roman history also fit in this category but are not generally mandatory but available in the undergraduate phase in many schools.

And finally there are many legal subjects one will find as electives and optional subjects and specifically in master (second Bologna cycle) programs: (im)migration law; public procurement; social security law; health law; construction law; corporate social responsibility; natural resources law; humanitarian law; interna-

1 Joint Statement on Qualifying Law Degrees (London, Law Society and the Council of Legal Education, August 1999) <www.sra.org.uk/documents/students/academic-stage/academic jointstate.pdf>.

2 <www.lawadmissions.vic.gov.au/admission_requirements>. There was also a Priestley 12 including practical subjects necessary for legal practice. They have however been replaced by a set of competency requirements developed by the Australasian Professional Legal Education Council (APLEC). (<www.aplec.asn.au/Pdf/Competency_Standards_for_Entry_Level_Lawyers.pdf>). See further chapter 7 about Skills.

tional criminal law; mediation and arbitration; forensics; consumer law; languages; etcetera.

It is at the discretion of the law school whether or not the second and third categories of courses are included in the curriculum. This will depend on the mission and focus of the school, the domestic requirements, the length of the curriculum, the space allotted to skills and comparative law and the quality of the intake.

The first category of courses seems to be imperative: students must be taught these courses. Leaving aside that students must also be trained to understand a legal system/legal systems; to understand and work with legal concepts; to apply legal doctrines to problems presented to them; to reason logically and convincingly, what does it mean that students must be taught the first category of courses? Students must be able to grasp contract law (entering into a contract, termination of a contract, execution of a contract, and the use of special contracts, such as employment contracts). They must recognize contractual issues when they arise; they must be able to relate to statutory provisions and the fundamental issues in the case law; they must be able to read and understand/have read and have understood the main textbook in this domain; and they must be able to research the (detailed) issues which they have not been taught. In short, students must be able to describe and apply the relevant and main doctrines of contract law, with its main rules and exceptions, understanding the workings of it. This same approach can be applied to the other first category legal domains: property law, tort, procedural law, constitutional and administrative law, criminal law and criminal procedure, company and business law, European law and international law.

One way to specify the first category knowledge informally is to (domestically) reach agreement not only about abstract statements defining the knowledge students must obtain but by defining and writing the textbooks which meet the criteria to covering the category 1 domains and doing so with the necessary depth, scope and academic problem solving. Such a description will be an indication to the labour market and set realistic expectations. Students can also easily check the level of their education. This will hopefully not lead to one textbook which fits all but a variety of textbooks, from which law schools can choose, while knowing that they generate the sufficient level of knowledge. The list of books, to be drawn up by groups of peers, will evidently be open to amendment: new books can be added. They do not provide an exhaustive list of knowledge obtained by graduates, nor of their skills, but they define the minimum and necessary level of legal knowledge in the category 1 domains, which are the domains prescribed by law (or understood through consensus among stakeholders) in a given country for educating lawyers.

The main question that always arises with professors of specific courses is about the level of detail. Courses tend to be filled increasingly with more cases and more in-depth details and intricacies. I do not believe that this is the way to go.[3] I do not deny that students must be taught how to discover and research exhaustively very specific details and exceptions and very detailed statutory rules, case law and subordinate regulation, but that serves as a lesson to learn how to do it and not as lessons to undertake in every course about every subject in every legal domain. It is more important that students acquire this skill rather than memorize knowledge. We know that the devil is always in the details, and that lesson must be taught to students, but we also know that details cannot be memorized in all domains of the law for proper application. Students will forget them after the exam; however what we can teach them is to be always aware of details and how to research them and, more importantly, how details fit in the grand scheme of things (the concepts and the legal domains). Once students realize the structure and oversee the whole picture, it will be easier for them to pick up and relate the details. Learning the details in all domains is an effort which might distract from the overall pictures; it is impossible to do for all legal concepts and will lead to useless knowledge, because precisely the details tend to change (the half-life of legal knowledge).

This issue is connected to my other arguments about pedagogy and teaching methodology, which impact upon understanding the structure of law, the application of legal concepts, and the creative interpretation and solution of issues. Once students can work with the fundamentals and structures and we have worked with them with examples and going into detail, as well as having also worked extensively on skills, the graduates will be skilful lawyers who will be qualified to work with black letter law, as well as with contextual issues and complex problems.

A curriculum must certainly reflect what one is aiming for. When we intend to educate students to grasp the basics of the above-mentioned legal domains, we have to seek ways how best to do it. Do we teach private law in one big course? Or do we cut it into smaller pieces? Or do we teach private law twice: the first time in the beginning at an introductory level and the second time at a later stage and at a more advanced level? These approaches all have their pros and cons. Teaching private law in one course has the advantage of conveying the internal consistency of private law and seeing the links between property, contracts and tort. Disadvantages certainly are that one big course is not easy to swallow for students, that it neglects the links with other legal domains, and that students can for compensate flaws in their knowledge of property law, for example, by doing better in the exam on contracts. I therefore tend to suggest the following: to offer an introductory course (introduction to law, which coherently introduces students into the basics of the legal system), and afterwards offer two courses at two levels on the various aspects of private law, first an introductory course and an advanced course at a later stage. This later stage has the advantage that students get the various subjects a second time and can deepen their knowledge of the introductory courses. The curriculum

3 In the previous chapter I referred in that respect to Sousa and his plea for pruning courses and a curriculum.

could be illustrated as two concentric circles, the first providing a foundation and the second allowing students to build upon earlier courses:

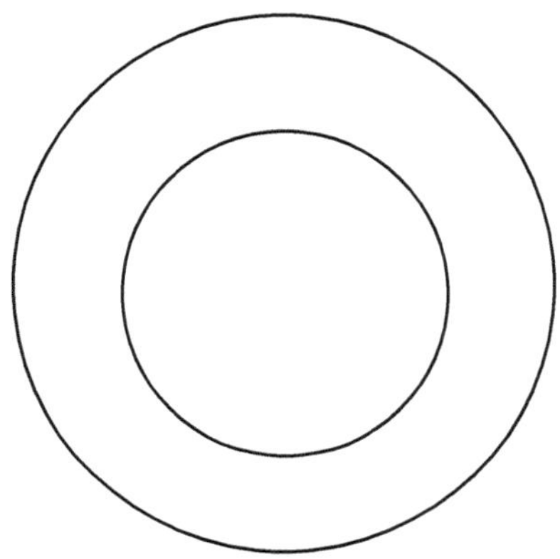

Secondly, I propose smaller courses/modules to teach the various aspects of private law, thereby limiting the possibilities for compensation and ensuring that all students have grasped all fundamental aspects of the different subjects of private law. These smaller courses assist the students to cope and a fail has limited consequences, more limited than a fail in a major one semester or whole-year course with one final end exam. It is also possible to concentrate the course and make it one coherent whole with an exam and writing and skills exercises, focusing the students' attention.

Electives can serve the purpose of allowing the students to choose a subject of one's particular liking, enabling them to carry out a more in-depth analysis and focus on one specific area. This approach certainly will raise the interests of the students and prepare them for later practice, where it is also expected of them to focus on a particular area. With electives, they are given the option to see what specialist domains are like, and how they are to be studied in a short period of time and how they link to the general body of law. Electives therefore serve as examples and as areas to test and exercise a student's ability to delve into a specific specialism, to link that to previous knowledge, and to be able to do so in a short time span. Electives therefore also do as much as training students' skills to study specifics and niches of the law. The offer of an elective, or at least of a course in which students train these skills, on top of regular basic category 1 courses, is for that matter a good part of a law curriculum. This is even more so the case when it leads to students crossing borders between legal domains and disciplines. In immigration law, for instance, students will have to combine international law (refugee law), European law (free movement of persons), domestic law (immigration law; family law), private international law and constitutional legal issues about pluriform legal systems and fundamental rights; and also it can be expected from the students to become familiar with demography, requirements of the labour market and migration patterns. Such a course therefore serves different purposes and can be useful in training skills, applying knowledge, seeking solutions and combining disciplines.

Superficially there appears to be a common perspective on the main subjects of study. The lists drawn up in that respect in many states are by and large very similar. However, they do not tell us what the domestic perspective is on the substance of these courses and the extent of details students have to acquire. The only possible comparison can be made in the EU Member States for European law; and for law schools in general, international law and international human rights. Even in these domains the differences are huge. European law differs greatly when we look at the number of ects credits as an absolute figure or related to the total number of credits for legal education. This also applies for international law: a compulsory important subject in some schools and in others a small, or only elective, course (or courses). I have added some data here indicating the number of credits in the bachelor (Bologna first cycle) program for European law and whether European law is a compulsory subject. Attention to European law ranges from the absence of a compulsory course (however with the possibility for students to pick EU law as an elective) to 6 ects courses and exceptionally to as much as 12 ects courses. This does not appear to be an awful lot, considering the growing impact of European Union law.

For European law schools, the text- or case books for European law also greatly differ, ranging from books in the domestic language or English text books.

The modes of delivery are also different: they range from classic lecture based teaching (with tutorials), to small scale teaching; and they range from a concentric-circles approach to offering chunks of legal domains, taught once; and there are differences between the sizes of courses (full year, one semester, modular).

Chapter 5

SKILLS

We are inclined to call good lawyers, skilful lawyers, people who master the skills of the trade. People who assist their clients and get the best deal for them and are capable of representing and defending their interests in negotiations, in litigation or in policy making and legislating.

In Chapter 2, I made a list of the 21 skills (competences) needed by all graduates and asked for by the labour market, and necessary for good employability. In this chapter I will raise the question how to convey, or train and educate students to obtain these skills.

A first question to be asked is whether to separate skills classes from substantive law classes, and to teach skills as such. I am not a proponent of a separate-classes doctrine. First of all there is a principled reason, because the skills have their added value in conjunction with the law and legal knowledge. We do not teach them only because we like them so much but because law and legal arguments and legal work improve with good skills. Secondly it saves time to teach skills always in connection with substantive law: students learn two lessons at the same time: a skills lesson about validity of arguments and precise reading and writing (or other skills) and about the law. Have students present an argument in class and it will help the student to learn the law better and give him the tools to present a paper.[1]

This means, however, that skills need to be carefully planned and fine-tuned in the curriculum annually and over the whole curriculum. Therein lies certainly one of the risks of this approach, that this fine-tuning might be difficult to achieve over all courses and the whole curriculum. It places high requirements on the organization and planning of the curriculum and the law school as a whole.

A second inherent danger is in the possibility that my preferred approach implies that all law teachers have all the necessary qualifications and desires to include an integrated skills approach, coordinated with other courses, in their own courses. They might, however, prefer to put more emphasis on the substance of the law, than on the relevant skills, or they might feel more at home in teaching the law

1 Christensen 2010, has noted that law students learn most effectively when doctrine and skills are combined. They learn more doctrine when it is placed within a skills or real-world context. Sullivan *et al.* 2007, have also argued for a bolder, more integrated approach of teaching doctrine and skills.

and less accustomed to give good feedback on skills. These risks or challenges could certainly be overcome with a good law school organization, a common and shared strategy, strong leadership and recruitment and promotion policy, and life-long learning and training for faculty as well.

We all have probably seen the examples of exams being graded where the examiner primarily takes into account the substance (does the student mention the right articles of the code; refers to the right cases; summarizes the proper arguments; and refers to the proper remedy or court procedure), neglecting at the same time that some writing errors have been committed, or that the student writes in sloppy language. What is the use of essay exams if we do not test the quality of the writing in the exam paper? However, to test the quality of the writing also requires the law teacher to correct students on the quality of their linguistic skills in class or to teach them the proper ways of formulating legal arguments.

Although I am a proponent of integrated skills, I can see the benefits of (sometimes) very specifically and separately addressing necessary skills, precisely in those cases where students demonstrably lack a sound basis for the integrated skills in law schools. Also, some skills could very well be taught by adjunct faculty or specialists, who target the relevant skills in particular. For instance, in moot court training, it seems wise to also have meetings in which students are being videotaped and are given feedback about their presentation skills: how they stand, move their hands, make eye contact with the judges etcetera. To have a specialist coming in to teach those lessons might be very worthwhile for the students. Another example of a special skills course could be to drill the (first year) students in the language of the program: if one finds that (some) students do not meet the necessary minimum linguistic requirements, it is obvious that such a situation has to be remedied as quickly as possible.

Integration of skills in the courses and the curriculum implies that one must organize a faculty-wide consensus on that approach, on the skills and their level, on how to distribute the skills in the curriculum and over the courses, on the expertise of the faculty to cope with skills and substantive law, on a consensus on how to test the skills and make it part of the exam requirements, and for which skills it might be necessary to have a separate track or course, because that might serve the interests of that skill in the best possible way.

Skills teaching generally is time consuming, requires exercises to be performed by the students, feedback by faculty, and a lot of intensive contacts between faculty and students. It therefore places burdens upon the finances of the school. Also, when one integrates skills and law courses, it implies small-scale teaching and small tutorial groups, not necessarily with the exclusion of lectures or larger educational settings, but educational settings must be created in which skills can be taught, trained and assessed properly.

It also implies that law schools are explicit in explaining the necessary skills to the students; where the skills are being given proper attention in the curriculum; how they are being assessed and that they are an important factor in the organization and content of classes, lectures, tests, and other work which must be performed by the students. The message must be conveyed that skills actually have to be learned, trained, rehearsed and maintained, in order to become part and parcel of the lawyer. The focus can and will shift during the curriculum: skills will become more sophisticated while the curriculum progresses. In the beginning of the first year the focus will be on reading and understanding legal texts and terminology and on library research, on oral presentations, discussions and on papers, while later in the curriculum skills might take the form of moot court training/participation in moot courts, negotiation games and writing a more elaborate essay (and defending it).

As the last example shows, many skills come in combinations: when we have students writing extensive essays, such as, for example, a bachelor or master essay, why not include in the process, and as part of the grading, a brief oral defence?

Generally, a large essay is considered to be a conclusion of a program and the final proof of graduation. I do not necessarily disagree, but I can also imagine that other final proofs, which very much link to skills and employability, can be devised. For example, ask students to work on a law in context project: provide them with a major or complicated societal issue and ask them to research it and to work together towards a final presentation or papers for stakeholders. Requiring students to carry out such a project in a collaborative and multidisciplinary manner could add to the learning benefits.

The 21[2] skills I have mentioned in Chapter 2 were the following:

1. critical thinking, reading and listening and reflection;
2. creative thinking and solution-oriented thinking;
3. clear writing;
4. oral skills and skills of persuasion;
5. research capabilities;
6. life-long learning;
7. negotiation skills;
8. advising clients, ceo's, ministers etcetera;
9. client counselling skills;
10. political and policy sensitivity;
11. social communication skills;
12. international communication skills;

2 The MacCrate Report (1992, American Bar Association's report on legal education: The MacCrate Report, Legal Education and Professional Development - An Educational Continuum, Report of the Task Force on Law Schools and the Profession: Narrowing the Gap 1992) listed ten Fundamental Lawyering Skills: problem solving; legal analysis; legal research; factual investigation; communication; counselling; negotiation; litigation and alternative dispute resolution; administrative skills to organize and manage legal work; recognizing and resolving ethical dilemmas. In Australia so-called competency requirements developed by the Australasian Professional Legal Education Council (APLEC) (<www.aplec.asn.au/Pdf/Competency_Standards_for_Entry_Level_Lawyers.pdf>).
The competencies include regular skills (problem solving, work management, business skills but also ethics, and professional responsibility.

13. ICT skills;
14. Sensitivity to other (legal) cultures and knowledge of more languages;
15. Basic understanding of other disciplines ((social) sciences and economics);
16. pro-activity;
17. curiosity and precision;
18. entrepreneurial skills (to set up one's own business);
19. understanding of the law in its context;
20. professional ethics;
21. collaborative skills.

The question to be addressed is how can a law school go about including them in a curriculum? The first five skills ought to be built into the regular substantive law courses. They ought to be part and parcel of studying law but must also be made a very explicit part of the exam and part of the classes and lectures. This can be done by having students write and present papers and do oral presentations; organizing small pleading contests and debates; having students do some independent research instead of solely asking them to read a text book.[3] Make the resolution of cases or problems part of a course and make it visible in class when students present different solutions or have different perspectives on the cases or problems. When comparative law is included, and this follows up on my arguments about the relevance of comparative law, make sure that it leads into a discussion about different legal solutions and the 'quality' of the domestic law, in the light of other solutions and aspects. Organizing active tutorial groups with plenty of student participation, also specifically when the composition of the classes is truly diverse and/or international, will improve communication skills.

In the book *Educating Lawyers*, the authors also propose an integrative model. In the concluding chapter[4] they summarize their findings as a three part model for a law school curriculum, with the following elements:

1. the teaching of legal doctrine and analysis, which provides the basis for professional growth;
2. introduction to the several facets of practice included under the rubric of lawyering, leading to acting with responsibility for clients;
3. a rhetorical and practical emphasis on inculcation of the identity, values, and dispositions consonant with the fundamental purposes of the legal profession.

I am not at all sure that this summary will be valid for all global law schools, because of the specific meaning of lawyering and its focus on judicial decision making, court cases and reasoning and interaction with clients. However, when we use that second aspect to mean, for other law schools in other jurisdictions (where

3 Wolski 2002, p. 287-302; the author not only analyses skills but also describes in a table how to make skills in a curriculum explicit and visible.
4 Sullivan *et al.* 2007, p. 194.

legal education is also and maybe even more so focused on educating academics who serve society in a wide variety of jobs), that we have to train our students in the skills necessary to interact with their 'clients' and 'bosses' (politicians, legislatures, CEO's etc.), the statement could be held to be valid as well. What, however, is ostensibly missing are, in my view, two things: the first is a 21st century perspective on global lawyering and transnational and international developments and the second is the link with the didactical method, which is, in the perspective of the authors, foremost (be it with adaptations and improvements) the case dialogue method.[5] What is missing in this book is a broader discussion of other pedagogical initiatives (law in context, problem-based learning, trans-systemic method) to achieve the goals law schools must set for themselves.

Skills related to moot courts, client counselling, negotiation, advising, and political and policy sensitivity, can be promoted in existing courses by weaving them into tutorial groups and courses.[6] I have witnessed many experiences of courses in which the professors made a small moot court part of the course, or set up an assignment requiring the students to write a specific piece of advice to a minister or other public figure, in a given political setting, or, to mention another example, students, as a conclusion of their program, participated in their own conference presenting the papers they wrote and commenting on other papers and asking questions to other presenters.

Ultimately, a law school could make a choice to have a large moot court, or a negotiation game, or a law in context project for the students, in which skills and content are combined and which will lead to an assessment of skills and substance, such as: a moot court in an area of the law; a negotiation game in which students do contract negotiations or work on an international treaty; or a law in context project. Students have to be subjected to collaboration, writing, defending a point of view/ party in a case, communicating with the opposing party/parties. They have to do so by relying upon their knowledge of the law and whatever else is necessary for the advancement of their case, upon their skills of persuasion and communication, and upon their written and oral skills. One could also envisage a 'game' in which students are being presented with a specific issue and subsequently must devise and execute a strategy, possibly culminating in a moot court. With such a 'game' we can reflect with students on legal and other strategies to best defend the interests of their clients.

Entrepreneurial skills possibly are best served with a separate course, taught with the help of professors from MBA programs. These skills involve many lessons on business, economics and marketing, and, although I named them skills, probably relate more to knowledge than to real skills: knowledge as to how small businesses

5 They do however also refer (in the context of professional education and pedagogy) to the practice of the 'case conference' in which students observe, stimulate, attempt, and then crucially reflect on their work or performance' (p. 9).

6 Sullivan *et al.* 2007, p. 13 also argues in favour of the integration of legal analysis, training for practice and development of professional identity.

are set up and run and what their legal and business rules and environment are, that is, what it takes to set up shop.

In literature about legal education and specifically when it deals with our future generation of lawyers and aspects of internationalization, reference is made to 'general practical skills'[7] or 'a wide range of skills going far beyond facility in linguistic exercises'.[8] To think like a lawyer, the Americans call it.[9] These references are extremely relevant but sketchy. They are relevant, because the more we expect from our students, in the sense that they can operate across borders, can work in one legal system, but also transnational, and can switch between domains, we can expect less concrete knowledge (that is not less in the absolute sense, but less in the sense that we want our students not so much to know of one system or one domain, but to have a feel for more legal systems and legal cultures). How must we define what concrete knowledge we expect from our students and of what and how much, and how do we ensure that we convey all the necessary skills enabling them to be professional lawyers? Here we are also plagued by our uncertainty about the future lawyers. It can safely be assumed that there will be a large diversity in lawyers: some will be specialists in one specific (small) domain; some will work in a predominantly local/domestic legal setting; others will work as policy makers and on an international level; quite a few will work trans-boundary with international colleagues and on international issues etcetera. How can we educate and train all these lawyers in one curriculum with the right mix of (the right) knowledge and (proper) skills, which will prepare the students for their future careers, and will also give them the necessary and valuable tools to adapt their careers during the 40 or so years that they will have to work and practice and adjust their careers and knowledge and skills to the future demands?

In this book I have already indicated that I do not favour a one-size-fits-all model. I strongly believe in diversity, not only between countries but also within countries between the law schools. Between US Law Schools there are enormous differences; they cater for different needs. Elite schools (the Ivy League) admit and educate other students than local law schools which train for the domestic state bar (exam). There is in the world an enormous difference between funding, domestic regulations and strategies of law schools.

I agree with Peter L. Strauss who wrote about the McGill curriculum and favours the McGill approach.[10] However, he concludes:

> 'not every school will make such a choice. Cities, states, and nations will continue to need lawyers whose training suits them to domestic practice. Columbia has never offered a course in New York practice [...]. Correspondingly, it may be that trans-systemia will have less appeal to schools serving local or even regional bars than to

7 Klabbers 2007, p. 198.

8 Reisman 1996.

9 Sullivan *et al.* 2007, p. 47.

10 Strauss 2006.

schools who invite the world and imagine their graduates dispersing widely throughout it. [..] All in all, I think this likely to be a market-driven choice.'

Market-driven means that law schools must have their eyes open to the changes in the market and the demands from the market. They must be able to predict and foresee future market demands and be able to adapt to them.

It does not by definition provide for an easy answer to the question about skills: it is obvious that a transsystemic (transnational/ international/comparative) law curriculum needs and trains other skills than a curriculum purely focused on domestic law. Or maybe the skills are per se not that different, but we train them differently and more in depth, because they must compensate for a less up-to-date and fully-fledged knowledge of one legal system. Instead we train the capability to solve problems and to find solutions to those issues that are common to many legal systems. Part of the curriculum will be filled with skills related to the perspectives of discussing, analysing and seeking solutions to problems and from the perspective of different legal systems that operate as examples and as sources of possible options. Only after the students have been immersed in this approach can they be taught specific aspects of specific legal systems but all the time with an open mind to other solutions and legal systems. This idea is opposite to a general perspective that students ought to be immersed first in one coherent legal system before they can engage in comparative legal exercises. That is that a student must be a lawyer first instead of being an academic first, who is open to problems, questions and responses, and then becomes a lawyer. The major question is whether a lawyer can only be defined as a person who is a fully-fledged domestic lawyer or that we can also educate academics who are trained in legal reasoning and in legal issues and who can do so with an understanding of different legal domains and legal systems.

In academic literature about legal education authors refer to lawyers and legal education with phrases such as lawyering skills, lawyer-statesmen and mastering what it takes to analyse, argue, write and litigate, and be creative and original, and be able to apply the law in order to solve problems. Even though these aspects presuppose the knowledge of law and of legal systems, the focus is on the range of skills to be applied in and through the legal domain.[11] Lawyers must have the skills

11 Supreme Court member Lord Sumption was quoted in the *Telegraph* (5 April 2012) saying: Lord Sumption told Counsel that the 'most difficult' thing about practising law was 'not the law but the facts'. 'Most arguments which pretend to be about law are actually arguments about the correct analysis and categorization of the facts,' he said. 'Once you've understood them it's usually obvious what the answer is. The difficulty then becomes to reason your way in a respectable way towards it.' He added: 'That's why the study of something involving the analysis of evidence, like history or classics, or the study of a subject which comes close to pure logic, like mathematics, is at least as valuable a preparation for legal practice as the study of law. Appreciating how to fit legal principles to particular facts is a real skill. Understanding the social or business background to legal problems is essential. I'm not sure current law degrees train you for that, nor really are they designed to. This is not a criticism of the course. It's simply a recognition of the fact that a command of reasoning skills, an ability to understand and use evidence, and broad literary culture are all tremendously →

to learn about the relevant and applicable laws, to have an overview of a legal system and a good eye for relevant and important details and risks and opportunities. Creativity in the application of the law presupposes a bird's eye view and a broad basic knowledge of the workings of a legal system. Specialization(s) will certainly be relevant, but the absence of a specialization does not detract from the fundamental lawyering skills.

When we have great lawyers in mind, it is likely that they had a general knowledge of the law, a sharp mind for analysis, analogies and solutions and, furthermore, an awareness for possibilities and a quick mind to research those possibilities with an intuitive feeling for solutions and this is combined simultaneously with the gift of communication skills.

It is apparent that knowledge of the law is indispensable, specifically of the concepts, coherence and issues, but absolute 100% knowledge of the law does not make good lawyers; it makes people with knowledge about rules and codes, but for lawyering we need certainly more. What distinguishes a legal mind from a good lawyer are the skills to apply the law, find and reason solutions, seek analogies and discover comparative solutions. The excellent lawyer combines these aspects and when law schools strive to educate these lawyers, they must set up the curriculum so that knowledge and skills and competences are fully addressed. Whether this can be done depends on the intake and the length of the curriculum. Whether it can be done for all students in a law school in the same manner might also be the question, implying the issue of diversity between schools and between students studying in the same school (for example special honours programs).

It is however imperative not to neglect skills and to address skills and what these entail in a legal curriculum. Training students in these skills will help to make the distinction between people with legal knowledge and capable and competent authoritative lawyers.

valuable to any advocate. If you don't have them you are going to find it difficult to practise. If you don't know any law that is not a problem; you can find out.' <http://www.telegraph.co.uk/news/uknews/law-and-order/9384619/The-best-lawyers-are-not-law-graduates-claims-judge.html>.

Chapter 6

SELECTION AND EXAMS

I believe not many students love exams; exam period is generally a period of tension and stress, with a fine line for some between deep failure and success, between misery (failing to achieve one's ambitions) and maybe frustration. Exams can also lead to 'medals' (high grades) which objectively show how well a student has performed and that the student is among the top of her/his class. We probably need exams for that purpose: to be able to praise the best and allow for a ranking of students. We seem also to need exams to ensure that those who do not deserve to become lawyers, those who do not meet the minimum requirements of skills and knowledge, indeed do not become lawyers. We need exam-like settings to inform the students about their knowledge and skills levels, in order to tell them that further study is needed in some domains. In that respect exams also have a function as instrument of feedback and information.

Exams (and the selection which takes place in and through exams) are a neglected issue in teaching law. We teach a course, write an exam (essay, multiple choice, problem based, take home), grade it and continue with our other work. In some cases exams are graded by two examiners; but in many cases only the teacher/professor grades an exam. Sometimes a student is given some feedback on why (s)he failed, by making available a 'model' answer and/or the criteria used by the grader when assessing the exam, or by talking with the student.

In general a distinction is made between formative and summative assessments. With the former we intend to give the student feedback on his/her progress: its purpose is educational. A summative assessment is used for passing a judgment on how a student has performed and implies consequences about being able to continue, or being among the top of the class, or being admitted to the honours program.

In *Educating Lawyers* the authors underline the importance of feedback to the students. They criticize the use of single end-of-semester essay exams, because they do not provide the students with any guidance until the course is over.[1] Their plea

1 Sullivan *et al.* 2007, chapter 5: Assessment and how to make it work. See also: Best Practices for legal education, chapter 7: Best Practices for Assessing Student Learning. Some of the principles the authors formulate are the following: the teacher uses assessments to inform students of their level of professional development; the teachers use multiple methods of →

is for differentiated forms of assessment and for law schools to take the idea of formative assessment as integral to its mission. The Best Practices for Legal Education formulates therefore as a principle for a law school to conduct multiple summative assessments of student learning throughout the term. Subsequently it formulates as a principle that (these) summative assessments are also formative.

There is a link between exams and learning; but there is also a link between exams and the intake of students and between exams and the output to the labour market. In the context of American Law Schools, selection is prior to the study of law through the LSAT and other criteria. It appears that American students (who are also fee paying) have been selected and are eager to graduate in a competitive and challenging atmosphere. In that respect exams, to a lesser extent, do fulfil the need to ensure that all students after a course meet the necessary requirements. In a context, as in many European countries, of open admission (and low fees!), exams have a (summative) function of testing the minimum threshold: whether students indeed did study and did make an effort and have the capabilities and competencies to progress through law school and complete the studies of law. Exams function in that setting as an instrument of selecting the competent and skilled students. This is an important function for it allows the schools to maintain the necessary level. That level might be maintained through other mechanisms, such as for instance instituting a more selective admission process and/or a higher tuition fee, but these are policy decisions which are in most countries outside the scope of universities' or law schools' decisions. Another aspect could be to incorporate in the teaching and learning process many formative assessment components which will help to stimulate the students' work attitude and improve their competences and skills. However, despite this approach, it will still not fully resolve the feature that some of the students (who had to be admitted through open admission) do not qualify and will not meet the standards and qualifications of an academically educated lawyer.

Techniques to be resorted to lie in the domain of formative assessments: during a course students will have to answer questions, solve cases, give presentations, and practice skills, with the aim to keep them focused upon the course and to be given the necessary feedback about their progress and efforts.

Exams are taken, or better students are assessed, on different levels in different countries. In Germany law school exams are for the school, but what really counts in the end are the state exams that determine the access to legal jobs in the civil service, bar and judiciary; students are assessed at the state level. In the US, the bar exams are the equivalent to the state exams and law schools are scored on pass rates of their students for the bar exam. In Italy, access to legal professions is on the basis of comparative country-wide exams for a limited number of places in the schools specializing in the legal profession (with the number of places set by the minister of education). In France access to the bar also requires students to pass an aptitude

assessing student learning; and the teachers conduct formative assessments throughout the term.

exam. In these countries studying law in a law school is not only a project in itself but also a preparation for a state/country-wide exam. These exams have the advantage of being assessed and graded by independent examiners, allowing for nationwide standards to be applied. That advantage can also turn into a disadvantage, because they impact upon the curriculum in law schools. When the exam focuses on specific domains of the law and not on others, law schools will be tempted not to offer and students will be tempted not to take these courses on these other domains. When these exams focus on black letter law knowledge and not or less so on skills or international law or comparative law, law schools will be inclined to focus on the national exam's requirements. Students will, specifically when studying at a law school is an expensive matter, also ask for a curriculum which properly prepares them for the exams, since passing the exams makes them employable and gives them value for their money. The latter aspect is specifically relevant for (high) fee-paying students.

Law schools are influenced by these after law school exams and will seek to prepare the students in the best possible way. It allows law schools to be compared with each other on the basis of pass rates. Whether this comparison is valid remains to be seen, since in situations such as in Germany students seek special guidance outside law school to prepare them for the *Staatsexam* (*repetitoren*). In the US, special bar exam books and 'prep' courses also exist for the students.

How about finding a way to have insight into law school exams and testing? In medical schools in the Netherlands all students must do a similar (progress) test which shows all students' knowledge at certain stages and allows for a comparative analysis of the quality of medical schools and their teaching. This could also be a solutions for law schools in those courses that are basic for all students as part of their law degree.

Another possibility is the UK solution of having external examiners come from other law schools and participate in grading and assessing the quality of the major exams. This practice promotes quality control and a balance in the level of exams and the quality of the graduates.

A third possibility is to have regular sessions with peers from other law schools during which exam questions are being made or assessed and the quality of each other's exams and grading criteria are being reviewed.

An issue that comes back in literature about (legal) education is the need for frequent, adequate and regular feedback. Testing students must have a formative function and education is about an interaction between students and faculty about learning performances, about effort and improvements, and about reflections and discussions with regard to academic knowledge and skills. Obviously students must also be tested on their qualifications and skills for a final assessment to determine whether they can graduate or pass the (bar) exam, but, prior to those tests, feedback is elementary for the acquisition of academic knowledge and skills.

According to Jan Klabbers, '[e]xams have degenerated into the ultimate measure of performance, the result being that much of the teaching is geared to help students to pass exams rather than helping them to become good lawyers…'.[2] He continues by stating that it appears that what matters is the production of lawyers per se, rather than the production of good, mature, independent lawyers.[3] Many of the skills I have discussed in this book do not lend themselves to easy, end of semester tests, but they require exercise and practice and feedback. In general, Martha Nussbaum argues that the ability to think and argue is difficult to measure through standardized tests. 'Only a much more nuanced qualitative assessment of classroom interactions and student writing could tell us to what extent students have learned skills of critical argument.'[4] Regular feedback implies a small scale setting (small groups, or small sections of students in courses) and it presupposes faculty who have been trained to give feedback.

The small-scale teaching, however without arguing that larger scale lectures are to be made redundant,[5] is of fundamental importance for a variety of aspects such as feedback, problem solving, and lawyering skills. Obviously this aspect might conflict with budgetary constraints and with the sheer size of the student body and student intake in a specific law school or program. For that purpose I will argue in Chapter 15 paragraph 3 that the involvement of assistants, graduate students and students, could be a possible solution.

The latter suggestion, involvement of students, revolves around the notion of peer assessment. This will also be discussed at a later stage (Chapter 15 paragraph 3). At this stage I will point out that variations of peer assessments, students commenting on each other's work, will serve two major educational purposes. One is learning to phrase comments constructively and to the point, and seeking the weak points in an argument or presentation made by another student (even, if one fully agrees!). A second is that learning by doing is also promoted here: students, both the commentator/reviewer and the presenter, exercise a skill in a subject matter. The subject matter and the skills are practiced. For faculty the accompanying advantage is that students assist in providing feedback and comments. This can be set up in the form of a moot court in which parties comment on each other's arguments and find out where they perceive the weak spots in the opponent's argument or what they felt was missing and it can include the involvement of student/judges informing the parties how they were struck by strengths and weaknesses and original findings and omissions. A real student conference is another option, (by and for the students in a specific course) with students performing the different roles in the workshops (presenting a paper, commenting on papers). These and other forms of peer assessment are perhaps not so much a form of assessment but rather feedback. It is not assessment in the sense that a grade is not being given. The goals achieved are however much more important in that the students mirror practice, train skills and perform different roles.

2 Klabbers 2007, p. 15.
3 Klabbers 2007, p. 16.
4 Nussbaum, p. 48.
5 I see diversity also within a curriculum.

In Chapter 8 I will discuss the didactics and introduce as a suggestion a combination of lectures and electronic lectures which students have to watch and understand before they come to interactive small scale class. In that respect one could combine the electronically available lectures, the study materials and the interactive (Socratic-based, or problem-based) classes (tutorials) for fine tuning where the students discuss the problems they have encountered and therefore can focus the tutorials on these issues. One step further could imply the development of questions (memory, application, solving cases) for the students to answer. The answers to these questions could be modelled in the shape of a spider web, indicating the issues in the course and the levels of knowledge (memorization, application, problem solving). In such a way students will have a picture of the growth of their knowledge and skills; and they see where lacunae exist and where the skills are less developed. They could then work on those aspects. When a student has shown that (s)he has developed the full scale spider web, (s)he can continue to the next course and consider this course to be fully mastered, with all the other requirements (presence and participation in class; handing in of papers etc.) also met. Would we then still need an end of course test which students can and will pass without necessarily having a full insight on all knowledge and skills and without the feedback which they can use in that same course?

The electronic spider web has the advantages of feedback and assessment on a number of testable aspects. What has to be ensured however is that students will not be able to fraud the system, by having another student log in under their name and provide all the answers. For that we either need a well observed honours code (we have here the same issue as take home exams) or that students can only do the questions in a controlled setting with nobody else present and that could contribute. Devising exams in this manner will certainly alleviate faculty (though the question banks have to be filled and need a critical mass of questions), and facilitate them to work on the tutorial groups and ensure interactivity and the necessary feedback on the quality of the skills. I do fully realize that a computerized question bank for all courses will not be a cure for all and will not assess and provide for feedback of all necessary skills and problem solving and pleading and writing skills. I do hope however that the latter skills will be given more time when we free staff and students from focusing on the acquisition of knowledge and the growth thereof in another setting, where a student can work at his/her own pace and take more or less time, and faculty can be involved in assuming that students will learn the necessities and can focus on the complexities, the application, the academic questions and the solving of problems and of cases.

As a final comment, I suggest that law schools seek possibilities and ways to integrate exams in their teaching and make them part of the learning process of students. Involving students and electronic assistance will greatly help the advancement of students' learning and will prepare students for life-long learning and for their professional lives.

PART C

CURRICULUM

Chapter 7

LENGTH OF CURRICULUM

Some decades ago a law curriculum in the Netherlands lasted five years; many students however took more time. This was not so much because studying law was extremely complicated but for other reasons. When I was a law student myself the 'eternal' student, students who studied for many more years, was not an uncommon figure. This has radically changed. The curriculum was reformed and shortened to last four years. That did not seem impossible, since most law curricula did not take a serious student a full-time working week, and 42 weeks a year. Five years were simply reduced into four years. It does not seem to have had an overall (negative) effect on the quality of the graduates. The question therefore is what can be said about the length of a law curriculum, given the demands of the labour market and the quality of the students.

After having focused upon the labour market and the employability of students/graduates as important factors for law schools to consider, and having linked those aspects to the quality of the first year students (the intake), now it is time to discuss the length of the curriculum. These three aspects together determine in my view what it is law schools can and should do and how they can best relate to all relevant factors and devise a 'best' curriculum which efficiently trains the incoming students in the allotted time to become graduates who fit the labour market and the general expectations. At a later stage I will come back to the substance and contents of a legal curriculum and discuss its academic nature and its role in shaping students into full-blown academics and responsible citizens.

The analysis of intake, length of curriculum and labour market might also lead a law school to discuss with the stakeholders determining these three aspects (because law schools themselves do not really, or maybe occasionally do not at all control these aspects) and to draw attention to gaps between intake and law schools' expectations; or between the allotted time for the curriculum and the expectations and demands from the labour market.

The length of legal studies range considerably from three years (US) to five years (many European countries opted for a 3+2 model under Bologna: three for a bachelor degree and two for a consecutive master degree). In the Netherlands the model opted for is 3+1. On top of this two tier structure, under the Bologna scheme, one has foreseen a third layer of three or four years for a PhD.

Length of Curriculum

US	3
UK	3
Belgium	5 (3+2)
France	5 (3+2)
Italy	5 (3+2)
Scandinavian countries	5 (3+2)
The Netherlands	4 (3+1)
Spain:	4
Germany:	8 semesters (4 years)

On the continent in Europe the general Bologna-proof format indeed appears to be 3+2. This format, on the face of it, bears no relationship to whether or not access to law school is selective. It is in some countries; in others it is not. That in itself seems odd; in a highly selective intake one could assume that intensity and/or length of study might differ. The Bologna model seems to have harmonized only superficially (ba+ma), and left all other major differences intact.[1]

The differences in length of the curriculum can be explained by the pre-Bologna lengths of law studies; they also have a relationship with the common law (3 years)/civil law (generally 5 years) divide (and correspondingly the selection in intake and in general no selection divide, with the exception of Scandinavia). In a few continental European law curricula, a lot of space is created for non-law courses, such as history, philosophy, sociology, psychology, economics(in Belgium) and roman law, ecclesiastical law and legal history (Italy).

There might also be, unofficially, a reason connected to the length of the curriculum and to how hard students in a given country study and prepare for classes and exams. Officially in most European countries the law curriculum, as are other academic studies, is set up according to the ects credit system: one academic year counts for 60 ects credits. These credits stand for contact hours and self-study hours (studying at home, in the library, writing papers etcetera). The study load must be assessed in ects credits. There is however something odd in this system. According to this system, 60 ects credits stand for the workload of a whole academic year which ranges from 1500 to 1800 hours per year depending on the country. This means that one credit corresponds to 25 to 30 hours of work.[2] In the Netherlands for instance one credit stands for 28 hours of work with a total of 1680 hours per year. This means that, depending on the length of an academic year in a specific country, students can be expected to do more. The difference amounts to five hours per credit, totalling to 300 in one given year. The ects system hides this inconsistency by enabling schools to equal courses for compensation purposes and acknowledgement of study abroad exchanges, through the equivalent of ects, while knowing that study hours might differ significantly. Between two courses of 6 ects the study load

1 I will discuss shortly the ects system which intended to harmonize study load and weight of courses, but also shows major deficiencies.

2 <Ec.europa.eu/education/lifelong-learning-policy/doc/ects/key_en.pdf>.

difference in hours can be up to 30 hours and this is not even taking into account that, since studying is not math, some courses might indeed require less study hours from the average student, or because the course is not asking the students to use their full potential.

A five year law curriculum of 25 hours per ects credit is 7,500 hours; a four year law curriculum with 30 hours per ects credit is 7,200 hours; and with 25 hours per ects credit it is 6,000; a three year curriculum with 30 hours is 5,400 hours. This is only theory, based upon official numbers, but what we should know (but many universities simply do not know) is really how much time on average students study. Do they really study the hours of credit in a law school/in all law schools? We do not know. What we do know is that there are large discrepancies in the academic year allotted for teaching and exams. In Europe teaching runs from anywhere from the end of August to the beginning of October and lasts until the end of May to the beginning of July. It is therefore highly speculative to compare years of study, without having insight into study hours and study load. Students in a five year curriculum might even study less than 25 hours per credit; assuming they do 20, that totals up to 6,000. On the other hand, students in a short, highly selective three year curriculum could study more, let's say 35 hours per credit, which will lead up to 6,300 hours in total. What does it really mean that some law curricula are set for three years and others for five years? When we really want to understand equivalence and depth, it is important to go into detail and research the courses and their exams.

This math is speculative, but my experience has taught me that in practice it holds true. Talking with many colleagues about their courses and the study discipline of the students, and confronting students with these findings, I have noted that in many instances of lengthy curricula (5 years, with many students studying even longer), students also take time or need time to have a job on the side, thus indeed reducing their effective study week to much less than it is supposed to be (20 hour working (=studying) weeks are not at all exceptional). Students tend to have part-time jobs, to fund their studies, and spend time in extra-curricular activities, for instance to include them on their CV. This is not an exclusively European aspect but is also to be found in Australia.[3]

It is therefore not only the length of the curriculum which counts, but also the number of hours students are really made to study and do study! Selection, and coherence of the student body, furthermore plays a role here. In an intellectually very diverse student body, a tendency is to lower standards in order for all students, or as many as possible, to catch up. Highly important is, in a relatively short period of the curriculum, to spend effectively as much time as possible to study and work with disciplined and eager students.

3 Goldsmith & Bamford 2010, p. 157: 'Compared with a generation ago, Australian law students are spending more time working and engaged in extracurricular activities. Financial pressures, as well as employer expectations, are playing a major part in shaping the law student environment.' This also applies to undergraduate students in the US; Arum & Roksa 2011, also blame the decline in learning on distractions from socializing and working.

I wish to point out here that it is important for schools to collect data about study patterns and study behaviour. These data could be used to improve study patterns and to align ects credits for courses with actual study behaviour. These could also be used for further discussion about design of law curricula and their substance.

In recent years we have experimented in Maastricht with a detailed and consistent evaluation questionnaire, which also asks students questions about contact hours and study hours. This has allowed us to spot the courses where the students on average seem to spend less time than they should, allowing the faculty to merge courses, or to increase contents or difficulty of assignments. The side effect was that it also gave us an argument when students complained about the difficulty of the exam. The best counter argument was to inform students that they found the exam difficult because they had not studied properly and had not studied for the required number of hours.

Because of the diversity in intake, in length of studies, in access to the professions, it is fair to say that a variety of content and a varied emphasis on issues of education will exist among law schools. When intake is less mature and a study span is relatively short, and there are relatively few hours per ects, some important issues will have to be neglected or left to post law school (professional) education or study while working (apprenticeship).This is the Dutch model: a relatively young student intake (18/19 years); four years of study and three years of bar internships and a growing phenomenon of traineeships. By being on the top of the scale of the hours per credit, this compensates for the four years curriculum as opposed to the five years in most of the civil law jurisdictions. Furthermore, a lot can also be done, as I have argued, by focusing strictly on the study hours per course!

A second aspect resides in the consequence that short academic legal studies (combined with a lesser mature intake: young students and no selection) and high labour market demands lead to either a brief focus on legal studies in the strict sense or to a neglect of important skills. In such a situation a law school will be tempted to teach the main subjects of law in courses and a few electives only with a focus on the basics. Might it be fair to qualify English legal education in this sense? (However, there is certainly a process of selection which takes place there and this shows how important that feature is when only a short study span is available and the labour market is demanding).

Also, strict adherence to rigid study patterns and study discipline and high standards of teaching can effectively compensate (with the intake selection or certainly the admission interviews or questionnaires!) for the short time span of the UK curriculum of only three years. Regular students enter law school (after a selection on the basis of secondary school results) and study law for three years and gain admission to the bar(s) afterwards for a further lengthy training.

There is also another route to the legal professions for students with another bachelor degree: they can opt for a program of approximately one year, which qualifies them for access to the training as barrister or solicitor. Here the academic education in law lasts for one year, which is enabled by the fact that these (mature) students have previously successfully undergone a three year undergraduate education.

Is it possible to formulate a general rule about the appropriate length of a legal curriculum? I am afraid not. The first obstacle is the difference in domestic regulation: the more courses and legal domains that are prescribed as compulsory for a law school curriculum, the lengthier the curriculum will be. The second reason is the way the intake of students is organized and what can be said about the quality of the incoming students; limited intake and a strict selection combined with an excellent secondary school system, are relevant aspects to take into account here.

At the least, it is important to note that in two common law countries (US and UK), legal education lasts (only?) for three years. In the US, this is after an undergraduate degree, but in the UK this is after secondary school, however with specific requirements. For the UK – continental Europe divide, one of the explanations is the relative recent development in the UK that legal education was taken over by academic institutions from the legal professions. On the continent legal education has a century-long tradition of being taught in universities and shares this long history of university teaching with theology and medicine.

Another aspect seems to be the different approaches to the law: common law versus civil law. On the continent lengthy codes became gradually the object of legal teaching, with extensive theoretical frameworks and concepts underlying these codes and the legal framework. With the growth of European law, and its impact in many domains of law in all European legal orders, this distinction will gradually dissolve. But the case method (or the study of cases) has left its mark as opposed to an extensive and exhaustive teaching of a legal domain as such.

What is important, however, to note from the experiences in the UK and the US is that a law curriculum can be made drastically shorter than is generally the case in Europe, when the students undergo a firm selection and the students pursued an undergraduate degree prior to their law school experience. This is self-explanatory, since these students have already obtained an academic qualification and have intellectually matured and chosen a career in law presumably after careful consideration and are well motivated.

Chapter 8

DIDACTICS

We all have memories of professors and courses where we were challenged and learned a lot: courses which gave us skills and expertise which we cherish and where we had fun learning. These outcomes were probably related to several aspects of the course, for example: the level of the course which was challenging but also relating to our previously acquired knowledge and skills; that the course was fun because the course appealed to our emotions and curiosity; the course was satisfying because the course took us to a higher level and we could perform better after the course than before and we could resolve more and more complicated issues after the course; we felt taken seriously because the course appealed to our self-esteem for it challenged us to train, exercise, apply and resolve; and we felt respected because the class or the professor took time to deal with students' questions and was interested in our progress.

Students generally know a good teacher and good course when they experience them. Most of the law professors were good law students themselves and have shown their excellence in research. Many of them might be (or are) good teachers, but we also know that the teaching quality of teachers and of courses and curricula can be improved, by reflecting on the design of courses and the skills of the teacher and by reflecting on the modes of delivery of the curriculum as a whole.

Didactics ought always to be an important aspect of curriculum design, because they are certainly the drivers of the efficiency and effectiveness of our teaching. We know that lecture-based teaching is less effective than more active ways of teaching or training and certainly an abundance of literature exists about teaching and how best to do it. Law schools and law faculties all over the globe seem not to be the best and foremost places to have experimented or imported massive didactical teaching reforms. I have come across many practices in which a curriculum consists of lectures with some small tutorial groups as well as some added skills training. Since 2008 Maastricht Law Faculty has participated in setting up a new law curriculum in Hasselt (Belgium) with two Belgian partners (Hasselt University and Leuven University) and in that respect a clash of teaching cultures became prominent. The Belgian professors assessed the importance of 'their' courses on the basis of the number of lectures available and the question whether they could lecture all their materials in the available hours. The Maastricht profes sors assumed that the most essential, relevant and important materials were dealt with in small tutorial groups, allowing for the professors to theorize about the law in the lectures, to provide other examples, to relate the course to topical and new developments, to critically discuss and analyse the law and to draw comparisons with other legal systems and to relate to other disciplines. Battles have been fought about whether a tutorial was to take place after the lecture (in the same week) or before. The Belgian professors insisted on scheduling the lectures before a tutorial group, assuming that the lecture had to be more prominent and had to lay out the structure and basics first, before a smaller tutorial group could proceed to go to work with the materials.

It is self-evident that to have a clear view not only as what to do and teach (the substantive aspect), but also how to do it (assuming also that a faculty will implement and needs a coherent design pertinent to contents and form) is essential, therefore, Chapters 9 and 15 paragraph 1 will discuss these aspects about coherent curriculum design and faculty leadership.

Another aspect is to relate teaching to research about how students learn and retain new knowledge. John Cafarella showed that it is better to have two intensive learning sessions of 20 minutes each, instead of one session of 40 minutes. He argued:

> 'As we shorten the learning episode, the down-time decreases faster than the prime times. This indicates that there is a higher probability of effective learning taking place if we can keep the learning episodes short and meaningful. Thus, teaching two 20-minute lessons provides 20% more prime time (approximately36 minutes) than one 40 minute lesson (approximately 30 minutes). Note, however, that a time period shorter than 20 minutes may not give the learner sufficient time to determine the pattern and organization of the new learning, and is thus of little benefit. The data confirm that more retention occurs when lessons are shorter. Lessons divided into 20 minute segments are more productive than one continuous lesson.'[1]

When we devise curricula and teaching formats, it is beneficial to take outcomes from research such as this one into account. Classes which last 20 minutes and subsequently have time to practice the newly acquired information will therefore be more effective than a 30 minute lecture.

It was my luck that I have worked for many years in a school (and a university) with a specific didactical perspective and inspiration (Problem-Based Learning). I have also been influenced by having been active in sports. One of the lessons in that respect which I carry with me and try to convey is that learning a sport and training others in a sport is related to a variety of things: interest and aptitude, learning from watching, but specifically from trainers who explain well, can show how to do it, but most of all, from doing and training and rehearsing again and again and again and practicing the technique and the execution of the exercises yourself. In Dutch it

1 <http://sciencegnus.com/Primacy%20Recency%20Effect.pdf>; see also Sousa 2011, p. 95-99.

says; *praatje, plaatje, daadje* which means explain, show and act/do! That is, let the students actively participate in doing what we want lawyers to do in real life: defend arguments; explain a solution, research a problem, select relevant facts, write papers, short and long, provide explanation or plead a case, give oral presentations. Learning is doing and learning is teaching others.

We can also learn from David A. Sousa and his book *How the brain learns*;[2] finding that retention after three days is 10% from lecturing and 20% from demonstration. 'No one doubts that the lecture method allows a lot of information to be presented in a short time. However, the question is not what is presented, but what is learned'. Then, what has to be done in order to improve retention rates and improve learning? Sousa recommends the following techniques:

1. interactive lecture and direct teaching; here the students have periodic opportunities during the lessons to give feedback on what they have learned;
2. visual material;
3. verbal and visual information;
4. learn by doing/practice ('Learning by doing also encourages problem-based learning, whereby students get a real-world problem to solve that involves using their new information and skills. The problem-based approach has the added advantage of boosting student motivation when compared to lecture-based instruction because students see how the learning can be used to directly address meaningful problems,'[3] and can actively restore information in their memory;
5. practice and teaching others.

The Learning Pyramid,[4] which provides a similar message about the effectiveness of different modes of teaching, is also instructive here:

2 Sousa 2011, p. 100.

3 Sousa 2011, p. 101.

4 The Learning Pyramid, devised by the NTL Institute of Alexandria (formerly the National Training Laboratories of Bethel, Maine), comes from studies on retention of learning after students were exposed to different teaching methods. The pyramid shows the percentage of new learning that students can recall after 24 hours as a result of being taught primarily by the teaching method indicated. Information recalled after 24 hours is presumed to be in long-term memory storage.

The Learning Pyramid

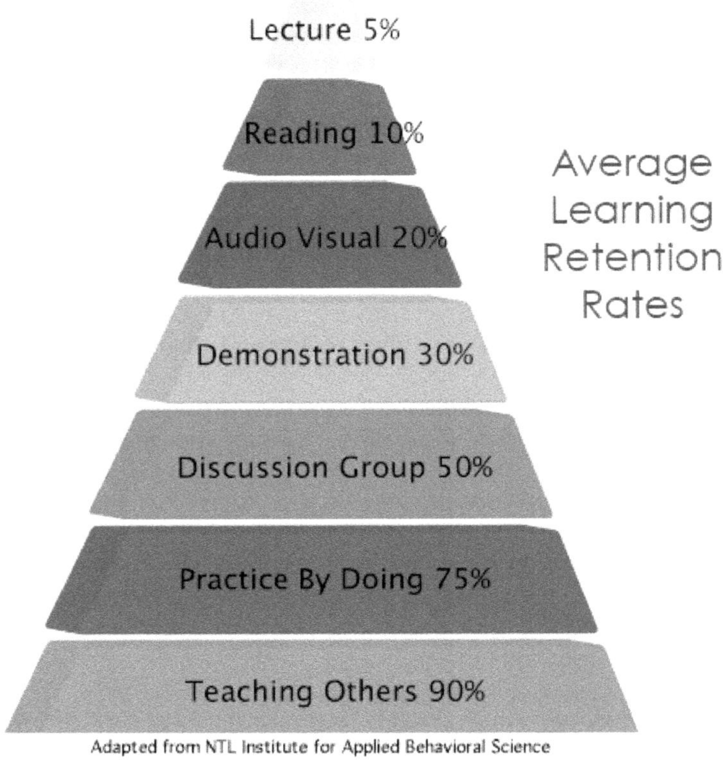

Another aspect to bear in mind is the need to prepare students for employment later in life, where collaboration with colleagues is indispensable: if that is so, we have to prepare students to be able to work collaboratively. In employment lawyers work with non-lawyers and have to relate to other disciplines: a corporate lawyer deals with marketing departments or with the CEO and has to advise and consult them on legal questions. This requires thinking alongside these professionals and explaining the legal issues.

Increasingly, students and the labour market rely on new ICT techniques for communication, social media, presentations, research and sources. The law might be stable, or so we think, but the world we live in is in a constant state of flux. 30 years ago the fax was a revolution; since about 15 years E-mail and text messages changed modes of work; smart phones, lap tops and I-Pad and the possibility for video conferences also changed our ways of work. Information is everywhere; we can have access to every bit of information, but how do we select the right information and how do we digest it for ourselves and make it available for our clients?

We prepare our students for a lawyering life by establishing moot courts and competitions and pleading contests, so why not prepare them (better) for life after law school; that is prepare them for all activities in employment and prepare them for an interactive professional life. How better to do that than in an integrated didactical approach in which substance and form are integrated. Practice what you preach. When we preach to train and educate active, participating, critical, self-reflective, communicative young lawyers, isn't that precisely how we should teach them? Practicing these features from day one in law school is necessary.

Following up on what I have argued before about the enormous diversity in the labour market and the changes in the labour market, it is of the utmost relevance to work with students on the skills they need to be good lawyers, whatever profession they choose. Whether they specialize, or do routine legal work, or work for a CEO or minister. Skills, and the skills I have described, are enormously necessary in that respect, and will assist them to do their jobs well. That is the reason that the didactical system must precisely meet those demands, to promote, culture, foster and enhance the skills and capabilities.

A didactical system must meet these needs as well as train the students in acquiring knowledge of the law and in the application of the law. In a paper published in Science by Louis Deslauriers and his colleagues at the University of British Columbia,[5] it is suggested that spending class time on problem solving, discussions and group work (with reading assignments before classes) is indeed more effective than traditional lecture-style teaching. Problem-Based Learning (PBL) is, in this respect, an approach to teaching, and specifically to learning, which aims precisely at focusing on the effective modes of learning.[6] Mckinnon states that little is written about the use of PBL in legal education, and unfortunately that statement is still true. She refers to Murdoch University School of Law (Australia) and to Maastricht University, Faculty of Law. In Maastricht PBL has been employed in the law school since its foundation in 1981, and the school still attaches great value to its values and characteristics, even though changes have been made and the model has been adapted to serve its purposes fully. Moens relates PBL in his Murdoch School of Law to successes in (international) moot court competitions, and I can indeed confirm that a similar feature applies to Maastricht. But it is also true that research about student skills, study attitudes, professional competences and academic preparation for the labour market has not been properly carried out and reported with respect to the legal domain. Here, work has to be done, possibly with collaboration between law schools which have made use of PBL.

5 <http://www.theglobeandmail.com/news/national/university-students-fare-better-with-interactive-learning-study-finds/article2020684/>; see also The Economist, 'Teaching methods. An alternative vote; Applying science to the teaching of science', 14 May 2011, p. 84.

6 About PBL in Law: Moens 2007; Mackinnon 2006. Maastricht University and also its Law Faculty have been completely set up as PBL settings. For law there is, for instance, also York University (law) and Uppsala (law).

There is another lesson which I have learned in practice and from experts and that is that it is essential (in legal education) to train students to select the essentials and not to try to remember all that has been presented to them. Sousa calls this the issue of fast and slower learners.[7] Fast learners

> 'learn the concept in less than the allotted time. During the remaining time their brains often sort the concept's sub-learnings into important and unimportant categories; that is they select the critical attributes for storage and discard what they decide is unimportant. This explains why fast learners are usually fast retrievers: They have not cluttered their memory networks with trivia'.

The slower learners need more time to learn the concept. If they do not have that time they lose part of the sub-learnings but also they 'do not have the time to do any sorting'. Sousa reports of studies in which the curriculum was sorted from the start, with a focus on the essentials and not on unimportant material. That showed better results. Sousa therefore recommends pruning the curriculum of the least important 20-25% and using the time gained by linking the concepts to previously taught material and to other concepts in the curriculum. That is to increase the level of complexity and go up from remembering to understanding, application, analysis, evaluation and creation. Diminishing the amount of information which students must remember gives more time and space to spend time on these other five more complex exercises.

Teachers must be trained and persuaded to consider these aspects useful; but also we must, as teachers, ensure that the appropriate material exists to teach essentials and to teach the students how to retrieve and remember the essence of concepts. Pruning the curriculum is first; pruning the substance of courses is a second; constructing the relevant teaching materials which assist students to understand the essence and how to perceive the core of concepts and of a specific course, is extremely helpful.

Certainly, we see the rise and increase of ICT developments which are and will be incorporated in curricula, such as virtual learning environments and e-learning tools. That means that faculty will need to be trained in the use of these tools and their implementation in the curriculum (that aspect will be dealt with in Chapter 15 paragraph 3). The incorporation of ICT aspects in our teaching serves a variety of purposes: first of all it increases our possibilities for (inter)active teaching and learning; secondly, sometimes our students come in with great skills of e-learning technology and ICT skills; thirdly, information is increasingly imparted through e-literature; and fourthly, the labour market has been discovering the assets of the new technologies for communication and doing business. It is an illusion that the legal labour market will be immune from these developments.

Technology has pervaded our lives: students register and apply through web based programs; communication with applicants is through these new channels;

[7] Sousa 2011, p. 264.

students can consult their courses and schedules through the Inter- (or: intra)net; they hand in assignments through computer programs, which automatically scan them for plagiarism. Students make sophisticated presentations in power point; they read E-books and E-journal articles; and can access case law from all over the globe in electronic ways.

The question is therefore how to incorporate E-learning in a curriculum, adapting it to the didactical needs and goals.[8] I define here three reasons for introducing E-learning aspects:

1. for distance-learning;
2. for 'remedial' teaching purposes: assisting students to improve learning and better understand and cope with problems;
3. to prepare the students for their future careers in which they will increasingly rely upon E-technology: this is therefore a skills-aspect; making students aware of the capabilities and possibilities, challenges and risks of ICT technology.

The latter aspect implies that we have to train students in those aspects, stimulating and training them to work paperless, do web research and become familiar with computer applications in businesses and in legal practice.

The first element applies for those schools, setting up distance learning programs and web conferencing for teaching purposes. This feature will enrich the curriculum and will allow a law school to reach out to more students and to assist students in studying more intensively. The idea here is that distance learning does not only facilitate 'virtual' students but also the students who enrol as regular students. They can also receive combinations of E-learning and on the spot education in class and through lectures.

The second element is a pertinent one, because it might also enable our third goal, training students to work with E-technology. Here, we have to specifically define what it is we want to do and for what purpose. We can video tape all lectures and make them available for all students but doing so implies a change in lectures and in study behaviour. Experiments in my School of Law have shown in this respect that lecture attendance decreased but that many more students watched (parts of) the lectures more than once, and also did so during the course. It is not unlikely that as a general effect it generated a better focus for the students. This poses another question, namely whether it might not be better to video tape small, let's say 15 minutes, lectures about a variety of doctrines and concepts, for beginners and advanced students, and store them in a library (focusing on the essentials, as we have learned from Sousa). This will allow students to be able to re-listen/re-watch lectures and do so whenever they feel the need. The real-life lectures will then be serving a different purpose: not so much explaining these basic concepts and doctrines, but discussing with students difficult issues and cases and

8 For instance, Donkers *et al.* 2010, Chapter 13.

applying the doctrines to cases and issues. Or the lectures will serve to link the concepts and doctrines to topical issues and the professor will discuss with students recent court decisions and developments. This approach will deepen the study of law; it will allow the students to watch basic lectures when they have the time to do so; they can listen to it more than once; and they will be better prepared for the real-life lectures and tutorial groups and can use those for application and problem solving.

These lectures are short and are a kind of video clip, to be watched and studied by the students before class. Watching them can be done outside class time, in the spare time of the students. Watching lectures can be done online, or on a smart phone or I-pad on the go. In real life a lecture can be listened to only once; lectures online can be re-listened to until the student understands it all. We know that lectures can only play a limited role in learning; only a small percentage of what is said during a lecture is actually retained and actively stored. New concepts, and many lectures are about new concepts, will be better memorized and truly understood when a student has to work with it and can and does recall the information. It will lead to application of knowledge and a better understanding. The short length of the video clips also relates to the time span for concentration and listening; after each video clip there are questions to be answered as a self-test for the students.

This method is already put into practice in some primary schools, and in that respect The Economist quoted Carl Wiesman, saying: 'good teaching must de-emphasize lecture and emphasize active problem solving'.[9] In line with other findings, lectures, or explanations, must be relatively short, and be followed by practical assignments, which allow the students to apply what has been explained in the lecture. Subsequently two explanations of two different concepts, with their separate applications by the students, can be followed by more creative exercises inviting the students to combine the two concepts; or to seek new solutions for new problems.

Another tool through ICT developments is to set up in a course a bank with a variety of questions, about facts, details and/or cases. These questions can be utilized by the students as self-help and study questions; or the teacher can use the test bank as a preparation tool for the students, for instance, by making it a requirement for the students to answer the questions electronically as a preparation for a tutorial meeting and answering before a specific time. This will allow the tutor to check everyone's input, the answers and the problems encountered by the students, which might help in the tutorial group meeting.

Such a bank full of questions could eventually, if so desired, also be used for exam purposes; the bank selects a certain number of questions randomly which the student has to answer.

9 The Economist, 'Flipping the classroom (Electronic education)', 17 September 2011, p. 42-43; this is in line with the Learning Pyramid.

Another feature might be to set up a virtual reality scheme for a negotiation game, or the practice of a lawyer with clients, or a consultancy business or a political game for instance with a political context. These are definitely not easy to make or maintain; in this domain collaborative efforts between law schools for building these games and practices, and with legal practice for their input, will be necessary.

Less far reaching are the 'simple' blackboard environments where faculty can post blogs and course information, where students can interact in discussion forums and where these forums can be moderated by the tutor (or a student/moderator).

When discussing didactics the design and choice of study materials is crucial. In the USA the Case Dialogue method and the Socratic teaching method have led to the development of a variety of case books which fit that teaching method. For most continental European law schools the study materials used were the Codes, text-books, possibly some readers with further and selected in-depth reading and court decisions, which shed light upon recent developments and doctrinal aspects. The textbooks might have been written for study purposes (students) and/or for legal practice. They can be characterized by a systematic, doctrinal treatise of the specific field of law. In the lecture/classroom format of teaching, these teaching materials might suffice: the incumbent professor lectures from his text book; the students duly learn this text book/lectures; they sit an exam answering questions, and continue their studies.

In case of a choice for a different teaching format, but also I suggest in the context of the lecture-based pedagogical design, law students do benefit when the teaching materials build upon psychological insights in the learning processes of students and their brains. One of the important Psychology handbooks is Peter Gray's *Psychology*.[10] The structure of this book is not untraditional: eight parts and 17 chapters about the different domains of psychology. But it is important to note how the material is presented: each chapter is preceded by a picture; paragraphs and subparagraphs headings are set in different colours; different parts of the chapters are concluded with a Section review ordering the preceding information. Regularly, the margins contain questions aiming to underline main issues in the main text. And all chapters are concluded with Concluding Thoughts (and also with Further Reading). The Concluding Thoughts interconnect issues within the chapter and between the various chapters. In his style writing, Gray also aims his book at students.

Writing books for students is a different skill than writing a book for professionals or other academics. We want students to master the essence and the essentials of a domain of law; we want them to become able to apply the knowledge learned; we endeavour to train them to solve problems; we want them to analyse critically what they have read and to gain creativity in resolving issues and finding solutions. These outcomes do require attention in the study materials, in the sense

10 Gray 2010.

that the materials show the students what is expected and provide them with an example of how it is being done.

Textbooks for students ought therefore to inform the students about the essence of the subject; this can be distinguished from the main text by separating it in separate paragraphs, in boxes, or in a schematic form. Pictures and tables and schemes are helpful because they appeal to other parts of the brain and serve the function of rehearsing information. Use the text to ask the students questions about what they have read: these questions can be related to memory or to an understanding of the text but also to invite the students to apply the text to a specific issue, to analyse and evaluate what they have read, and to seek new solutions to specific problems.

Crucial in the context of textbooks and casebooks and other materials is that they also are in line with the pedagogy and the content (comparative, international, transsystemic). That is a reason for my argument elsewhere in this book to work on study materials and books in the context of teaching. It is necessary and also a necessary scholarly endeavour, because textbooks and casebooks in this domain are relatively rare. There are therefore two reasons for parallel work on books and curricula: the pedagogy (adapting the materials to interactive study and to how students learn, memorize and can apply and build upon) and the content, which constantly has to be updated and adapted to internationalization trends and a comparative legal approach. Furthermore there is a need for integration with other disciplines and for a focus on skills and the ability to work critically with the law and reflect upon the law. Many European textbooks do not do that: they state the law as it is and as it has been developed, without commenting on the quality, or on other better approaches or directions. Generally there is no, or only a very limited treatment of what other sciences have to say about the law, or about the law in practice. Those textbooks fulfil the function of telling the reader what the law is, but they do not lead the student in analysing and reflecting upon the quality of the law, the impact of the law, possible alternatives or other approaches and solutions, or work with the student on how to use the law (and other disciplines) to resolve legal disputes.

In an earlier chapter I have discussed the labour market developments and the adaptations to (global) competition and IT (the Flat World). Also reference has been made to globalization of law and legal issues and the increase of trans-boundary issues and of the use of the English language as a lingua franca. We have to be aware that globalization and internationalization lead us to search for a common language (or common languages) which will assist us in international dialogues, in the use of internationally understood and accepted concepts and terminology and in international (legal) communication. For those purposes knowledge of languages is, to say the least, convenient: when one wants to conduct business in and with China, learning Mandarin is an asset and so is Spanish for Argentina and Russian for Russia. But we are not all geniuses when it comes to languages and we have to diversify and seek our needs and niches. For many, legal English will be a good vehicle as a lingua franca and communication tool at the international level. In that respect we have to pay attention in law schools to delivering that basic feature.

What is important here is to ensure that law students will be trained in studying legal courses and that they do so with the use of comparative law and international/European law in English using English terminology. I do not deny the importance of the domestic legal language, nor the use of other major international languages (Mandarin, Russian, Spanish, French, Portuguese), but the flattening world will lead (also) to the relevance of a common lingua. We may not always be in favour of it, or regret that other languages will hereby decrease in global importance, but the trend will be unmistaken and towards an English-ification caused by the global competition/collaboration and IT. Law schools must prepare their students for the future legal businesses and can therefore not escape these trends.[11]

The common language is a consequence and a pre-condition (facilitator) of global lawyering and collaboration. Will this endeavour be without traps and risks? Certainly not; law and language and (legal) culture are interwoven. English terminology does have specific meanings in specific domestic legal settings, and the simple transplant of a word (and the concept that lies behind it) to (different) international legal concepts and terms is indeed not always possible or doable. However, it is a process that is already occurring within international organizations and the European Union, developing their own legal concepts in the English language. Maybe not the English-English with the common law meaning, or not the American-English with the meaning under US law, but a Euro-English or global English, with specific concepts, meanings and terminology. The best way to teach this terminology is for students to learn, and be taught, read and study European, international, and also comparative law (also) in English, with due attention to linguistic issues. Let us train students to express themselves in English, be aware of the pitfalls and questions of terminology; that awareness can only be created by using the language and reflect on the (different) meanings of concepts.

Another question is still on the table, which is how to teach and educate students to be prepared for the skills of creativity and innovation, which are crucial in the global competition for creative creators and creative servers. I dealt with this question in Chapter 5 (Skills) but allow me to make a few comments here in this chapter about didactics.

The top scale of knowledge and skill is to be able to work with it; not only to apply what one has learned, but also to invent new solutions, combine findings from different disciplines, or to connect distinct domains of the law. We have to include in our teaching to train students to be able to reflect on new issues and to try to contribute to solutions with new ideas and suggestions. The mode of delivery of courses has to be immersed in precisely that. When we want our students to work on new ideas and on seeking solutions, a curriculum must be set up in a way that precisely this can be achieved and to challenge the students to reflect and solve

11 In this respect also: Kornet 2012, p. 313: 'English is emerging as the common language' in the context of Europeanization.

and to comment and connect. The strength and competitiveness of legal education and of law schools reside in the ways and the extent they can and do deliver these essentials.

Elsewhere in this book I will deal with liberal arts colleges/education and the relationship with (professional) legal education. I agree with Martha Nussbaum that it is desirable to superimpose legal education after liberal arts education in which students have acquired an inquisitive mind and critical reflection and insight in other disciplines.[12] That focus will improve legal education and educate students who are better in the skills needed in the flat world and in the global competition. If that seems not to be as possible in given systems of education in general, and legal education in particular, it has to be for law schools to include as many of those aspects of creativity, innovation and multi-disciplinarity and collaboration in their programs. For these reasons in chapters that follow I will analyse skills, other disciplines, comparative law and academic training in general.

In recent years we have increasingly noted that students have a different methodology of learning and studying: some of my colleagues have called it 'zapping': students acquire bits and pieces of information and find it difficult to gain oversight and to see and understand the (main) structures and the main picture. I am not aware of research available in this domain but, when this is indeed a generally shared picture and is confirmed in research or in exam results, we have to work out schemes to counter and remedy this feature. It will necessitate spending time and energy in the first courses in the first year to train the students to develop a sense for legal structures and general concepts. We will have to teach them how to apply details and examples as parts of a broader structure and to perceive this overall structure and the common features of similar issues. The idea of studying law is to be able to recognize and solve legal problems, but to do so requires the understanding of the fabric of a legal system, which in turn facilitates the understanding of the details and also how they fit in the whole system.

Structure and details are key issues in legal education and in understanding law. Without a proper perception of the context and of the structure(s) of legal domains and of the interactions of concepts and legal systems, details do not fall in their proper places and are difficult to memorize and to see how they fit. Legal structures come to life with and through the details and examples. It is therefore a constant interaction which must be taught to and trained with students constantly, combined with a critical analysis of the two levels, and with a permanent component of skills, as is illustrated in the following picture.

12 However, Arum & Roksa 2011, have shown that 45% of undergraduates demonstrate no significant improvement in a range of skills, such as critical thinking, complex reasoning and writing. In a study for the Accrediting Council for Independent Colleges and Schools (ACICS) (<www.acics.org>), published December 2011, it was reported that many employers say that college students lack job skills. See also The Chronicle of Higher Education 13 December 2011.

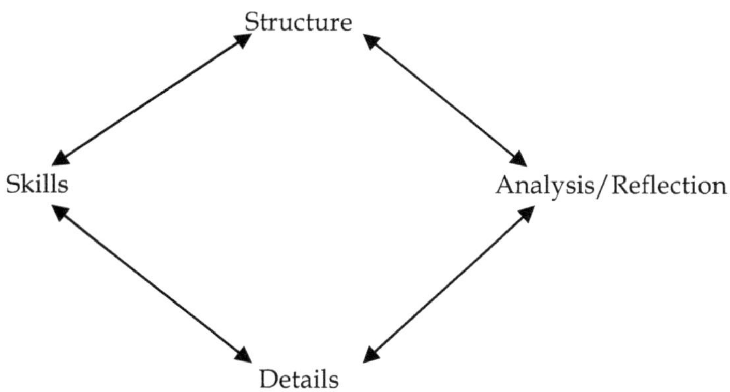

For an effective and smooth transfer of knowledge and skills to the students, enabling them to acquire the relevant knowledge and to enable them to apply what they have learned in practice creatively and become academic problem solvers, law schools must seek a coherent pedagogy which is consistently implemented and executed. This requires the formulation of what it is one wants the students to be able to do after graduation, which means we have to define their competences and skills. We also have to reflect on the best ways to deliver teaching and skills. I am convinced that law schools must take into account the employment settings and evolutions taking place in the labour market in this process. Mimicking some aspects of the labour market in teaching formats can be useful, in that ICT possibilities are an integral part of education, and that students are trained to apply knowledge and skills creatively and are trained to communicate with their peers and can constructively collaborate.

The markets for legal education in many countries are a prerogative of accredited law schools. In accreditation and the formulation of quality criteria, the traditional legal professions, specifically the bar, play an important role. Sometimes limited access to law schools is related to a limitation of access to the bar, in the sense that limiting numbers of prospective lawyers also influences the competition between lawyers and affect the costs. Most of the traditional legal education is through and in traditional law schools offering in-house, on campus teaching. The question is however whether this model of limited capacity and reliance upon traditional learning and teaching will be there forever.

The introduction of E-learning components in regular law schools, as well as the increased need for life-long learning programs will push demands for an E-learning solution. Also, it could be perceived that increasingly legal education programs will be offered through E-learning or through hybrid models of various mixes of E-learning and learning on the spot. When private companies will be admitted to the markets of legal education through online learning this could change the balance. In US Higher Education one can witness the rise of E-providers, offering online and cheaper education. They have no costs of buildings, campuses, or research time of their staff and can, for that matter, compete with regular universities, whose costs have risen. For legal education in Europe the cost factor is less relevant for students since legal education (with the exception of the UK and Sweden) is (for the students!) relatively cheap. However, students might want to add to their CV that they did a course (or courses) offered by a high-ranking law school, albeit online, but still an option which is relevant and cost effective.

Law schools could seek to diversify their teaching profile by adding E-courses and online learning facilities. I suggest that law schools might add to their attractiveness by offering hybrid products and enabling non-campus students to take courses and programs (which could be accredited by a home university - let's call this virtual exchange - or which could lead to full degrees). That is programs designed for students/professionals who have studied other sciences. Law schools could offer legal courses to scientists, business students, economists and others who want to integrate legal issues in their work as consultants, counsels, accountants, managers, patent officers and other professions. That in itself will constitute competition for lawyers who have no knowledge in these other fields of expertise.

Many facets of the law and the study of the law are linked to human contact (negotiations, client counselling, pleading and mooting, debate and the exchange of oral arguments), but many other aspects relate to paper work (drafting contracts, writing memoranda, analyzing texts) and can be done, monitored and graded online.

These factors, when done in a hybrid setting, will influence the didactics of teaching. One has to investigate how the pedagogy for face-to-face teaching and online teaching fit together. The school has to assess whether it wants to work in these markets and offer courses, modules or programs online. It will allow a school to expand its name and generate more alumni and maybe establish its brand. It does not necessarily, however, add to the internationalization of the classroom (experience). But a law school might feel forced to do it, for instance when other schools are seen to be offering online courses and students respond to those and less so to schools without an online course offering. Hybrid forms of teaching could meet students demands of having a study abroad experience, being able to a flexible program and study hours and studying parts of the programs from home, as well as saving on costs (travel, renting a residence abroad for a year, fee), and still acquiring a desired degree.

E-learning features could also be made part of the regular curriculum, containing for instance remedial teaching components (extra assignments, questions for self-study and quick tests for the students to help with self-study); or to re-listen/re-watch lectures; or for papers and feedback; or for pre-class preparation purposes, allowing the teacher to get an idea of where the students have encountered problems in preparing for class.

Chapter 9

CURRICULUM DESIGN

A curriculum is more than just a few (or many) modules or courses. It is imperative that a curriculum defines precisely what the goals are and how these goals can be achieved. Modules and courses are all building blocks contributing towards the overall purposes of the whole curriculum. One has therefore to develop a coherent curriculum design[1] about law, skills, attitude and critical analysis. A curriculum must be more than the mere sum of its parts: if well designed and structured the building blocks of a curriculum build upon one another, are well tuned and build upon the foregoing and are systematically ordered. Substantive courses lead from introductory to advanced, and so must skills be placed in such an order that students and professors know the sequence, the prior knowledge, the focus in their specific course, and the ultimate final goals of the curriculum. Curricula must be designed to serve the purpose of educating and training incoming students, to become highly qualified employment seekers and truly academic citizens.

This is all the more relevant because law and lawyers play a fundamental role in society: the stability and sophistication of a legal system contribute to legal certainty and inspire confidence and are major factors in generating economic growth, investment and jobs. The rule of law is not merely a hobby of lawyers or civil rights activists but is one of the important devices for security, certainty, economic prosperity, growth and stability.

In some sciences the half-life of knowledge is a very short time span. For law we also witness an increasing multitude of new rules, decisions, regulations, contracts, restatements, and even in multi-layered settings, so that lawyers increasingly are incapable of learning them by heart and of staying updated. Even the half-life of legal knowledge is shortening. This requires new and different skills from our students and graduates and this by definition has implications for legal curricula.

Another aspect is the growing need for interdisciplinarity: major and many societal problems seem to be so complex and interwoven with other disciplines that they require multidisciplinary solutions. Climate change; issues of crime and terrorism; the multi-cultural society; the stability of financial and economic systems and of states; the role of hedge funds and investors: these and many others require

1 See for a thorough and in-depth example: Schwartz 2001.

multidisciplinary approaches and solutions. Lawyers need to understand areas such as forensic disciplines, economics, financial markets, computer software, money laundering through real estate, nanotechnology in order to be able to design appropriate (if necessary) regulation and resolution of disputes. I am not so sure that we do a good job in law schools in preparing our students for these new challenges. Do we train them enough in working in multidisciplinary groups, such as think tanks, working together towards solutions? Or do we train them sufficiently in those other disciplines so that they can have a meaningful discussion with a psychiatrist about a forensic study of a psychopath killer, or with an investment banker or accountant about money laundering or stability of financial institutions, seeking appropriate regulation and supervisory mechanisms? Do we train our students sufficiently for client counselling or negotiations or problem solving or advising a minister on policies?

I submit that, taking into account the half-life of law(s) and the exponential increase of the multitude of multi-level regulations, laws, court decisions, dispute resolution, arbitration, treaties and so forth, we have to address the issue as to how to incorporate attention for lawyering sills and the demands from and in modern day society in a curriculum.

A curriculum is not something which is simply there or ought to reflect the way things have been done for many years. Curriculum design is imperative to fulfil the needs of legal education. A curriculum must be designed because it is in the end a compromise as to how best to achieve all goals of teaching skills, academic attitude and knowledge that is appropriate for the students entering law schools and best suited to allow them to enter the labour market(s) and the subsequent legal trainings. The labour market(s) has (have) been in constant and rapid change. Since our first-year students grow up in a world completely different from ours (us teachers) and will very soon have no knowledge of the 20th century and since the law and the legal challenges have drastically changed, it is imperative to thoroughly reflect upon legal education and what it means.

This is extremely complicated for the following reasons. In a law school professors have their chairs and their decades-old courses; any change in the order or the size will therefore be difficult to achieve and be opposed by those who will have less hours or a less prominent place in the curriculum. It is easy to conceive that incumbent professors in the abstract might be willing to reflect upon legal education and curriculum changes but, at the same time, feel that their course and expertise is indeed essential.

Lawyers in general, and this is an obvious generalization, are conservative and inclined to be careful with modernizations and changes. This, combined with the self-interest reason, leads to a complicated situation. However, careful analysis of the labour market, reflection on didactics, upon modern approaches of teaching and learning, and on the changes of the general landscape of university education and the reliance on benchmarks and the experiences of students in student exchanges and study abroad programs, will contribute to an opening-up of the discussion about curriculum design. The markets of legal education will, be it possibly slower than in other domains, also open up for competition and students will express their preferences with their feet. Law schools will find themselves open to competition by private competitors, or will be affected by lower places in international rankings, or they will see competitors doing better in (inter)national moot courts.

The only solution in that respect is to work towards a fully-fledged curriculum design, which takes into account the labour markets, the students, experiences of other schools, skills and competences, and the developments in the law.

Curriculum design implies many things; not only what to teach, how to teach, in what sequence to teach what, but also how to structure the school around the curriculum and to ensure that quality is measured and improvement cycles are introduced.

Curriculum design must also be related to the nature of the school (professionally oriented or academic/university) and to how legal education is set in the domestic teaching structure: undergraduate /graduate/ postgraduate. Schools have possibilities to choose between various strategies for how to go about their programs and programmatic offers. Is there a market for a specific LLM, considering the point of view of the students and the labour market? Which intellectual skills and legal knowledge do we want to focus on and what is the likely perspective for our graduates on the labour market? Transplanting legal education models from one country to another is unlikely, but learning from each other's experiences and expertise is possible. We can benefit from experiences elsewhere and implement them in a curriculum or new course and thereby improve legal education in a specific setting. This learning from others is indeed possible and absolutely necessary. This also requires a law school to be explicit about the goals of a legal education: what do we want to teach and convey and how do we want to do it? Do we focus on a specific segment of the labour market (for example, litigators), or do we want to educate learned legal academics? What is the proportion of (intellectual and/or professional) skills and knowledge? These questions relate to the student intake market and the labour market for the graduates and they are not easy questions, for a variety of reasons. One is that the answers to the questions are also related to resources and staff abilities. In that respect a thorough focus on intellectual skills might be helpful, since those skills are certainly more durable than pure knowledge of specific domains of the law. Another issue is that when we consider teaching law (also) an academic enterprise, the teachers and professors should be expected to engage in research and to have a connection with what is being taught and the subjects of research.[2] This might be particularly true in LLM

2 The link between teaching and research is for many scholars/teachers self evident: they teach and they do research. As I will discuss later in this book, for an academic study of the law, a link between research and education is essential, specifically (but not only) for master students. It is necessary because a research attitude and research skills are indeed indispensable for law students and legal professionals. That having been said, in some jurisdictions such as the US, there is certainly a debate about this issue. Some authors do engage scholarly work in the US and its impact upon law schools, law students and law curricula, is considered as →

courses but it is also true for undergraduate law programs. My starting point that the focus must be on intellectual skills presupposes a development of research skills in the students. For that purpose, an academic atmosphere of research and writing and the involvement of students in research projects is a clear necessity.

But to come back to the subject of this chapter: a curriculum needs a design and a coherent philosophy and perspective connected to the law school's mission and role. There is certainly no one-size-fits-all model.

Is it possible to formulate some common denominators for all law schools? On a certain level of abstraction this is certainly possible, though it raises the question whether it will give all of us engaged in legal education sufficient substance to rely upon.

In the previous chapters I have attempted to provide issues which law schools ought to take into account when drafting a curriculum. One certainly was to appreciate the relationship between knowledge and skills. I have argued that law is about both and that good lawyers master both.

Another lesson was to set up effective didactics and ensure that students primarily acquaint themselves with an overview of the legal system: without structural insight details will not stick. Structural knowledge will remain and details tend to change. Professors do want students to identify with their knowledge as experts and tend to over-estimate the need to focus very much on details instead of underlining the structure and concepts and the application to problems, stimulating the students to combine, create, reflect, defend, argue and discuss. In this learning process the students will come across further details and thereby learn the relevance and importance.

The preceding chapters lead me to propose procedural and substantive aspects for a curriculum design. The main gist is to reason from the perspective of what we think or predict our graduates must master for 40 years after they have graduated. Do they indeed benefit from a course on contracts, another course on comparative contracts and a separate course on international contracts? Or might it be better to combine aspects from these three domains in one course, training the students to switch between the domestic legal systems, be inspired from foreign legal systems, and also to learn about international issues? In law schools we tend to distinguish sharply between legal domains, because these distinctions match the different chairs and indeed frequently have specific concepts and approaches. But seen from the perspective of the application and later employment, different domains come together in actual practice: for instance in the example that a company wishes to start a marketing campaign for the launch of a new product the legal counsel will be

being too far away and having lost touch with legal practice (law schools hiring impractical scholars; focus on theoretical articles and the neglect of practical articles); see e.g. Newton 2010. European research is, to my knowledge, certainly different from scholarly legal research in the US, and also has regard for legal practice. Many European journals are co-edited with legal professionals and also have a function of informing legal practice.
These differences however do underline my point that we have to be careful to draw uniform conclusions which fit legal education all over the globe.

called upon to assess product liability issues, possible IP questions, codes of conduct relating to publicity campaigns, privacy infringements, possible competition issues and similar questions. If that is required by actual practice, we have to prepare our students and also reflect upon curricular issues meeting those challenges.

Many issues about the curriculum are still to be dealt with in the chapters to follow and the outcomes of those chapters will therefore have to be added to the preliminary conclusions listed below as lessons for curriculum development.

The following 15 important lessons/common denominators for law schools can be used as a checklist on the basis of the preceding findings. They have in common the necessity to consider a curriculum as a coherent whole, to be reflected upon, and to be considered as a means to reach specific aims (which must be identified), and targeted for a specific intake in the context of a specific society and legal system.

The following checklist can serve as a reminder in this respect:

1. adapt the curriculum to the input level (competences and skills of intake);
2. adapt the curriculum to the required output level (requirements of the labour market(s) and or continued education);
3. ensure to integrate law and (intellectual) skills;
4. include 'reflective' aspects (thinking about the law);
5. adopt an effective and productive pedagogy, which relies more on science than on tradition, and involves the students in their learning exercise;
6. make curriculum issues a law school policy and not a policy of individual faculty;
7. integrate and combine research and teaching;
8. evaluate the effectiveness and quality of the programs delivered and make the necessary changes: in general: build in a continuous process of innovation;
9. participate in national and international legal education networks;
10. develop a law school profile in legal education;
11. make stakeholders (students, alumni, labour market, faculty) part of the process of reflecting about education;
12. teach law not only as separate and distinct domains, but (also) in its context and in connection with other disciplines;
13. raise awareness of ethical and professional attitudes and professional standards;
14. adapt HRM policies to support your educational ambitions, programs and policies;
15. be fair and consistent in feedback to students and in exams and connect tests and exams and other assessments to the pedagogical philosophy.

Chapter 10

BLACK LETTER LAW AND EVALUATION: ACADEMIC TRAINING

Are lawyers simply professionals or legal technicians, or are lawyers more and do we want them to be more? More, in the sense that they cannot only apply rules to easy cases but can also think about rules and law in hard cases and difficult facts, and find new solutions to new problems and issues. These questions relate to issues pertinent to the labour market and the wide diversity of employment for people with a legal education. These issues also relate to the place of legal education in the educational framework of a specific country. These issues seem to have a link with the debate whether law is a science or merely a profession, and how to qualify legal research. Is it similar to social sciences, or economic studies, or has it more similarities with theology or philosophy, or does law share characteristics with these other domains? The labour market for lawyers is considered by many to be the legal professions proper (judges, prosecutors, notaries, solicitors/barristers/attorneys). But even within these professions there are huge differences between top law firms, which work with complicated issues and have to work in advanced domains, and on the other hand small local firms, specializing in serving private clients. We also see lawyers working in law making, policy advice and on corporate issues: they also have to work on the edge of legal work drafting and negotiating new rules for new problems, and creatively solving highly complex problems. In the top legal sector, we can also witness the importance of having had a broad academic background, because that brings along a critical mind and an open mind to other academic disciplines. There is therefore ample reason to link legal education to academic training and to an academic setting.

Students do not always seem to appreciate the courses which sharpen critical minds and reflection: legal theory, legal philosophy, sociology, ethics have not gained huge popularity. When students are allowed to choose between courses, they are inclined to opt for the courses that prepare them for practice and sit in the hard core legal domains. That is in many instances also what labour markets have asked law schools to do. However if one accepts my arguments about legal creativity and inventive solutions, it does seem imperative that law students are also trained in modes and methods of reflection. There are different ways that this can be done, but there is certainly a need to insert academic attitudes and the development of a creative and critical mind in the legal curriculum.

A difficult question in legal education is therefore what precisely do we teach and, linked to that, what are we teaching and what do we offer? Is legal education primarily a professional training or an academic education? The answer to the latter question seems to determine the first. When we consider legal education as the most important gateway to professional life, this could be taken to mean that we must teach all knowledge and skills, which has a direct and important impact upon the exercise of professional legal work. One of the problems here, which I have raised before, is that in many countries and settings, we do not precisely know for what profession we educate our students, because the possible employment possibilities differ vastly. A second problem here is that, even if we know that we would train students for the bar, there is still a great discrepancy in the requirements of different law firms: some work in family law, others in labour law and/or social security, others in taxes and again others in competition, public procurement; and others in mergers or financial law. And this list could be expanded with many more examples.

It is indeed an impossible task to educate people and make them learn all disciplines and sub disciplines and areas of the law. This would be impossible for reasons of limited time, but it would also be a waste of intellectual effort and it would contradict what, in my opinion, law schools are supposed to be doing. It is a waste of effort because of the half-life of legal knowledge. Studying and learning by heart many of these (sub) disciplines would imply learning much knowledge which will be outdated and redundant when (if) one, at some point in the future, is asked to work with it. Law changes and, in some domains, it does indeed change very rapidly.

Instead of teaching all the law there is, law schools must educate and train their students to be able to immerse themselves in a new area of the law quickly. We need to teach students to acquire the tools to constantly develop and update themselves. Because we simply do not know in which domains of the law our students will work, and they also most of the time do not know it, and probably they will change careers and switch areas of the law during their professional lives, we as educators cannot teach them all that the law comprises.

However, as I argued before, we must give them the tools for further study and problem solving, and teach them these tools, and let them practice using these tools during their studies, for instance by picking a specialized subject and delving into that subject. It does not really matter what subject is chosen; what matters is that students learn how one quickly immerses oneself in a new area; where the information can be sourced; how that specialized subject fits in the grand picture of the law. The lesson is in the exercise.

I have called this chapter, somewhat rhetorically, and suggesting a contradiction, 'black letter law and academic training'. For arguments sake, there is a contradiction, however, I do not want to suggest that academic training can do without knowledge of statutes, rules and cases; nor do I want to argue that such knowledge can do without academic context. For that purpose I have added the concept of evaluation. Law schools must endeavour to seek the proper balance between teaching positive law, on the one hand, and educating students to obtain the skills to evaluate the law(s) they are studying and study these/it with an open, critical and academic mind, on the other hand. Students must be able to evaluate what they are studying and seek alternatives and benchmarks for it. The notion 'evaluation'[1] handily summarizes what I mean.

It goes without saying that lawyers without any relevant knowledge, or with insufficient knowledge, of the law in the books will have difficulties being a good lawyer. The extent to which we have to force upon our students the details of the law is also related to the brightness of the students. As Tamar Frankel put it: when a school attracts the brightest students, it can be better than others schools in organizing learning under concepts and theory, for the students can and do learn the details of the law themselves. 'For them, learning the theoretical basis for judicial and other decisions is more important.'[2] She argues that great schools are fundamentally different in the focus of teaching the subjects of law, because they prepare students for different roles in their careers.

Let me argue, however, why all law schools have to devote time and effort in a legal curriculum to evaluation and/or academic aspects and the underlying concepts, doctrine and theory.

The first response is that lawyers without this academic flavour cannot and will not be good academic lawyers. They might be able to do good executive work, or work as paralegals, or assist lawyers for routine work, but they will miss the necessary qualifications to draft complicated contracts, to assist in mergers, or to work for high demanding clients in complicated cases. This first response indicates one of the themes in this book which is that the market for legal education must be more diverse and must and should allow for a variety of different kinds of legal education, training students for different jobs and different kinds of lawyers. Some schools may allow for top academic, internationally-competitive legal education and, on the other end of the spectrum of schools, professional schools could opt for training their students for routine legal work.

The argument for this first response is that lawyers will be better lawyers when they have been trained in critical and evaluative analysis. The idea is that they will find it easier to delve into complicated multi-issue problems, that they have been trained to creatively resolve complex issues and can pro-actively service clients. The academic flavour has given them skills and tools.

The second response is that the academic flavour makes the curriculum much more challenging and intellectually stimulating and thereby enhances the quality of the work of the students.

The third response lies in the half-life of many parts of the law. Learning positive law and cases might give students the impression that that is what counts, whereas we might better teach them the transferable skills as to how the law is structured, how to fit in new domains of knowledge, and how to work with the law

1 I borrow this word in this concept from my colleague Jaap Hage.
2 Frankel 2001.

and ensure that advice to the client is not only conform the law but also the best solution-oriented, inventive, persuasive, and fitting into the client's strategy, advice the client can get.

This still leaves the question unresolved what the proper demarcation is between black letter law and academic evaluation (and we may add the time and efforts spent on skills). This question however raises another one: might there be a good/better sequence as to how to teach positive law and the academic and skill aspects, or is there no sequence? And is the best way to mix positive law, skills and academic evaluation in one great bowl and teach this soup full of ingredients to the students from day one?

In continental Europe there has been less a discussion about the distinction between the academic component and the lawyering skills than in the UK and the US. The most important factor why this is so is that for the UK legal education has only recently (half a century ago) been taken over by university law schools from on-the-job training by the legal profession.[3] In the US the academization of legal education took place earlier and is generally referred to as the Langedellian revolution, after the Harvard professor Langdell who introduced the Socratic case method of teaching. On the European continent legal education (the study of law) has been a part of universities for many centuries. There seems to me, therefore, to be less a debate about the two concepts: legal education as a professional training or as an academic undergraduate (and postgraduate) study.

In another comparison J.H.A. Lokin has equalled modern day legal education to a walking buffet: many practice-oriented courses to be consumed by the students, one after the other.[4] And N.C. van Oostrum-Sneep also pleads in that respect for 'moral education of the students', values and ethics.[5] In the same vein Jan Klabbers argued that (legal) education should serve two functions: prepare for professional life and for public life, the life as a citizen. In the globalization discussion the latter should mean that we ought to train our students to become (global) lawyers and global citizens.[6]

Kronman[7] has called it the quest for educating lawyer-statesmen (the lawyer-statesmen ideal): lawyers who can become statesmen in the republic and apply their skills and knowledge for the common good. Martha Nussbaum[8] links education to democracy and specifically the education in humanities. The need, she argues, for education is to train students to approach world problems as a "citizen of the world". Education is for citizenship, for employment and for meaningful lives. Her argument holds specifically true for those countries in which university or professional education is not preceded with a Liberal Arts education, such as is the

3 An interesting description of the development and of the present situation is by Boon & Webb 2010.
4 Lokin 2005.
5 Van Oostrum-Sneep 2009, p. 31.
6 Klabbers 2008, p. 17-18.
7 Kronman 1994, p. 5.
8 Nussbaum 2010, p. 7 & 9. See also: Shapiro 2005, for instance, on p. 95.

case in Europe. The quality of education is not only to teach and incorporate in the curriculum what is needed for economic growth or is directly linked to the requirements of applicable knowledge relevant for the labour market but also to educate critical skills, argumentative skills, ethics and other reflexive competences. Content must be present in a curriculum to educate and force students to think critically for themselves and to be able to engage in discussions about a variety of social, political, ethical and legal issues. As I have argued these skills must be incorporated in a legal curriculum; they must be an indispensable part specifically when they are lacking in the preceding school system. Nussbaum also links the content to pedagogy and deals in that respect with the Socratic pedagogy: students interactively participating in their teaching and class discussions and writing papers. For law I will urge in that respect for the comparative legal method/the transsystemic 'McGill' method to be considered as another mode to achieve similar goals of (inter)activity and critical argument. I have argued in another chapter in favour of problem-based learning, which is helpful. I propose that anything other than a pedagogy in which lectures are given and students listen, try to remember and learn by heart and to digest is a better direction to follow.

Nussbaum links education to the other 'Not for Profit' skills, with less focus on pure economic growth education but also on critical thinking and discussion and therefore of humanities, as a democratic need. For lawyers there is also another, related, need. The need to uphold the rule of law, the responsibility for the fabric of law and the (democratic) institutions in a country, with due regard to human rights and elementary fairness and equality, are values to instil in our students through our legal education. For that reason law schools must pay due attention to these values and to other notions than making money for the firm or the client. Accountancy and financial banking scandals have led us to put on the agenda how and to what extent business schools must incorporate professional ethics in their curricula. In medical school students are trained with skills on how to deal with patients, complex life and death issues and medical interventions. In the same vein I urge for a similar approach for law: professional ethics, surely, but also democratic values, the role of law and interventions through law and regulation, and skills of critical analysis and independent (legal) thinking and wisdom in arguments.

In a few articles Mikael Rask Madsen[9] introduced the notion of legal diplomacy and legal diplomats for (judges in) the European Court of Human Rights during the first years of its case law. With that qualification he referred to a similar feature as propagated by Nussbaum and Kronman: lawyers with an eye on international relations, with a feel for diplomacy, with knowledge of the law, and with a sensitivety for wise adjudication, steering between the protection of human rights and the necessary promotion of the stature of the Court vis à vis the states parties to the European Convention of Human Rights. Similarly, the European Court of Justice also can be seen to have built its authority not only with judicial craftsmanship but also with authority derived from the wisdom of its judgments.

[9] Madsen 2011a; Madsen 2011b.

For all these reasons legal curricula, the 'legal' pedagogy, the skills and academic spirit in a law school must be more than knowledge of the law and of rules and judgments. They must, in the setting of academic/university law schools add, or better, start from the perspective that it is necessary to educate academics, with a critical mind, with an open spirit and well-reasoned and argued opinions, linked with a political and social sensitivity and desire to promote the rule and quality of the law.

These arguments, combined with the enormous diversity in the labour markets for law graduates and the developments in legal work in the future and the half-life of the body of law, call for an approach with a focus on transferable skills, reflection, and critical qualities, to be exercised in the legal domain. But this has to be done with due regard for society, the rule of law and other legal cultures. The latter will be the subject of the following chapter.

The question about black letter law and the knowledge of all, or many, domains of the law is an issue which will lead to different answers according to the pre-law school knowledge of students, the extent of professional training after law school, and the profile of the law school (what kind of lawyers for which segments of the labour markets does one intend to educate). Clearly the length of the curriculum (and legislative requirements about substance and credits) is highly relevant. Attention for other disciplines (law and X courses or minors) will detract from the intensity of the study of all legal domains in depth. The addition of skills has the same effect. The less credits are available in legal education, the more difficult an integral approach will be. In those circumstances a focus on the basics of the main legal domains is self-evident, combined with skills and links to other scientific areas.

Chapter 11

GLOBALIZATION AND COMPARATIVE LAW

In recent centuries, with an emphasis upon codification, the nation states and national sovereignty, we have witnessed the development of law as a predominantly domestic discipline. Central in studying law was the focus upon national codification, national case law and domestic legal culture. The curriculum of law schools was governed by domestic stakeholders such as bar associations and national legislatures. The only courses which might have had a transnational content were international law (if at all present!) and possibly courses focusing on legal theory or philosophy, where students were invited to read texts from non-national writers. Also in civil law jurisdictions in continental Europe, students could be confronted with Roman Law and legal history. Finally, electives did occasionally appear focusing on comparative law, as a methodological course (the theories of comparative law), or as a substantive course (or mixed) about major legal systems or comparing major legal institutions and concepts.

Recent decades have shown an evolution in this respect. Due to the developments of globalization (and Europeanization), international collaboration, the growth of international organizations and courts, the increasing importance of international rules and student exchanges between universities (accompanied with staff exchange, international collaboration between universities and law schools), curricula of law schools have been amended and in some cases transformed. Furthermore, research in law schools has become much more international. There even exists a Global Connectedness Index![1]

The questions must be posed if and how globalization and internationalization trends (in practice and in research) have been taken up in curricula,[2] and in that respect, how this has impacted comparative law, and if and how comparative law, and its impact upon legal practice and the making of law (specifically but not only

1 Made by DHL: <http://www.dhl.com/en/about_us/logistics_insights/global_connectedness_index_2012.html>. According to this index, edition 29012, the Netherlands is the most globalized country, followed by Singapore!

2 Minow 2010, mentioned the undeniably global context of law practice, law, economies, and competition between law schools as one of the four features of the current moment, suggesting that legal education could be on the brink of the most dramatic changes in 140 years.

within the European Union), has gained importance in law curricula. Have law schools managed to escape the domestic rules of bar associations and legislatures, and do they sufficiently prepare themselves for the future and future developments of legal challenges and the labour markets? And how must law schools seek to mediate between domestic and global demands? Has the labour market already accommodated globalization and do law schools pro-actively orient themselves to the future, or are these perspectives farfetched and unrealistic?

In this chapter I will deal with the two subjects of this chapter (globalization and comparative law) in two separate paragraphs. In the final paragraph of this chapter I will tie them together. The two issues are interrelated because globalization (and its various regional siblings, such as Europeanization) does show the urgency for the teaching of comparative law. However, apart from the globalization component of comparative law, there is also another factor which in itself makes comparative law an indispensable tool in legal education, as such, and that relates to the function of comparative law as a lawyer's laboratory and as a didactical tool. These aspects will be addressed in paragraph 2 as well as in relevant other chapters of this book.

1. Globalization (and Europeanization)

Without wanting to deny that some local disputes are indeed still purely local, it is sure that modern-day lawyering has obtained increasingly more international components. There are many reasons for this development (and there will undoubtedly be more to come or they will become more pressing). One of the most obvious reasons is that a variety of legal issues are indeed transboundary and have transfrontier implications and effects: international crime; international financial issues; environmental climate issues; international trade; international transports; migration; severe crimes; cyber crime and warfare; issues of nationality and family law; and others. For the resolution of these problems, states have resorted to international treaties, agreements and settlements. These international resolutions undoubtedly have a gradual and deep impact upon domestic law: domestic law had to be changed in order to make the international rules more effective and have them implemented into domestic law; international collaboration exported and imported foreign experiences and practices; before introducing policies, states resorted to international consultation and comparative research; international networks were set up in which policy makers and lawyers concerted their actions and agreed upon practices and regulations to ensure effective international collaboration and action.

This is even more prominent on the European level, within the context of the Council of Europe and specifically within the European Union. In the many domains of competence of the EU, domestic legislation is intertwined with EU regulations, directives and decisions. An intricate web has been spun of multi-level governance and consultations and collaboration. Many civil servants of Member States meet in Brussels with their counterparts from the other Member States to discuss policies, implementation, collaboration and harmonization.

European law making is an amalgam of legal concepts and legal cultures of the Member States, which has gradually evolved into Euro English and Euro law and legal culture. Whether the EU was initially to a large extent inspired by the domestic legal systems, and whether it initially resorted to domestic legal concepts which it transformed and knitted into EU legal concepts, now the time has certainly come to consider EU law in many domains as a distinct legal system, and one which heavily impacts upon the legal systems of the Member States,[3] but still as a legal system which has many of its roots in domestic legal systems.

Globally, authors have also argued in favour of the need to adapt the legal curricula of law schools to globalization and trans-border issues. In that perspective W. Michael Reisman stated that the legal curriculum should be based upon a notion of a comprehensive transnational legal system, rather than an autonomous national system.[4] He described the McGill curriculum, teaching transsystemic law, and considered it a valuable experience of characteristics and learning outcomes of a transnational focus. Jan Smits has also argued in favour of preparing students for global citizenship.[5] His arguments are threefold: first of all that the law itself is no longer a national phenomenon; secondly, that it better meets the requirements of an academic study: preparing students for global citizenship and training them in legal ways of thinking (to think like a lawyer); and finally that an international legal education will attract better motivated students.

This means that legal education has to reflect this reality and, more so, has to take into account that the present state of affairs will most likely be one of more intensive collaboration and internationalization in the immediate future. Since law schools do not educate lawyers for the present or the past, but for the future, we have to take the globalization trend into account.[6]

The above also holds true from a more theoretical point of view. Globalization does impact upon what we have to teach so that our lawyers will have the knowledge and skills to cope with the globalizing issues which will be on their plates and which they will have to deal with in their working lives. 'The era of globalization ... presents us with a new set of ethical challenges', as Shapiro has argued. These challenges require 'a much improved knowledge of the empirical

3 It is telling in this respect that the 2010 edition of the General Part of the textbook on *Principles of Belgian Private Law* (*Beginselen van Belgisch Privaatrecht*, Kluwer 2010, by Walter van Gerven & Steven Lierman) sets Belgian private law in the framework of international law, and European law, and describes Belgian private law in the context of multi-layered modern-day legal systems. This book is a very interesting way of perceiving domestic law in this multi-layered context and interacting with other domains of the law and globalization/ Europeanization trends.

4 Reisman 1996; about the need of legal education to focus more on the lawyers of tomorrow (who often need to be able to switch from one jurisdiction to the other and need to switch across issue areas); Klabbers 2007.

5 Smits 2011, p. 43-64.

6 In this respect also: Van Zandt 2004.

state of the world'.[7] These empirical data and ethical challenges must be(come) part of general education and of professional legal education.

In an edited volume about the Internationalization of Law the editors Mary Hiscock and William Van Caenegem very aptly and timely analyzed the need for law schools to internationalize their education.[8]

> '[W]e have moved from a perception of a palette of disparate and 'sovereign' systems tangentially connected to the perception of a single underlying system or structure [...] [a]lthough we still speak and think in terms of sovereignty and think primarily up-from-sovereignty, that view no longer represents a reality where the interconnections, correspondence, collaboration and so forth between systems is so intense that there is in fact only one, global system.'

That trend has been illustrated neatly in the book in a variety of contributions and is also reflected, as Hiscock and Van Caeneghem argue, by increasing international student bodies in (some) law schools and programs, by the growth of English taught LL.M's and by a growing collaboration between law schools in double and joint programs.[9]

Internationalization and globalization can easily be constructed as vague concepts, which detract students from the study of domestic legal concepts and issues. That certainly is not intended. Internationalizing curricula will serve the purpose of educating students, in various domains of the law, in the impact the internationalization labour markets, legal and societal issue and markets and commerce have on the law itself and on how to conduct legal business and offer legal services. Seeking to partly[10] escape state centric approaches in a law curriculum and expose students to transnational legal issues will enhance the students' competences.

2. Comparative Law

One of the arguments in this book is that we will have to train lawyers who will have the knowledge and the skills to be operative for the many decades to come. Purely training in the knowledge of domestic black letter law is not good enough and even a waste of time. In order to be able to train lawyers with the necessary lawyering and academic skills it is necessary to reduce the attention on the black letter law and to focus in our curricula upon solutions and reasoning and analysis.

7 Shapiro 2005, p. 111.
8 Hiscock & Van Caenegem 2010.
9 In that respect see also: Lo 2010.
10 Partly, indeed, because in many law schools and for a variety of legal domains, domestic law is a primary source of law and must be educated. The issue here is to present students with the non-state centric approach also, where appropriate and to do so in an international classroom setting, which will also contribute to a lawyer's cross (legal) cultural competences and cross-border lawyering skills. Partly, this also implies that diversity between law schools can result in some law schools establishing different profiles and having a different emphasis on the scope of globalization in a curriculum.

Let's train legal minds and not legal encyclopaedia. Let's focus on skills on how to handle disputes and problems; how to interact with other disciplines and with clients and employers. Let's focus upon academic skills: training our students to reflect creatively and critically on legal approaches. That, in my opinion, is the first reason, and a very important one, to rely heavily upon comparative law.

The main didactical tool in my experience for creativity and academization of the study of law is to introduce a substantial focus on comparative law. Comparative law serves as a basic attitude in legal training. We have all been raised in first and second year courses in contracts, torts, property, company law, constitutional law and criminal law by learning the basic domestic concepts. Why not reverse this approach and move to teaching approaches to these areas of law in the first year and do so comparatively: asking general questions, such as what constitutes a contract? Let students research that question by delving into comparative law, researching different methodologies and countries and concepts? Let us use the world as a laboratory and as a world of reflection and inspiration.

The world encounters so many issues and problems that are common to many states and legal systems. Research into those issues, and particularly into how states have resolved those issues, or have drafted legislation in those areas, might assist other states and policy makers and lawyers in drafting and assessing one's own rules and policies. On a more fundamental level it will help all lawyers and students to ask fundamental and pertinent questions about the quality of their own legal system. It will also enable students and lawyers to evaluate legal concepts and legal resolutions.[11]

Comparative law in this sense is *not* about copying and pasting foreign legal solutions and concepts. It is instead about learning from each other and about investigating legal solutions and legal concepts, as well as assessing these and being inspired by other legal systems when one seeks a solution or has to draft a law or regulation or judgment. By looking across borders students (and legal professionals and researchers) can seek inspiration, or can engage in a discussion about good or even 'best' practices and best solutions. Human imagination is less creative than what occurs in the real world and, therefore, to find out which obstacles a legal rule can meet, or which aspects might be relevant to assess the quality of a judgment, it is certainly helpful to look across borders at similar rules and judgments and see what these have brought about in legal and factual effects. Comparative law can serve as an indicator to look for effects and impacts of legal constructs, enhancing our creativity; it makes comparative law a tool for lawyers to have a real world laboratory at their disposal.

11 To quote Chesterman 2009, p. 887-888: 'The content of the basic law degree will continue to emphasize the traditional subjects, but the move away from the memorization of black-letter law will become irresistible: faculties will seek ways to ensure that their graduates are both intellectually and culturally flexible, capable of adapting not merely to new laws, but to new jurisdictions. Comparative and international subjects will receive greater emphasis, with comparative and international perspectives also being introduced to a wider range of subjects.' See also Chesterman 2008, p. 58-67.

A second reason for allowing ample space for comparative law is that it is a technique to train research and linguistic skills. Comparative law requires: research skills in foreign legal systems; a feel for legal sources, terminology and system. It provides an experience of not only being satisfied with finding and understanding the legal rules but also researching the law in action, as well as the effects of the rules on the behaviour of people and its side effects, whilst also trying to assess the 'quality' of the rule in question with regard to its costs, (side) effects, and impact.

When progressing through law school, after students have acquired the skills to do research, to approach what they have found and how they have evaluated their findings critically, they can eventually learn the workings and precise doctrines of one specific legal system. That will then be a lot easier to do with a critical and evaluative mind and with a mind open to new solutions and creative new ideas.

The comparative approach also fits in well with skills training and exercises, because when discussing and comparing solutions and variations, one is compelled to define 'best' and to examine the quality of rules and regulations and concepts. It will also assist the students to conduct research, to understand other legal systems and value them and, later, when working in an international environment, to engage in exchanges with foreign lawyers. These will be assets which will be cherished increasingly.

The third reason for reliance upon comparative law is a more practical one, and it rests upon the present-day situation that legal systems interact and that therefore domestic lawyers interact. When systems and people interact, it is always good to know the other system and the frame of reference of the other lawyer.

In Europe, the de facto trend is towards Europeanizing the legal domain and the legal professions. Or, it is at least towards exchanges of opinions and practices, the search for joint solutions and the search towards commonalities. The 27 (in 2013: 28) EU Member States are increasingly under the legal influence of European rules, decisions, directives and regulations. They are also involved in a permanent exchange of information and in a mutual collaboration and in meetings. Many legal issues are the subject of European, or combined European/domestic solutions or at least a subject for consultation. This implies that lawyers from 27 (28) jurisdictions sit together and draft new legal regimes and draft rules or discuss white papers or common issues. This by definition means an exchange and a mixture of legal cultures and legal concepts. An identical process occurs on the global level, maybe less intense and less pervasive but increasingly so. Lawyers with skills in comparative law, with abilities to understand and switch between legal cultures, and who master (legal) languages, will be much in demand.

Lawyers will have to work with foreign legal rules and with foreign lawyers: whenever they meet in Brussels and discuss new rules and policies and draft documents and contracts; when they are confronted with issues of cross-boundary relevance in regional areas; when they consult on mergers and takeovers, or product liability issues; when they apply company law and consumer law, which are to a large extent European law; when they work as criminal lawyers or a prosecutors and a case is part of an international investigation, etcetera. For those purposes, and many others, linguistic capabilities (legal English?!) are a great asset. as is a basic understanding of one another's legal systems and legal cultures. That will certainly enhance the quality and the smooth operation of the process one is involved in, and it will enable better advice and quality work for the client.

Here, the same lesson applies as it does for studying (domestic) law: we train lawyers who know what they do not know. For knowledge of foreign legal systems, we will have to train graduates who know when it is time to hire a foreign lawyer and know how to communicate with him/her and how to avoid legal misunderstandings.

For those reasons, a more in-depth training of comparative law is indispensable, as part of the regular legal curriculum.

Many of the aspects which I have described *supra* have been taken up by the Faculty of Law of Maastricht University. We have designed an English taught international, European and transnational legal curriculum, inspired by the European developments of exchanges of students and staff and of a 'common law' of Europe. Special teaching materials[12] and a Journal[13] have been written and set up. Skills trainings and moot courts were developed and will be developed. The didactic formula is based upon the Maastricht University-wide utilized 'Problem-Based Learning'. Those who have an interest, I kindly refer to our website: <www.maastrichtuniversity.nl/law>. I kindly invite those with an interest in pursuing similar approaches of curriculum reform to contact us, for an exchange of experiences and for networking.

In the end of this book I have described this project and my proposals in this respect in more depth. I will also comment there on the common objection that it is impossible to design a European, international comparative law curriculum, because a law student ought to master the domestic legal system first, before embarking upon comparative exercises.[14]

3. Comments

Bénédicte Fauvarque-Cosson argued for a (further) development of European legal scholarship, based upon the existence of a new European legal culture, and therefore the creation of a new European legal science. This is based, so to speak upon an empirical analysis: noting that this European legal culture is shaping and is followed by academics who at the same time participate in its formation. She notes, however, at the same time that the strength and durability of European legal thinking largely depend on the place it will (note the future tense of the verb) be

12 For example: Heringa & Kiiver 2012; Kiiver & Kornet 2010; currently work is undertaken under the supervision of Jaap Hage (editor) of a book about Introduction to Law as well as by the criminal law department, about comparative criminal law and criminal procedure.

13 *Maastricht Journal of European and Comparative Law*, (<http://www.maastrichtuniversity.nl/web/Institutes/METRO/MaastrichtJournal.htm>).

14 For example, Van Oostrum-Streep 2009, p. 28.

granted in universities. She even goes so far as to state that legal education may well be the flaw of the whole process of Europeanization, since in many European countries legal education is still very nationalistic. This leads her to argue in favour of a reorganization of law faculty programs with a less national and more European perspective.[15]

I agree with this analysis and reasoning, however, in my perspective the teaching of comparative law also contributes to the aim of the academization of legal education. This implies training students in a critical analysis of legal rules and the resolution of disputes as well as training them in cross-national/European/global practice and scholarship. Claudio Grossman formulated a perspective on the need to build the world community through legal education, which entails and necessitates the following: establishing links between the study of domestic law and international law; focusing on different legal systems; and including cultural issues.[16]

Backer has analysed the various models as to how to internationalize the curriculum of (American) law schools, with many examples and models.[17] He has also pointed to many practical aspects such as the need to carefully tailor internationalization efforts to consensus among faculty; abilities of the faculty, and the available resources.

In order to give credit where credit is due, McGill Law School has been among the first schools to come up with a trans-nationalized legal curriculum.[18] This curriculum aims to do 'much more than simply open the doors to worldwide legal practice. Rather, the ambition is to create cosmopolitan jurists'.[19] The approach is to adopt an entirely new approach to teaching: 'By working with different legal traditions having distinct historical and methodological underpinnings, students are exposed to a variety of perspectives and a contextual analysis of legal problems.'[20] Peter L. Strauss noted that the way to do it is to approach the matter from the perspective of human problems and desired outcomes; 'the question of how one got from point A to point B was just a system whose particulars could be learned'.[21] Dedek and Mistral defined the aspiration of the program as to 'transcend the fixation on the study of law as the study of "legal systems"- hence the label "transsystemic" legal education'. The McGill program is about more than the mastery of positive rules. The students, as Dedek and Mistral argue, cease to think in terms of a single national legal paradigm and are instinctively prepared to cope with several jurisdictions. They also conclude that the concern that the comparative

15 Fauvarque-Cosson 2007. As a consequence the author also pleads in favour of the development of relevant (comparative/European) textbooks, collection of materials, case books, commentaries etc.

16 Grossman 2008, p. 21-35.

17 Backer 2008.

18 See: Jukier 2006; Strauss 2006; Dedek & De Mestral 2009.

19 Jukier 2006, p. 174.

20 Jukier, p. 177; see also the Strauss 2006.

21 Strauss 2006, p. 169.

approach might have been purchased at the price of a less thorough training in the positive law, has appeared to be unfounded.

The experiences described above, coupled with the internationalization of law and the source of inspiration in foreign legal systems, show that it is necessary and possible to draw more on comparative law in a law curriculum. As to the how, there are many possibilities, varying according to the profile of the law school. The McGill approach and the Maastricht European Law School have integrated foreign law and globalization aspects as an inherent feature in their curricula. They do not take one specific domestic legal system as a starting point but seek to focus on issues and problems and the search for legal solutions and legal concepts. A more moderate approach would be to indeed teach domestic law but with a constant comparative law aspect as part of all courses. Another possibility is to offer a (compulsory) course to students about comparative law.

However it is being done, students' ability to work with the law and a legal system will improve with the aid of comparative law; through comparative law, lawyers will have a laboratory available to examine laws, solutions, approaches, which can assist him/her in doing the job in the legal domain. Comparative law will also allow for reflection on the quality of the law and a discussion of possible and feasible solutions, in which theoretical and conceptual arguments can be enriched with foreign experiences.[22] This will enhance the academic flavour of the curriculum. A basic knowledge of foreign law and legal systems will further allow for international legal work and legal communication and collaboration. Finally, the knowledge of comparative law and of foreign languages will be a competitive advantage in the global lawyering markets. We already witness the benefits for students who pick an extra master degree abroad after their domestic graduation. Similarly, the success of student exchanges on the European level shows the feasibility to incorporate a foreign legal study experience in a law curriculum. This incorporation can be enhanced through adapting legal curricula to include more outward looking/comparative law aspects.

Comparative law fits in the trends of the labour markets which I have described before - demanded by globalization and/or Europeanization.[23] Familiarity with globalization and comparative law will be/is in demand. On top of the issue of employability, comparative law will increase the academic depth and quality of the legal curriculum.

22 See also Hage 2011. Ault & Glendon 1975 call it giving students a kind of perspective on the operation of their own legal system, by exposing them to a range of legal techniques which differ from those familiar to them from their common law training. They argue that since there is a constant need for new and alternative models of solutions to social problems, comparative law is a source of such models. It helps (as do legal history and legal philosophy) in providing perspective but also in enabling students to think more creatively about legal problems which they will encounter in law school and in practice.

23 Also: Chesterman 2009: 'At least some international experience will increasingly be seen as essential to the practice of law at the upper echelons.'

4. International and Comparative Flavour

In the previous paragraphs I have discussed the impact and the utilization of globalization, Europeanization and of comparative law. Important in that respect is furthermore the internationalization of the classroom (and of the faculty). Collaboration, exchanges, international rankings and benchmarks, international exchanges of perspectives and experiences in teaching law and skills, are key words. Many parts of the law are truly international; other parts of the law undergo the influence of other legal systems; and for skills training we can learn from each other. This means that, not only is it urgent and relevant to learn from each other domestically and continuously improve but also globally law schools must open their doors and windows to international experiences and lessons to be learned.

In Chapter 13 I will refer to the practices of business schools and their international accreditation procedures. For law a similar international accreditation standard does not exist but, apart from that, the lessons to be learned from membership of and participation in such organizations are of enormous importance. An organization such as the American Association of Law Schools (AALS)[24] is an example of how globally and/or regionally international collaboration might develop.

In Europe the European Law Faculties Association (ELFA) sprung up and globally IALS (International Association of Law Schools) came into being some years ago. But work has to be done here to make them as prestigious and relevant as AALS or as the three business schools organizations.

Specifically I am impressed by the example of the AALS, as an organization, which offers a platform to discuss and reflect about legal education. An organization through which faculty from all law schools meet, exchange best practices and seek and give assistance, and have a forum to publish about legal education.[25] In the UK there is also a very active Association of Law Teachers (ALT)[26] which also publishes a journal called *The Law Teacher: The International Journal of Legal Education*.[27] Forming associations and setting up networks through which to discuss legal education domestically, regionally and internationally is extremely important, the more so with the AALS and ALT format that these associations are very much teacher driven. Within AALS many sections exist, allowing experts in specific domains or faculty with certain interests to meet and to pursue research and improve upon education. That is certainly a format for networks about international, transnational, regional and domestic legal education. I do believe that law schools benefit by participating through their faculty and their leaders in such networks, organizations and conferences.

These organizations do and might play a role in developing benchmarks and standards and good practices for legal education. Not primarily with the purpose to

24 <http://www.aals.org/>.
25 *Journal of Legal Education*: <www.aals.org/resources_journal.php>.
26 <www.lawteacher.ac.uk/>.
27 <www.lawteacher.ac.uk/journal>.

set up new benchmarking or accreditation processes but to make visible what is happening in law schools and what schools can learn from one another, and where changes and investments are needed because a law school (or the law schools in a specific country or setting) appear to be missing the quality indicators. League tables, (inter)national rankings and accreditation mechanisms might also fulfil the need of benchmarking, facilitating transparency and therefore guide states, universities, stakeholders and law schools to make more resources available or invest in quality. Professional organizations of law deans and law schools also have a role to play here. In the legal domain there is a lot to be gained in that respect. Only recently lawyers and law schools are increasingly accustomed to invest in and think in European and international terms and perspectives. Although we have to take into account that law has been a primarily domestic discipline, this perspective is however also drastically changing. Law schools, law professors and law deans must organize themselves actively internationally and reap the benefits from international assistance, exchange and standards.

I have given this paragraph the title 'International and Comparative Flavor' in order not to create the impression that all law schools must have a fully-fledged international and comparative mission and profile; that would go against the diversity of contexts and roles of law schools I have proposed and that I envisage. That does not mean on the other hand that law schools ought to ignore the international and transnational components of law and must set aside comparative law as a didactical concept and as a means of improving substance. Law schools must play a role in developing the best teaching concepts and in preparing their students for the legal profession in the future and serving society in being schools in which legal academics and future leaders of a country are being educated. These functions all demand that legal education is embedded in domestic and international and comparative law and that students have the opportunity to study in international settings such as with and through exchanges, international classrooms, that is in a proper curriculum which facilitates internationalization of the courses and the contents, and which prepares the students to work with different legal cultures and legal professionals. For these reasons I have given this chapter the name 'International and Comparative Flavor'.

There is a lot that law schools can do here, also assisted with the development of the Internet. Literature is increasingly electronically available and so are lectures, placed on the web. These can, as I have argued before, also play a role in didactical adaptations of a curriculum, but might also play a role for law schools to offer lectures from other schools and from abroad to their students. This could well lead to a very basic quality boost and internationalization of course content. I do hope that international associations will play a role here to facilitate these Internet-based applications and the availability of lectures. I would look forward to IALS and ELFA for instance facilitating on their websites links to accessible and free lectures, made available by law schools.

In the context of a law school with international ambitions or an international curriculum, or trying to build courses with an international or transnational substance, the exchange of information about modes of delivery, materials and structures of courses is helpful. International networks and organizations are relevant in that respect. It would be certainly interesting to have a platform through which educational innovations could be made public and be made available for discussion and evaluation.

International flavor in a law school and a program is injected furthermore through faculty, in their courses, and through their teaching. The international networking and conferences about teaching must therefore be something for faculty, as is the AALS model. Law schools have a role in making it possible for faculty to participate, or certainly for law schools to stimulate their faculty to attend and participate and share experiences.

In addition to a law school's own faculty, a feature is to regularly host visiting faculty and enable guest lectures to be held (either delivered in person or through video lectures). These facilities confront students with foreign legal thinking and teaching and allow faculty to be inspired and to engage in collaborative projects.

Another aspect of international flavor is through the content and the format or profile of the courses and programs which a law school has on offer. Internationalization of and in a law school must have a match between the policies, the faculty (and their research!) and the programs/courses as well as the students. An international flavor must be linked with the substance of the teaching. Courses about domestic law, which incorporate a comparative approach and programs about international legal issues, are relevant ingredients for internationalizing a law school.

Another aspect relates to student exchanges (see also paragraph 5 of this chapter) and for the present context specifically the value of also having incoming students. Student exchanges will inject a law school with foreign experiences and enrich a classroom with a foreign legal approach. Student exchanges are valuable for one's own outgoing students but also for the law school which hosts students from abroad. European universities have experienced this incoming aspect of exchanges in a positive way and it has led law schools to add (English taught) new courses in the curriculum; to add an international flavor in classrooms, also for those domestic students who do not participate in international exchanges and do not study an international legal program. That is certainly one of the great benefits: to confront even the home students in their own familiar study setting with the influx of foreign law students. They bring along different approaches to the law, ask different questions, will suggest different solutions and they enrich class life in a law school.

A law school, which embarks fully on the path towards an international law school, ought to meet many of the aspects referred to above: international and comparative courses and programs with international literature; international faculty; student exchanges; international visiting staff and guest lectures. The law school must be infused with different nationalities, cultures, backgrounds and substance. All these aspects will in the end lead towards a truly international classroom experience.

This in itself may sound easy but also leads to softer characteristics. It is one thing to have an internationally diversified faculty and students and to have an international and comparative content; another aspect is that international diversity also challenges a law school. Students from different backgrounds have different expectations; they have different learning backgrounds and experiences; foreign students have crossed a border for a study and will inevitably stumble upon cultural or other aspects with which they are not familiar; some might take some time to adapt in the very beginning of the program, learning to cope with the language or needing time to establish friendships and social contacts.

At the same time faculty needs to develop sensitivity to these aspects or to cultural aspects in a tutorial group. The law school has to take into account in their communication with students the different backgrounds and questions. Study counselors and mentors might need to be more engaged and more available to give guidance and support.

The route of internationalization does need investments in facilities, faculty, courses, support, international networks and connections to the (international) labour markets (see Chapter 14). It requires resources for faculty training and their participation in the necessary networks and it sets an agenda for the leadership of a law school to embrace fully the international profile, if one has chosen that option for the school as (one of) the routes to follow.

It is, however, not necessarily an all or nothing approach. Gradually a new development can be started, but also then one has to be aware that even gradually resources have to be made available and priorities must be set. This gradual approach is very visible in China. China is a country with a massive growth in numbers of law students, law schools and a gradual internationalization policy of a few schools, but with many more to follow.

In China the following initiatives are worth mentioning as primary examples of the internationalization of programs and schools. In Peking University (Shenzhen) School of Transnational Law since 2008 an American JD (Juris Doctor) program is offered and taught by American professors. Furthermore Tsinghua University School of Law and Temple University Beasley School of Law set up an LLM program in 2002. In 2008 the China-EU School of law (CESL) set up shop in Beijing, largely funded by the EU and operated in a consortium of 13 European law schools and three Chinese Law Schools. The CESL is established at the campus of one of the Chinese partners, the Chinese University of Politics and Law (CUPL) in Beijing. Students study for two years in a CUPL Juris master and subsequently one year in a master of European and International law (MEIL); it is therefore a double master. Recently some Law Schools (Tsinghua, Peking University, CESL/CUPL, Shanghai Jiao Tong KoGuan and Renmin) started programs about Chinese law, and taught in English, aiming at foreign students.

5. Exchanges and Study Abroad

The idea of student exchange (and for staff as well) has greatly been influenced by European Union policies: initially under the ERASMUS exchanges, later re-baptized as Socrates. The active policy to pursue intra-EU exchanges and collaboration has had a great impact upon our students, our curricula and our academic staff. Exchange of students led many law schools to developing courses (also in English) for those students; it influenced our own students who returned after a study abroad experience with ideas about how to improve things in their home university. The influx of foreign students had its impact upon courses and the interaction with students and in the classroom. It brought faculty into contact with teaching experiences elsewhere and promoted teaching collaboration. For a comparative flavor, interaction between, and understanding of, other legal cultures, and collaboration between students from different backgrounds, exchanges and study abroad are essential. Also with respect to language this is a key issue, because it stimulates living in a foreign residence, interacting with foreign students and studying in a foreign language. These aspects prepare for future work surroundings and international collaboration. For law schools international exchanges and study abroad projects facilitate the comparative input, which I have advanced as an element in modern-day law schools and which improve the academic nature of legal education. They also impact the internationalization of the classroom and of law schools. These features contribute to quality, reflection and intensity of legal debate.

Exchanges and study abroad not only ought to involve students but also faculty. Features of European programs such as ERASMUS and Marie Curie facilitate teachers and researchers to have international collaboration, work on joint teaching materials and courses/programs, and internationalize their research. The effects of these efforts will trickle down in education. These faculty aspects are all the more relevant because they enhance sensitivity among faculty for cultural issues and for the essence of international exchanges and they will improve international and comparative research which will benefit the quality of education and will have an impact upon the students.

In many schools international exchange is voluntary; students can opt for an exchange experience. They will have the relevant guidance and assistance and their grades and courses obtained elsewhere at the host institution will be acknowledged and be a part of the final diploma at the home institution. In some specific cases the experience abroad is mandatory, for instance, in the Erasmus Mundus joint programs and in double degree programs. An example of the former is the European Master in Law and Economics (EMLE).[28] An example of the latter is the King's College and Paris 1 (Panthéon-Sorbonne) program in French and English law.[29]

28 <http://www.emle.org/_EMLE_Main_rubric/index.php?rubric=Home& PHPSESSID=4tfjqg8i9c2v9mo39kcci1c9k7>.

29 <http://www.kcl.ac.uk/prospectus/undergraduate/english-law-and-french-law>.

The relevant question is whether one might have to go so far as to make an international exchange/study abroad experience mandatory for *all* students in the basic law program (for Europe under the Bologna system this would then take place in the three year bachelor program). Is it desirable and feasible to have a scheme under which all students must study abroad for one semester (approximately 20-30 ects)? The first question is whether it is desirable (for the students and their education). I believe it is, and it is even more so for those law schools and students with an international ambition, curriculum and perspective. Programs with an international outlook must certainly have a component in which this outlook is reflected in a study abroad experience. When one teaches internationalization, and preaches the importance of it, it must also be put into practice (practice what you preach). Clearly a lot of the international experiences for the students could and maybe should also be reflected in an international classroom and a truly international diversified student body and substance of the curriculum as well as international staff! However, I believe there is also the component of personal student experiences in having to move abroad, to integrate in another culture and a foreign law school, and being confronted with the teaching of law in another foreign setting, which makes an international study experience the necessary icing on the cake.

Experiences with the Socrates scheme and the schemes of student exchanges make me confident that it is certainly feasible. It will be even more so when many law schools will adopt grand-scale student exchanges. In other words, when all law schools participate in large-scale compulsory international student exchanges, it might be a possibility. Or, when a group of like-minded law schools will adapt to such a scheme, it might also be a possibility. It does however require many changes for exchange and student accommodation.

It will be a big step for most law schools to engage in such a project and I propose that at least the law schools with international programs and ambitions must embrace compulsory study abroad experiences for their students in the programs with an international flavor. This will allow for networks of like-minded law schools to come into being, in order to facilitate the process.

It is however absolutely necessary to make this study abroad experience a useful experience for personal reasons but also related to the content and structure of the curriculum. That is, when time allotted for law programs is limited, or studying law is expensive for the students, or maybe even both, making a study abroad compulsory requires a very precise definition of what is to be studied abroad and which courses must be available and have an added value for the programs of all individual students. In the case of a mandatory study abroad, the law schools must make sure that study delay is limited, that the coherence of the program is protected and that relevant courses are available (with all necessary quality assurance) in the host institutions. For this reason I argue in favour of networks of like-minded or similar institutions which will facilitate the necessary alignment of study progress and courses and will therefore make student exchanges easier and allow the students to complete a coherent curriculum with an intensive study abroad experience.

In these networks and in other multilateral or bilateral exchange agreements, law schools have to resolve issues such as time frames and semester/trimester structures and other practical matters, and the substance of the study abroad programs must also be determined. Which courses will be the best fit for which students? Will it be courses on domestic law and legal culture (and language), or courses on international and European law, or courses of comparative law? This will certainly be a puzzle, possibly not so much when the exchange focuses on domestic law (see for instance the double degree programs about two legal systems). However, it is most likely that this kind of double degree program will find sufficient numbers of students when they combine two large legal systems (UK and France/France and Germany). The option is much less probable with a small legal system or with a legal system with a less globally relevant language (in most cases these two criteria coincide). Smaller legal systems will therefore opt for offering courses in English, which therefore will relate to international and/or European law or to comparative law. However, it is precisely these courses that might as well be on offer in the home institution.

For all the above, we have to reflect on the possibilities under the domestic law of the land. To what extent does it facilitate study abroad experiences, or, on the contrary, hinder them. It is certainly a long shot but, when labour markets do appreciate study abroad experiences, it is to be recommended that these experiences are made public and made an integral part of the selection and admission process. Allow, for instance in the context of bar exams or *Staatsexams*, the students to relate to their study abroad, or hand in a portfolio about their study abroad, a curriculum vitae and grades. It is one thing to underline international experience as a valuable asset but another to make it a part of the selection process.

Chapter 12

OTHER DISCIPLINES

In some jurisdictions the study of law is a professional graduate training for those who have completed an undergraduate academic program.[1] In this format law students have been confronted, prior to entering law school, with other academic disciplines and other sciences. They have already mastered an academic education with all that entails. In many other (civil law) jurisdictions students enter law school after secondary school, without any prior academic training and without a study of (some selected) other academic disciplines.[2] This distinction in the format of the educational model can have its impact upon the need to introduce other relevant disciplines in the law curriculum or not.[3]

The issue is related to a perception of the necessary qualifications of lawyers, the needs and demands of the labour markets, and the essence of an academic training and education. A fundamental question really is whether lawyers, specifically those working in the higher segments of the legal labour markets, can do without education in other disciplines, as an academic exercise, per se, and as a much needed preparation for future employment.

Law is not an isolated issue, it relates to the rule of law; costs and benefits of regulation; difficult markets (telecommunications, cure and care, energy, mergers, financial regulation, to name but a few); and also to the design of public regulation, private regulation, international regulation, and politics. In corporate law, law relates to doing business and running a company. In criminal law, lawyers have to work with psychologists and forensic experts.

1 For instance, USA and South Korea.

2 Continental Europe.

3 In the UK and in China the two models exist as parallel possibilities: law can be studied as an undergraduate degree, allowing for access to the legal professions afterwards as well as a route for students with another undergraduate degree who can opt for a law program and a legal career (UK); or, as is the case in China: law as undergraduate and post graduate gives access to the legal professions, but there is also the possibility for students, with another undergraduate degree than law, to take legal studies as a post-graduate program and gain access to the legal professions. In my opinion it is unfortunate that in many (civil law) jurisdictions the second possibility is not really provided for, whereas the experience with lawyers, who have obtained a non-law undergraduate degree, such as in the UK and the USA, seems to be positive.

Lawyers might have been in a position that they could analyze facts for their legal relevance and reduce reality to legally relevant issues but, increasingly in modern societies, the law and regulation pervade almost all aspects of our lives. Lawyers certainly cannot solve all issues that are at stake in a society, but they might do a better job when other disciplines for the resolution of problems are also part of their toolbox. In advising a client, it is good to know about the client's business model and strategy in order to make the legal advice fit and further his interests. Or, in order to draft a regulation for a minister, it seems advisable to include a cost-benefit analysis, or a prediction about the possible effects and side effects, or an analysis about the fit of this proposal and the political agenda of the minister's party.

Does the study of law only imply that legal texts, doctrines and concepts, and related skills, have to be learned? I submit that law is an academic discipline which operates in a societal (or many different) context(s). Law orders different worlds, such as the interactions between humans; the corporate world; the financial world; international relations and trade; and human and corporate behaviour. The regulation through law intends to pursue certain goals: to protect human life and bodily integrity or morals; to protect individuals against damaging behaviour by others; to protect the environment and to free trade and competition further; to protect freedom of services and people; to regulate the power of states and state organs. In sum, law is there to protect and regulate those interests which deserve protection against arbitrary and intrusive behaviour. The 'when and the how' are the domain of (an interaction between) lawyers and society and politics. Legislators decide on the policies on, for example, the freedom of the markets and the competition rules and decide on the resolution of conflicting interests and policy choices; lawyers draft the rules. Lawyers also ensure that a legal system functions as much as possible as a coherent system (or maybe better: systems) and that 'eternal' interests are shielded from interferences - the rule of law and human rights.

However, how the law protects interests or regulates certain aspects of society is still often a question of choices. Suppose we agree on the protection of a specific interest, the question remains how that interest can be best pursued: through punishing certain behaviour or by rewarding 'good behaviour'? By concluding contracts with a sector or by imposing binding rules? And must we undertake action on the national, regional, local or international level? Here, the lawmaker has choices to make and for that purpose, if we also value efficiency and effectiveness of the law and of legal rules, it is opportune to understand the patterns of human behaviour in order to design the best rules and regulations possible.

Law and lawyers operate in a context. Law schools must, from that perspective, also teach those contexts and teach the students to understand those contexts and the sciences which help us to understand a context. In many legal systems, in criminal law, rules have been made to take the mental state of a defendant/suspect into account. We let experts in the domain of mental states of minds (psychologists, psychiatrists, even with specializations such as forensic psychologists) make the determination and write an expert opinion but, in most cases, we have judges (people who studied the law) finally deciding.[4] They therefore have to decode and understand the expert's report. Do the expert's findings indeed lead to the conclusion that a suspect at the time he committed the crime was of an unsound mind?

In an article entitled 'Building the World community Through Legal Education' Claudio Grossman argued that

> '(t)oday new skills are required in legal education as exemplified by the development of practical and experiential training methodologies. Clinical programs, moot court competitions, study-abroad courses, debate clubs, and an increased reliance on non-legal disciplines such as economics, psychology, political science, anthropology, and sociology have made the study of law based exclusively on reading cases obsolete'.[5]

Therefore he argued in favour of incorporating the perspective of other disciplines in the legal curriculum. The idea of law in context, the need to be able to reflect on the quality of law and legal rules, and the always present interrelationship between law and human behaviour, make it indispensable for law students to acquaint themselves with other sciences. Comparative law can assist us in acquiring knowledge and insight in variations of legal rules and concepts, and in how issues are being tackled in different settings. But in order to pass judgment on the variations observed, one has to acquire an understanding of how a specific rule or case judgment affects human behaviour and how they might impact upon the social fabric and what the costs are which are involved in certain types of regulation. Or in deciding how to assess setting up schemes for public procurement or the distribution of scarce goods such as phone frequencies or emission rights, one might have to work with experts in game theory. Criminal lawyers will benefit when they have expertise in forensic sciences. Researchers might do well when they have skills in statistical and/or economic analysis in order to set their research in an empirical setting or benefit from empirical studies.

It will be a lot to ask when we require all students to study all these and possibly other disciplines. In the same vein, it would be impossible to make law students experts in one of these domains, let alone in some of them. In order to assess the modes of including these other disciplines in a law curriculum, I propose to reflect further on the reasons for incorporating them. These are related to the notion of law in context: the idea that law students must be sensitized to the fact that law impacts upon human behaviour and is set in a specific cultural context. We do not aim at making law students experts in social sciences or cultural anthropology. What is necessary however is that they will have the tools to understand human behaviour and society.

4 With the exception of those systems where this is a decision for the jury to decide.

5 In: Klabbers & Sellers 2008, p. 30.

The same holds true for the relationship between law and business/economics and subjects such as trade, commerce, insurance, corporate governance, business law, are set in the context of doing business and seeking profit for a corporation or business. Insight into the fields of business, marketing, financing and others will make a lawyer a better lawyer.

The purpose of introducing other disciplines is therefore not to educate legal economists, or legal scientists, or legal psychologists, or legal philosophers, but to educate legal academics who have learned that these other sciences do impact on law and legal relations and who have been trained in the concepts of these disciplines, so as to make them useful for their lawyering. I think lawyers will make better lawyers with these skills than without.[6]

A second issue is how to educate or train law students in an awareness of other sciences and in being able to cope with the outcomes and methods of other sciences. Unlike in the case of double degree programs such as Law and Business, Law and Forensics or Law and Economics, in regular law degree programs the purpose is not to train students in two domains, and the interaction between these two domains, but to educate law students who will have basic knowledge as to how to approach other disciplines, which they will likely be confronted with in legal practice after law school.

For that reason I have a preference for the integration, or parallel teaching with law courses, of courses which relate to the other disciplines and can show the interaction and the desirability to have a basic applicable knowledge of the other science and its concepts. Certainly, as in a double degree, links can be made with a minor – law as the major and another discipline in a minor – that will allow for an in-depth confrontation in the minor of a science and a thorough treatment of that field. However, I am inclined to add here that either in the minor itself, or immediately after the minor, in the major, a direct link must be established between law and the minor. It is important that students are immersed in the connections and can apply the multidisciplinary knowledge in solving legal disputes.

These other disciplines can also be taught pre-law school (liberal arts college) or after law school (professional training programs); however these options seem less preferable. The main reason is my argument to establish links between law and the other disciplines when solving disputes or problems. The interaction and the application of the combination of disciplines are important. On the other hand, when a law school is set in a domestic setting after liberal arts college, law schools ought to benefit a lot from the expertise and knowledge students have acquired in college!

The intensity and the scale with which other non-legal disciplines are included in a law curriculum are dependent on the length of the overall curriculum and the legal requirements under domestic law. In the US setting, law schools can build upon pre-law school knowledge; in Europe many domestic systems consist of a

6 Hyatt 2007 wrote that what was missing in legal education is, among others, how to understand the multidisciplinary nature of most transactions.

five-year long legal training (3+2). This would allow for some substantial multidisciplinary training, the extent of which is determined by the intake level of the students, the domestic legal requirements, and the access to the labour market. But even considering these aspects, five years would leave ample room for substantial multidisciplinarity, skills and internationalization/comparative law.

In many European law schools extensive attention is paid to legal history (including Roman legal history), legal philosophy and legal theory, economy, ethics and sociology of law. One also finds criminology and business as available courses, in many cases linked to criminal law and business law. Not very present are political science, international relations, statistics, psychology, forensic psychology and psychiatry, and accountancy. Occasionally one finds also logic, criminalistics, and literature.

Since law is about humans, human behaviour, markets and financial markets, and about regulating/influencing human and organizational patterns, the inclusion of relevant disciplines and their basic study seems relevant to me. More specifically, educating lawyers in specializations such as criminal law, without a relevant notion of forensic disciplines and the ability to apply these disciplines in the exercise of criminal law, seems out of date to me. The same applies for company and business lawyers without adequate reliance upon how to conduct a business, and knowledge of corporate economics, financial transactions and in cases of mergers the definition of markets. To give another example, when studying contract law and tort, law and economics and behavioural expertise are extremely helpful in reflecting on these two domains of the law.

This chapter about other disciplines concurs with the other chapters about skills, academic legal knowledge and internationalization and comparative law. They lead to considerable requirements in the quality and content of the different courses and modules. They lead to a huge impact on the faculty, who have to teach a domain of the law with regard to substance, comparative methods, skills and other relevant disciplines. There is also a second issue: could this not lead to courses with too heavy a work load for students and faculty, with too many problems, issues, concepts to grasp and to be able to apply in cases?

This is certainly an important issue. The ultimate outcome, that students must be able to work with complicated, multidisciplinary issues, has to be reached at the end of the program. The integrated approach must therefore be present at least, when we work in concentric circles, at the second phase, at the end of the program. On the other hand, it can also be argued that a full integration in an early stage of skills, comparative law and other disciplines with substantive law, will make this approach a natural perspective for students. When we train students to switch from substantive law, to comparative law, to skills, to a multidisciplinary issue, it will come natural to them. That does leave however unaffected the claim that in order to be able to do just that, students might need a separate introduction in basic legal concepts and in the concepts of the other sciences first.

I believe that here there is not one best solution and I would leave it to the wisdom and knowledge of faculty and curriculum structures to balance the interests involved, taking into account the quality of the students and the expertise of the faculty to deliver integrated courses. However, with the caveat, ultimately we should aim for students who, upon graduation, can cope with integrated approaches to legal issues and complex social problems.

Earlier in this book I have paid attention to the increasing labour market demand for specialists who, as Morgan has put it, 'can make themselves the best available go-to person in a combined law-and-substantive field and who market themselves accordingly'.[7] This option must be made available by law schools for their students, in major and minor constructs. Students must be trained to be lawyers that will increasingly operate in multidisciplinary settings and will be required to have knowledge of specific relevance other disciplines. If lawyers are not prepared to do that, accountants, business experts, economists, scientists, health scientists and others will acquire legal knowledge in their specific domains and make the presence of lawyers less necessary for highly complicated and specialist cases. But even then, clients will want assistance and services that make the link between the legal and the substantive business domain. To be able to advise and work with hospitals and mergers (and the ensuing competition controls), a lawyer needs not only to be well aware of competition law but also of the peculiarities of the health care sector and how it is being financed and of the developments of standards of medical care and the development towards an increasing specialization and therefore coordination of care.

In the same vein, as I have argued that law schools will have to offer law courses and programs for non-lawyers, they will have to establish law and X programs for law students, as part of the regular curriculum. This is not a new plea, but one[8] also already tabled by Shapiro who, in his book A Larger Sense of Purpose, has argued for a more intimate connection between professional training and the liberal arts and a closer collaboration within universities.

7 Morgan 2010.
8 Shapiro 2005, p. 116.

PART D

EVALUATION AND ORGANIZATION

Chapter 13

EVALUATIONS, BENCHMARKS AND RANKINGS

There is a Dutch saying *meten is weten* which means 'to measure is to know'. Indeed, data about curricula and student performance and progress are relevant to know. Do we achieve our goals with a specific curriculum design? What stumbling blocks, if any, does the curriculum have? What is the failure rate of students? How many hours do students really study? What is the quality of courses and exams? What do students, or graduates value about their legal education and what do they specifically reject?

In order to improve legal education it is important to set objectives, criteria and standards and also to collect relevant data. Suppose, one wishes to reform a master program on Dutch law, to do so there are of course many options, a few of which I have indicated:

- one can describe what expertise and courses are available and put them together in a master program;
- one can collect data about the popularity of courses and put the most popular courses in the master program;
- one could take the courses which have been evaluated as the best courses;
- one could enquire among the most relevant labour market stakeholders and involve them in asking what they feel are the courses that might fit best;
- one could interview the students.

These options have in common that one needs data. Clearly, which data would certainly depend on the goals of the program, and defining those will also lead to a definition of the data one would need. My option would be to collect information from the employment perspective, because the assumption is that a master program is certainly tailored to a specific kind of employment. I would personally least favour the data about availability of courses, because such an approach does lead to maintaining the status quo. Since my central argument in this book is that law schools must educate lawyers for the future, the status quo is not the best indicator.

Leaving that aside for a while, data can also assist deans and leaders of law schools to conduct a personnel policy, to set a mission for the school, to define financial priorities and investments etcetera. For these reasons this chapter is devoted to a range of issues linked to data collection, the use of data, benchmarking and league tables and rankings.

1. Course and Curriculum Evaluation

Quality of legal education is one of the pervasive themes of this book: to ensure that the education and training offered are optimal and meet the demands and needs of students and the labour market and fit the (changing) circumstances. Basically, that is one of the messages in this book.

One of the important tools in that respect is to evaluate the separate courses continuously as well as the curriculum as a whole, and for the management of the school to have and collect all relevant data about the school, the students and the educational process (management information system-MIS). The need for an MIS will come back in Chapter 15. In this chapter I will devote some attention to course and curriculum evaluation.

Evaluation as an isolated effort is useless: evaluation only makes sense if it evaluates the right things and is done continuously and long term; and it is only useful when tools are available to implement changes and adaptations generated by course and curriculum evaluation. These aspects have to do with faculty organization and leadership and with the faculty itself. Are they willing to support course and curriculum evaluation, and in general quality assurance processes, and do they embed the outcomes in their teaching? The effectiveness of quality assurance, benchmarks and evaluations is not only dependent on the quality of these processes but also on the structure of a law school and the willingness of leadership and staff to implement and carry out the findings as important and meaningful. I strongly believe that a law school must have a strong mission and vision, a coherent strategy of teaching and research, a clear perception of quality and what it stands for and wants to pursue, and does so on the basis of a joint, common effort of all staff to work towards these goals. Setting goals and defining goals for education also allows for an evaluation to be meaningful. For course and curriculum evaluation, it is necessary for staff to share the common goals of the courses and the curriculum and the evaluations, whether these goals are met or not, and to share a joint perspective about how to improve them. Courses might be linked to individual professors, but a curriculum must be a whole and a joint coherent endeavour to educate students and take them to a certain level.

When these conditions have been met and faculty is involved in and/or accepts the evaluative approaches, one of the tools to be used is to evaluate all courses, always, and to do the same with the curriculum (or specific years) as a whole.

Evaluation of a specific course can and must include the following aspects:

1. class and lecture attendance;
2. exam statistics: pass/fail, grades;
3. link between exam results/grades and gpa's/secondary school grades/selection procedures;

4. evaluation by the students;
5. evaluation by the teachers;
6. consideration of the electronic learning environment (does it exist and if so what does it include);
7. the skills included in the course and how it fits in the faculty skills strategy;
8. the legal knowledge and its fit in the build-up of the curriculum.

Aspects 7 and 8 listed above do not have to be assessed every year, because generally they will probably be largely unaffected, unless a course or curriculum is amended drastically. They are important however to make explicit because they lead to important information about the curriculum. Aspect 6 might also be unaltered and only needs to be filled out when changed.

The aspects to be assessed annually are 1-5. The first two are fairly simple and self-evident. Aspect number 3 is important because it enables, specifically when also done on a curriculum level, to evaluate the quality of intake and selection procedures and also to adapt courses prospectively to intake levels and to remedy gaps and to refer students in an early stage to a mentor or study counsellor.

Aspects 4 and 5 leave room for discussion, interpretation and definition of content, and are of a subjective nature, though when one manages to have a large group of students filling out the course evaluation questionnaires, the outcomes will have an objective foundation, enabling conclusions to be drawn.

What is it one wants to evaluate? The teaching materials; the clarity and productivity of the tutorial groups and the lectures; the ability of the teachers to explain, clarify and elucidate, allow the students to participate and to have interactive student engagement, according to the law school's didactical philosophy; the quality and fit of the exam; the number of hours studied; the organization and clarity and design of the course. Correspondingly, staff teachers could be asked their opinion about the same aspects, related to their perspectives and the goals they set for the course.

In line with my argument in earlier sections of this book, I also suggest to have evaluation questions on the 'well-being' of the students, related to their 'academic fit' which, as we have seen, is one of the factors contributing to the success of students.

Important is also to evaluate courses annually and to do so in a systematic manner with the same aspects and questions: it shows progress over time; the effect of interventions and curriculum and course changes; and in general the development of a curriculum and will therefore alert leadership of a law school at an early stage when trends show a deterioration or mismatches and wrong developments.

Having information on the evaluation of courses is one thing. The second is to act upon it and to implement the necessary changes and improvements, and the third is to have insight into the qualities, impact and effectiveness and efficiency of the curriculum as a whole.

The data about the courses must, in order to allow for an assessment of the curriculum as a whole, be aggregated on the curriculum level. That however is not enough. It is indispensable to also have an insight into how students perceive the curriculum as a whole, as it were, when looking back. Did the curriculum as a whole teach them the proper skills effectively; do they have the right tools to be prepared for the labour market; did the separate courses match and lead to a coherent program; were some courses stumbling blocks; did the program offer a proper preparation for the labour market/bar exam/professional training; did the program foster and promote an academic culture and 'academic fit'; was the program well-structured and well organized?

For the curriculum evaluation and course evaluations one could go so far as to ask the students to give the course and/or program an overall grade. Those grades might lead to a simplification of the evaluation (or to a simple resorting to the grade for a course without looking into the other data), however, I certainly believe that it is helpful. It triggers the attention and is a helpful tool for a first glance at the appreciation of the students of the courses and programs.

What happens the moment we have collected all evaluation data and summarized them in easy-to-read tables and statistics? There are certainly many things that could be and ought to be done.

1. The first issue always is whether or not to publish all course evaluations and in what detail and to make these available for whom. In order to generate a public and shared commitment for evaluations and for the quality of the curriculum it is important to make all course evaluations available to all faculty. This appeals to a joint responsibility of all staff members for the program and the well-being of the law school. It also stimulates all course coordinators to work towards better evaluations and could assist staff in discussing best practices and learning from each other when they see that colleagues obtain good evaluations for their course books or lectures, for example. It is my experience that faculty want to deliver outstanding courses and want to learn from and be helped by colleagues. Public data about the quality of courses will generate a debate on the program and will make faculty aware of strengths and weaknesses in their courses and in their teaching performances. When one openly resorts to course evaluations in a positive manner, as a tool for continuous innovation and improvement and as a common and joint endeavour, faculty will engage in a discussion and assume a common/joint responsibility. Another question is whether the publication of all data for each course ought to be available for students as well. My perspective here is that transparency will involve the student community and will see them as responsible actors and stakeholders. In the quest for transparency and public responsibility for the quality of public and state funded services, I am convinced that openness and accountability are important and can and do serve the law school.

2. An analysis has to be made of the outcomes: what went wrong; what went well; which improvements can be made; what other changes have to be set in motion etcetera. Data must be interpreted and put into proper perspective. To

give an example: in a survey students assessed a course and its exam as very (too) difficult and containing too much reading and preparation. However, the same questionnaire revealed that on average the study hours did not indicate that students indeed had to work and worked (many) more hours than allotted to the course. In that case, it would have been too simple to reduce the amount of study materials, and instead what was done was that the coordinator provided an explanation in the course book about the structure of the course and the necessity of proper preparation and participation. In another course we were once confronted with students complaining about the textbook used in that course – it happened to be an English text book in a Dutch law course – and by delving into this we found out that the complaints were related to the English language of that book. Since it was our policy also to have English language study materials where possible and relevant, we kept this book but instead explained to the students the reasons and the need for our insistence and the advantages for the students to also be trained in legal English and English textbooks.

3. Act upon the analysis with the coordinator of the course and/or the program coordinator in order to implement the necessary changes. As I have tried to indicate in the previous examples, data needs interpretation and a discussion in many cases with students and the course coordinator about how to interpret the data, what to do and what not to do and why. For the discussion with the course coordinator it is important that the coordinator is aware of the profile of the school and the goals and remit of the program and how the specific course fits in, and follows those aspects. This is relevant in order to be able to search constructively for the best solutions, in the light of the curriculum and the strategy of the school, to what the evaluation might have shown. An implementation discussion must not go about the basics concerning the strategy and mission and didactical philosophy but must instead deal with the specific course.

4. Check after an agreed time whether the changes have been made and whether one has acted upon the recommendations and findings. This is crucial to an evaluation system. When we set up evaluations and plans for implementation, it is self-evident to check also whether the changes are implemented and whether they will have the intended and desired effects.

5. Make explicit to faculty and students to what changes evaluations of courses and programs have led. This is an important step, for evaluation purposes and to keep all stake holders involved; being transparent on the consequences and impact of evaluation exercises will keep everybody alert and will make it visible that the school is responsive to evaluations and that this has produced interesting and good results. That as such is a stimulus for staff and students.

Specifically for the students, this is an incentive to fill out the evaluation questionnaires and to keep on contributing to the evaluation exercises.

Course and curriculum evaluation are certainly joint efforts by faculty, students and deans or boards of law schools. They are an indispensable element of accountability and transparency about the law school and its quality of teaching. In my many years as dean I have been confronted with many arguments about reasons why not to rely upon frequent and regular evaluations. It has been called 'evalu-it-is' or a simplistic reduction of the realities of teaching, or as a giving in to students, or mistrusting students, thinking that they punish professors for hard work and strict exams. In my experiences I have not found any clues that students will give a bad evaluation to a great but very difficult course which really put them to the test. On the contrary, students show fairness in their evaluations and know how to distinguish between well-taught courses and lower quality courses; they appreciate efforts by teachers and they resent sloppy teaching. They recognize a lecture which is given by an inspired professor, or a lecture which is identical to the lectures of recent years. Naturally, we have to treat evaluations carefully and when we reduce evaluations to simple scores on a given scale we must make sure to indeed look behind these figures and analyze the other data. Indeed, evaluations do show occasional inconsistencies: students complaining about too much work, but at the same time indicating that they studied fewer hours than allotted for the course. Or we see students evaluating the lectures and tutorials highly but the course as a whole less. These inconsistencies mean that one has to explore what has occurred and how to communicate better with the students about the course, or that a textbook or the course book or the organization of the course was below standards.

Course and curriculum evaluation are at the heart of a law school. For effective use, I recommend regular and systematic incorporation in a law school's procedures. They cannot and should not replace the meetings one might have among faculty and with (delegations of) students about their legal education experiences. These meetings are important because they shed light on apparent inconsistencies or different expectations. The other advantage is that in these meetings management, students and faculty are seen to be involved in the common interest: excellent legal education. Evaluation fares well with enabling students also to engage in meetings with faculty about the outcomes of the evaluations. Sometimes an individual experience will give meaning and content to evaluation findings. Or students can elucidate the reality behind the figures and statistics and engage in a debate with the responsible teacher. Therefore, make evaluation also into a real dialogue between faculty and students.

2. Benchmarks and Rankings

Recently I googled for 'best European law schools' and happened to access the following site (the third website on google's hit list): <http://www.llm-guide.

com/most-popular/europe>. It shows the most popular European law schools, but in a very specific meaning of the term: according to that website:

> 'The monthly rankings in the Most Popular LLM Programs section are determined by the number of user page views per LL.M. program listing. Therefore, the "most popular" LL.M. programs are simply the programs that LLM GUIDE users have viewed most frequently. The number of user page views also determines the "popularity" of LL.M. programs in the geographic-based program searches.'

Similarly a popularity ranking is established by LLM Guide for global law schools and for other regions: <http://www.llm-guide.com/law-school-rankings>.

Although this might offer a nice perspective on the popularity of the website of law schools, it is not a good benchmark or ranking. For Law there are in many countries no good rankings, let alone that there exists a European-wide or global ranking of law programs or law schools. And even worse: no systematic method has yet been devised to benchmark law schools on a variety of important parameters. Though we might feel we can do without simple rankings, as in the league tables, it seems to be a good idea for law schools to learn from one another and therefore to have access to benchmarks and data, which will allow students to make rational and well-founded choices and which will enable university managers and law school deans to assess the qualities of his/her school and to assist him/her in making choices for improvement and setting priorities.

For law schools not that many league tables or rankings exist: globally and European wide the only ranking I found was the 'popularity' contest I started this chapter with. Within some countries rankings of universities and law schools do exist. In the United Kingdom there were two: one by the Guardian[1] and the other the Complete University Guide.[2] In Germany there is the CHE ranking, which also has a separate category for law schools.[3] In the US there is the long-standing ranking of US News.[4] For the Netherlands there is: <Studychoice123.nl/Studiekeuze123.nl>, which is an indication of quality of university programs including law programs.[5]

University wide there is indeed much more. First the global league tables and rankings:

- Shanghai Jiao Tong (SJTU) Academic Ranking of World Universities (ARWU);
- Times Higher education Supplement (THE);
- QS (Quacquarelli Symonds Ltd) Top Universities;
- Leiden Ranking;

1 <http://www.guardian.co.uk/education/table/2011/may/17/university-guide-law>.

2 <http://www.thecompleteuniversityguide.co.uk/league-tables/rankings/?s=Law>.

3 <http://ranking.zeit.de/che2011/de/?module=Hitliste&do=show_l1&esb=5&hstyp=1&ab=>.

4 <http://grad-schools.usnews.rankingsandreviews.com/best-graduate-schools/top-law-schools/law-rankings>.

5 <www.studiekeuze123.nl / www.studychoice123.nl>.

- Within Europe work is ongoing in a project called U-multirank,[6] a multi-dimensional global university ranking.

Nationally there are league tables and rankings, such as the ones I mentioned for law schools. Globally there are a few specialized league tables and rankings:

- Financial Times ranking of business schools and programs;
- Business Week (business schools);
- The Economist (business schools);
- QS Ranking of special domains (and one is Law!).[7]

Finally some classifications have been developed:

- Carnegie classification (USA)[8] and
- U-Map (Europe), an on-going project under construction.[9],[10]

Rankings and classifications can and do serve multiple functions and have various side effects[11] and consequences. First, let it be clear that transparency in performance is an absolute essential feature. The stakeholders involved, such as students, alumni, funding agencies/states, employers, do have a legitimate interest in knowing how their institution/law school is doing and what the quality of education and research is. Deans and faculty, and university leaders, also have an interest in having a clear picture what the management information data (see Chapter 15) leads to in terms of benchmarks: how does a school do in relation to others? This comparison will aid in doing better and performing better in those areas where competing schools show better performance. However, what is essential is that the data in the rankings are indeed comparable; that the data are correct; that the data meet the needs of the different stakeholders; that the data collected paint a realistic and transparent picture of educational quality; and that the different elements in a ranking do have the appropriate weight in the final outcome. And finally, we have to be aware of strategic behaviour of institutions. We ought not to be surprised that,

6 <http://www.u-multirank.eu/>.

7 <http://www.topuniversities.com/university-rankings/world-university-rankings/2011/subject-rankings/social-sciences/law>.

8 <http://classifications.carnegiefoundation.org/>.

9 <http://www.u-map.eu/>.

10 Browsing the web I also discovered Google college rankings: <http://googlecollegerankings.com/>, but I am under the impression that this ranking attempt has been terminated.

11 One of them is that institutions and schools will do what it takes to improve in the rankings. In Transfer (September 2011, p. 12/13) Gerald Schut gives some tips on how to improve the ranking in the Shanghai-ranking (and QS and THE); some examples: mergers (specifically with research institutes); buy and hire researchers who rank high in citation indexes; do not publish chapters in books, but stimulate articles in journals; cut down in expenditure for social sciences and languages because they do not count in these indexes and spend money in the sciences.

when rankings show how we do in comparison to others, we will look for ways to do better and a business wisdom will have it that one first goes after the so-called 'quick wins' or 'low-hanging fruit'.[12]

One of my arguments in this book is that law schools exist in many variations, serve different purposes and labour markets, sit in different environments and in different legal cultures and will have different profiles and strategies and aim for different markets in terms of students and the labour market. Maybe one of the fairest ways to assess quality of schools is by having comparative exams (but difficult to perceive in the domain of law where predominantly domestic law is being taught in law schools; this might possibly change for some selected law schools which will opt for an international profile), or by setting up and competing in national and international moot court competitions. Schools which do well in that domain might likely be a good school in teaching the relevant law and the necessary skills. But here, it might be difficult for a school to have all or many of its students participate in international competitions; and too many competitions will have a disruptive effect on the curriculum and the scope of teaching.

Rankings, however, are of relevance and are here to stay and will even expand. This means that law schools have to work with the rankers to ensure that law school rankings will be adequate and will be informative and accurate, with relevant categories of information for all stakeholders.

Rankings, classifications and other benchmarks must contain the information necessary for the relevant stakeholders. PhD students will look for the best research place in the domain of expertise and interest and will therefore be interested in a category classifying and ranking law schools with regard to domains of research, research facilities, PhD performances, citation index etcetera. A student will look for law schools, also possibly from different perspectives: small scale and very focused on student mentoring and guidance; or highly demanding and focused on top students with a very international classroom and many international exchanges and possibilities; or very focused on law in context and serving the local community; etcetera.

When we agree upon the basic idea that law schools are, will be and must be different in outlook and perspective, one simple ranking might not serve this perspective.

Classifications or statistics ought also to provide statistical and objective information: student/staff ratio; library (E-journal subscriptions); electronic learning environment; participation in moot courts and performances; completion rate; labour market perspectives; honours program; student satisfaction; contact hours; number of students (first year bachelor) intake; master intake; total size; mentoring system; career guidance; internship office; and staff composition.

The German CHE Ranking has a format which shows flexibility in this respect. The classification has five categories: research reputation; research funding; university education coaching; quality of teachers; and a total for the study situation in a

12 For some critical comments about rankings: Klabbers 2008.

school. Each school will receive a green, yellow or blue (top, middle, bottom) for each of the categories. When one clicks on a school, specific information is provided as to the number of staff and students.

- FAKTEN

Hauptfach-Studierende insgesamt [?]	
An Lehre beteiligte Professoren [?]	
Anteil Lehre durch Praktiker [?]	%
Gastprofessoren incoming [?]	
Gastprofessoren outgoing [?]	
Repetitoriumsbesuch [?]	%
Forschungsgelder pro Wissenschaftler [?]	T€
Promotionen pro Professor [?]	↓
Habilitationen pro Jahr [?]	

STUDIERENDEN-URTEILE GRUNDSTÄNDIGE PRÄSENZSTUDIENGÄNGE

Betreuung durch Lehrende [?]
Kontakt zu Studierenden [?]
Lehrangebot [?]
Studierbarkeit [?]
Einbeziehung in Lehrevaluation [?]
E-Learning [?]
Bibliotheksausstattung [?]
Räume [?]
IT-Infrastruktur [?]
Universitätsrepetitorien [?]
Unterstützung für Auslandsstudium [?]
Studiensituation insgesamt [?]

- REPUTATION

Forschungsreputation [?]1%

  - BESONDERHEITEN (ANGABEN DES FACHBEREICHS)

In this last category a summing up is given of special characteristics of the law school (special programs, library facilities, student body composition, research expertise, etc.). The CHE ranking has in other disciplines but law admitted foreign schools to participate in their classification schemes. For psychology, business and medicine for instance Austrian, Swiss and Dutch universities participate, showing the generality and transparency and neutrality of the criteria employed. When one researches these criteria, they do also seem to show a good fit for law schools and foreign law schools. The criteria, and the information behind the criteria, are not linked to the substance of the law but to the modes of teaching and can therefore be of a general nature.

In the European U-Multirank project, the CHE approach is implemented further and elaborated upon. In the U-Multirank Final Report the proposed design has been tested and submitted to the general public of universities and European decision makers.[13] The tool that has been developed is *multi-dimensional* (recognizing that higher education institutions serve multiple purposes and perform a range of different activities); it is a ranking of university *performances* (but not in the sense of an aggregated league table); and it is *user-driven* (as a stakeholder with particular interests one is enabled to rank institutions with comparable profiles according to the criteria that are important to the stakeholder).[14] The U-Multirank will contain five categories: Teaching and Learning; Research; Knowledge Transfer; International Orientation; and Regional Engagement. Two types of rankings will be produced: Focused institutional rankings (rankings on the indicators of the five performance dimensions at the institutional level); and Field-based rankings (rankings on the indicators of the five performance dimensions in a specific field (for instance law).[15] At the field level the Final Report proposes 'field-tables'. In these tables relative performance is indicated by a colour dot (green indicating top group; yellow indicating a middle group and red indicating a bottom group). The idea is to facilitate the user to sort the institutions on all of the indicators; and they may also choose the indicators on which they want to rank the institutions selected.[16] For our purposes

13 Van Vught & Ziegele 2011. The U-Multirank is now ready for implementation. The European Commission has announced it will launch U-Multirank: a new performance-based ranking and information tool for profiling higher education institutions, aiming to radically improve the transparency of the higher education sector, with first results in 2013. By moving beyond the research focus of current rankings and performance indicators, and by allowing users to create individualized multidimensional rankings, this independently run tool will inform choice and decision making by all higher education stakeholders (European Commission Communication 20-9-2011, COM (2011) 567 final: Supporting growth and jobs, an agenda for the modernization of Europe's higher education systems.

14 U-Multirank 2011, Final Report, p. 17.

15 U-Multirank 2011, Final Report, p. 18.

16 U-Multirank 2011, Final Report, p. 19. The Report further proposes to have multi-dimensional performance charts at the institutional level (called sunburst charts: 'In the sunburst charts, the performance on all indicators at the institutional level is represented by the size of →

the Teaching and learning component for the field-based tables will include aspects such as: student/staff ratio; graduation rate; qualification of academic staff; percentage graduating within normal period; relative rate of graduate unemployment; interdisciplinarity of programs; inclusion of work experience; gender balance; organization of program; inclusion of work experience; evaluation of teaching; social climate; quality of courses; support by teachers; computer facilities; overall judgment; libraries; laboratories. In the International Orientation domain, the following relevant (from the perspective of legal education) indicators have been proposed: percentage of international students; incoming and outgoing students; opportunities to study abroad; international orientation of programs; and international academic staff.

Students might also select law schools on the basis of research qualities and profiles since they are also part of the U-Multirank proposals.

The collection of data will be of the utmost importance and will constitute an effort for schools. This is even more so the case because accreditation agencies and other ranking organizations, or other benchmarks requested or imposed by other stake-holders, also expect schools to provide data and statistics. With an introduction of a well-accepted classification scheme, it is urgent that other stakeholders and 'rankers' will rely upon these new classification schemes and will rely upon the performance data collected or that they might even acknowledge a top group position of a school as a relevant fact in the accreditation process. Linking U-Multirank data and national accreditation processes is of the essence.

For universities and schools, whatever the format of a classification scheme, it remains important not to consider the outcome of such a scheme as the only reality. I certainly do not underestimate the role classification schemes will play but it will remain of crucial importance for university leaders and law school deans to set their policies and strategies and the ensuing priorities. For instance, certain aspects could still, though not included in benchmarks, be considered important. To name but a few: E-learning, skills training, moot courts, gender balance in staff, quality of teaching materials and the electronic learning environment, quality of mentoring and study counselling, elements of freedom of choice, selectivity of the program, the composition of the student body. Although aspects as these will weigh in (some of) the other indicators, they can determine a law school's profile and mission and be thoroughly relevant.

For research rankings a problematic aspect in the legal domain is that, unlike, for instance, in business and medicine, no generally accepted citation indexes, Hirsch index or rankings of peer reviewed journals, exists. This makes a domestic statistical analysis of quality of legal research impossible. It explains why research assessment of law schools on a national level takes the form of committees of experts who analyze the publications and research strategies of schools and give a ranking according to their findings. It would immensely help if law schools would

the rays of the "sun": a larger ray means a higher performance on that indicator. The colour of a ray reflects the dimension to which it belongs.'

work towards trying to achieve a system of peer reviewed journals (and/or a ranking according to the prestige of the journals) or find agreement in assessing the evaluation of the relevance of SSRN publications and downloads and the validity of key-note papers in conferences and visiting professorships and other recognitions of academic excellence.

For soccer clubs, a table has been made linking performance to the size of the budget,[17] showing that clubs are more successful according to their budget:

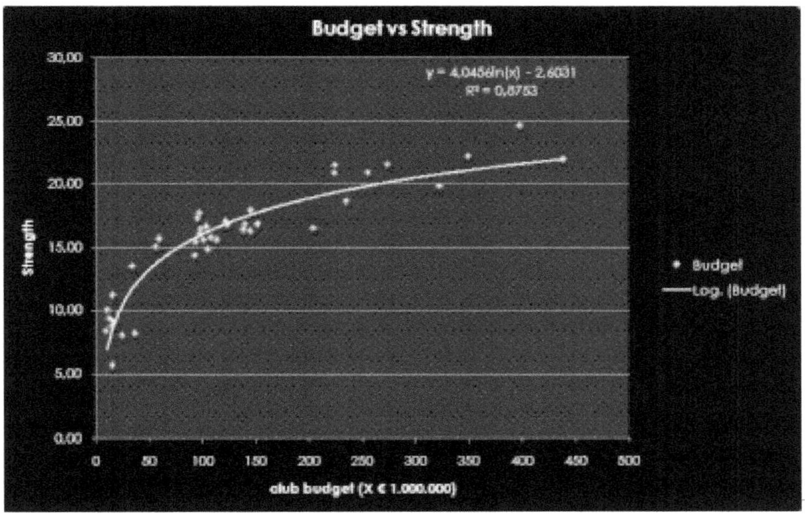

The answer to similar questions about the link between the budget and ranking position of a university or law school is probably the same in the sense that a high position on the present university rankings reflects a high budget and that the budget size decreases as one goes down the list or that budget decreases will eventually lead to a downward tendency in the rankings. Quality is for sale, in soccer and in education.

For international comparisons in the domain of education, it remains very much relevant to enable prospective students to search for quality programs on a level playing field. We can safely assume that in many countries, in which state

17 <http://www.voetbaldokter.nl/news.php?readmore=62>; this website provides the following explanation: 'For 41 clubs, the relation between club budget and strength (see three year list elsewhere on this site) has been modelled, yielding an R^2 of 0,875. Which means the relationship between budget and strength has become stronger compared to earlier attempts (winter 2011) to analyse this relation. In other words, budget becomes more and more the leading determinant for strength, making the outcome of the tournaments (Champions League and Europa League) more and more predictable. And even though this may benefit the quality of the soccer for a few clubs, it takes away the excitement of improbable winners making Cinderalla runs...'.

funding for universities is the standard, this is done on equal parameters. That allows for a fair competition, in which all schools have a similar starting position. Private schools, when not funded by the state, might benefit from not being state schools, or might suffer from it. For those reasons I believe that classifications ought to express the situation in a given country as to funding. That will allow stakeholders to even better assess the performances of schools and universities.

Let's have a closer look at the 2011 and 2012 QS Ranking table (referred to in footnote 161) with respect to Law. The first fifty law schools are ranked as 1-50; the second tier of fifty schools are ranked in an alphabetical order. There is only a small number of countries that appear on these two lists. The second point that shows very well is that schools in English-speaking countries dominate. The composition of the first group of 50 schools is as follows:

	2011	**2012**
Top 50		
North America	*(22)*	*(19)*
USA	16	16
Canada	6	3
South America	*(–)*	*(1)*
Chili	–	1
Europe	*(16)*	*(20)*
Germany	4	5
Belgium	1	1
The Netherlands	1	3
Italy	1	1
Spain	0	2
UK	9	8
Asia	*(3)*	*(3)*
China	1	1
Singapore	1	1
Hong Kong	1	1
Oceania	*(9)*	*(7)*
Australia	6	5
New Zealand	3	2
50-100		
North America	*(11)*	*(17)*
USA	7	13
Canada	4	4
South America	*(1)*	*(1)*
Chili	1	1
Europe	*(32)*	*(22)*
Germany	4	2

The Netherlands	5	3
Italy	2	1
Spain	1	2
UK	8	6
Ireland	3	1
Switzerland	2	1
Denmark	1	1
Finland	1	1
Sweden	2	2
Norway	1	1
Israel	2	1
Oceania	*(4)*	*(5)*
Australia	4	4
New Zealand	0	1
Asia	*(1)*	*(4)*
China	0	3
Hong Kong	1	1
Africa	*(1)*	*(1)*
South Africa	1	1

This leads to an overall score within the 'best' 100 law schools:

	2011	**2012**
USA	24%	29%
UK	17%	14%
Australia	10%	10%
Canada	10%	7%
Germany	8%	7%
The Netherlands	6%	6%
Ireland	3%	1%
New Zealand	3%	3%
Israel	2%	1%
Hong Kong	2%	2%
Italy	2%	1%
Switzerland	2%	1%
Sweden	2%	2%
China	1%	4%
Spain	1%	4%
Chili	0%	2%
Belgium	1%	1%
Denmark	1%	1%
Finland	1%	1%
Norway	1%	1%

Singapore	1%	1%
South Africa	1%	1%

In the overall list, English speaking countries accounted for 58% in 2011 and even 70% in 2012 (counting Hong Kong, Israel and South-Africa as English speaking). Many European countries are notably absent or (population wise and law school numbers wise) underrepresented, such as France, Italy, Spain, and Germany. However, with 41% Europe is not doing badly, even considering that 27% is from European countries not counting the UK! The underrepresentation also applies to South America, China and Africa. Overrepresented are Hong Kong (two out of three law schools on the list), Singapore (one out of two); and the Netherlands (six out of nine). The latter can be partly explained by the fact that all Dutch law schools offer a variety of programs in English and have moved also to publishing in English.

QS prepared the ranking in 2011 on the basis of three criteria: Academic, Employer and Citations. The first category came about from surveys among academics and the second among employers. On the website QS provides some information about the responses. There were 16,785 responses from employers, out of which 1.2% were in Law (= 201 responses for Law). The Academic Survey generated 33,744 responses, out of which 3.6% were in Law (1315 for Law). The QS website also indicated in 2011 which regions/countries the responses were from, however, without discriminating with regard to domain; however if Law is consistent with the overall distribution we can see that the US counts for 10.2% of the responses; and the UK for 7.1%. Less than their overall scores in the top 100 list, but it is another indication that English-speaking academics (and employers) do determine the rankings.

For 2012 the QS website indicated that for Law there were 986 responses from Academics and 2020 from Employers. For the overall count, Academics determined 60% of the score; Employers 30% and Citations 10%. It is therefore important to note that the QS ranking focuses on academic surveys and citation, and therefore on scholarly work of faculty and on the employability of the students (in an international labour market with larger employers, probably). This implies for law schools and their position on the QS list to have programs taught in English, educating students for the major (English-speaking international) labour markets, with English-taught programs and academics who publish in English in international journals. What it does not do is assess the quality of education, or the link to domestic legal practice, or the contribution to the local, domestic, regional labour market. The focus of QS, in a domain such as the law, is on those law schools with (a combination of) a couple of characteristics:

1. modus operandi in English (teaching and publishing);
2. educating for an international labour market;

3. large size and old age (culminating in many alumni...; a small school will probably generate less citations and less alumni and therefore less responses from the labour market);
4. involve in post-graduate training and professional training (spreading the name of the school in the professional domain);
5. publish, co-author, articles; organize conferences and mingle and be actively present (giving key note speeches and delivering papers) in conferences.

These conclusions also determine strategies to climb in the ranking, if one wants to do that: hire scholars and academics with high citation scores (even on a visiting scholar basis; all it takes is that they mention this affiliation in their academic work); set up some international, English-taught programs; grow in size and numbers of students and staff and/or merge with another law school; connect closely with the labour market and international organizations and corporations and set up a policy of career assistance/job placement/internships/and guest lectures of those employers in law school career events. The better and the more the labour market knows about and is involved in a law school, the more favourable they might report in international surveys about that law school.

The five aspects *supra* can and should, if one decides to pursue these goals, also be made a structural part of a coherent strategy and HRM policy (recruitment and promotion of faculty. See in that respect Chapter 15).

Christensen and Eyring have declared that phenomenon as 'You Get What You Measure'.[18] Rankings and benchmarks will lead to policies and adaptations in behaviour of universities and law schools. When the indicators focus on class size, PhD's, scholarly articles and facilities, institutions and schools will focus on and invest in these parameters in order to do well and even better in the rankings. They mention the recent change in the US that government regulators ask for accountability for the educational benefits of universities and their efficiency.

> 'What does college [law school] cost? How many students are admitted? How many graduate? How long does it take them to graduate? How many get good jobs? And at the same time, accrediting bodies have changed their measurement emphasis from inputs and activities to outcomes.'[19]

And indeed, rankings, accreditation criteria determine outcomes and they intend to do so. However, it is useful to realize that they do. Schools will not want to be seen as ranking low on rankings and benchmarks. They will therefore do whatever is necessary to meet criteria and a ranking's objectives. When rankings and benchmarks allow only for one dimensional criteria, which are imposed upon all schools, we indeed run the risk that success is identical for all schools and that all schools, however, different their resources and setting, strive for the same. Christensen and

18 Christensen & Eyring, p. 389-390.
19 Christensen & Eyring, p. 390.

Eyring plead therefore in favour of new 'meaningful success measures'.[20] They have devised a list of additional success measures which could inspire universities and law schools. For students they put on the list data such as: percentage of students graduating within x years; and student and institutional cost per degree earned; for subjects: the degree of student engagement in learning; and student learning outcomes. I would add for law issues such as moot court competitions, legal clinics and multi disciplinarity and integration of skills. For scholarship the authors added the degree of student involvement in scholarly activities and of inclusion of scholarship in the curriculum. They call it a shift from quantity to quality and from outputs to efficiency and effectiveness ratios.

Their attempt to focus on these measures puts efforts to rank and benchmark in uniform systems into perspective; it also does justice to the non-uniformity of schools and universities, and their additional success measures, focusing on quality, creating room for schools to be different, but yet to putting an effort into teaching, and leading schools to innovate and reflect on outcomes and the costs.

The CHE ranking and the European multi-map ranking under construction are certainly huge improvements when we compare them to the simplistic QS and similar rankings. They do enable universities and law schools to strategize and focus on educational strategies.[21] Rankings should assist schools and not hinder them or force them into a uniform straitjacket which is copied from the most successful and well-funded top schools in the pack.

3. Accreditation

Many schools need an accreditation from a state agency or a bar association, or other institution. Accreditation is needed for programs and/or for schools. This is to be distinguished from (educational or research) assessment exercises, though they might certainly coincide, in the sense that a site visit and assessment procedure are part of the official accreditation process.

Some countries have their law schools assessed, and leave it to the schools to 'accredit' (approve) their own programs which they offer; in other situations a state decides upon which schools/universities it admits to the system of higher education (and the accompanying state funding) and leaves it to an accreditation agency to approve each and every separate program (with regular intervals).

Apart from that (and on top of that) in the field of business schools (private) organizations have set up accreditations. They do not lead to state funding, or state recognition, but indicate an (international) quality check and approval from panels

20 Christensen & Eyring, p. 391.

21 Leiter 2006 conveyed a similar message: 'We should produce more rankings that unleash academic talent and ambition, not rankings that reward decanal connivance at manipulating ranking schemes cooked up by journalists.' He argues that the ranking of academic institutions should emphasize and reward academic values, such as, scholarly excellence, pedagogical skills and students' ability and achievements.

of experts. For business schools these are: AACSB,[22] EQUIS[23] and Association of MBA's (AMBA).[24]

It is probably undisputed that education (as an important social and economic product) has to meet (minimum) quality standards and that educational products which are flawed or defect ought to be taken from the market, or at least must not be government funded and must be exposed. In the context of government funding a process of accreditation is a sensible thing to do: checking upon the quality of the product delivered with tax money! When no tax money is involved the case for accreditation is less apparent, because one might then leave it to the market to set up quality designs and accreditation structures. A prominent example is the three business schools accreditations. They are well respected and serve as quality control mechanisms allowing the market to assess the value for money. In the same vein rankings (see paragraph 2 in this chapter) also work; the Economist ranking[25] of business schools is probably as good at being a quality indicator as sheer accreditation mechanisms and probably even better, because these rankings also compare and allow markets to compare schools and programs for different aspects and to search for the best value for money and for the best goal they want to achieve with a specific program.

For law the picture might still be somehow unclear in the sense that they are being accredited (domestically) and at the same time being ranked (sometimes in a variety of rankings). Accreditation sets the minimum standards: student/staff ratio; number of hours/credits taught; skills trainings; library; building; classrooms; quality assurance mechanisms etcetera. The rankings do rank and compare those who meet accreditation standards. It is like the admission of cars to a domestic market: all cars admitted meet minimum standards of safety, clean engines, and handling. The rankings and comparisons in the market and the magazines do the rest: they classify on prize, size, luxury, service, durability and other aspects so that the clients can make up their mind which car best suits their needs and wallet.

All doctors working in a hospital have passed their exams and have been admitted to the profession. Hospitals also seek accreditation in order to meet minimum standards of quality in care but that does not mean that all hospitals deliver the same quality of care or that all doctors are as good as their colleagues. To gain insight into the relative quality we need rankings and benchmarks. To be assured that hospitals and doctors deliver at least a minimum level of services we have accreditation (and continued education and quality assurance). So accreditation (or admission to the playing field) is certainly necessary. However, there is still the question about the relationship between (official) accreditation and rankings (and unofficial accreditations and reviews by peers). For instance, why not link rankings

22 <http://www.aacsb.edu/accreditation/>.

23 <http://www.efmd.org/index.php/accreditation-main/equis>.

24 <http://www.mbaworld.com/accreditation/accreditedprogrammes>.

25 <www.economist.com/whichmba>.

(and peer accreditations by private organizations) and (formal/official) accreditation?

Again, the business schools provide a good example (and we might add to the three accreditations referred to the Economist ranking). Why not link the latter accreditations with the former official one? This could be done in the sense that we strive for the former to incorporate the findings of (one of) the others? States might even go so far as to say that they will not accredit a school which ends in the lowest tiers of peer rankings?

For law the example of the (internationally competitive) business is difficult to realize, however, I do believe that it might be the way forward for those schools that offer programs with an international flavour or content and who want to attract international students. Let's call them the 'international law schools'. It is certainly imaginable to have an international framework of a peer organization, which sets up an accreditation/ranking procedure assessing the international programs of these schools. That will provide the international student market with an insight in the qualities of schools and programs. It will enable a fair competition and transparency of quality and quality assurance mechanisms, and it will connect the labour market to those schools and their international programs.

That leads to an international organization of international law schools or, maybe better, law schools with international programs (the schools might be assessed or accredited, or solely those programs they offer, which have a distinct international profile and mission). Unlike many national domestic accreditation processes, which also focus on the substance of the programs (number of credits/ teaching hours for specific courses), the international accreditation I have in mind will only accept those programs/schools offering programs with a distinctly international scope; schools/programs meeting this criterion will subsequently be assessed on a variety of quality criteria. In my experience the present situation is that domestic accrediting actors have to focus on substance (the content of the curriculum) as well as the quality and everything that entails. Their focus is, however, domestic; but what about the programs which are tailored for an international labour market and student body? They fall somehow beyond the scope of national accreditation agencies or are being assessed with the domestic criteria, which might limit student exchange, the input of visiting professors, different teaching styles and do not suit the international nature of the program.

What would count as an international school or program? For a start I think of criteria relating to the content of what is being taught: not a primary or exclusive focus on domestic law, but programs about international law, European law, comparative law, transnational legal issues, transsystemic programs, for which the school wants to attract an international student body and which purports to prepare the students for international practice, international academia, jobs with an international flavour. The accreditation would have to work out precise criteria and also assess to what extent the school with that specific program meets its own characteristics, definitions and mission and goals.

The second aspect of the process would obviously relate to the quality of all facilities, faculty, teaching materials, coherence of the program, extra-curricular activities, employability of the students, library, teaching materials, delivery of education, academic environment.

For national accreditation of schools and programs, the accreditation criteria differ according to the context in specific states, and the existence of other systems of quality assurance. Accreditation systems have in common with ranking/benchmarking systems that quality parameters will be set and will be assessed by independent/impartial experts/peers. For the sake of efficiency it is wise to coordinate these systems and criteria and to align them so as to set equivalent criteria and standards. They could rely upon each others' findings whenever possible. When one looks at the different evaluation systems, accreditation and rankings, it is noticeable that there seems to be very little mutual use of data and findings. That is a burden for the schools, which have to make the data available and probably different data, according to who asks for what.

I suggest that a distinction should be made between accreditation and quality assurance systems. Accreditation is about guaranteeing the minimum level of quality based upon a specific set of parameters and it is about allowing schools to be in the educational system and delivering degrees, with a recognized status. These aspects would mean that criteria must be set about output, throughput and facilities, in short, about the minimum quality to be met.

Rankings, benchmarks, quality assurance systems, and international 'accreditation' organizations, perform the function of distinguishing further between all schools which have met the basic domestic minimum standards. They will add to the minimum criteria and put emphasis on specific aspects; they can also distinguish between different schools and profiles.

Setting easy-to-measure criteria seems comfortable: student-staff ratio, completion rates, bar exam pass rates, grade point average, library subscriptions and library space, contact hours and others. However, many quality aspects are better assessed by measuring study progress, competencies acquired by the students, their skills and capabilities. These aspects require different questions and teams of experts delving into the curriculum, talking with students and reading essays and skills products.

Relevant in this respect is to take into account whether a school has an open and transparent quality assurance system and cycles of evaluation, adaptation and implementation to improve and innovate continuously. My first accreditation standard for schools would be to describe and apply such a system with examples. Secondly, the involvement of faculty, students and peers/outsiders/labour market in the continuous reflection on the curriculum could be clarified. Thirdly, the apparent presence of curricular innovation and adaptation to demands from students, labour market and developments in the sector has to be described and illustrated/shown with examples. Fourthly: the proof of faculty writing about and being engaged in educational developments in their domain of expertise, as well as the link between research and teaching, in the sense that students are involved in research activities, cannot be measured in hard figures, but are certainly highly relevant for improvements and curricular developments.

4. Conclusion

It is self-evident that the stakeholders of law schools ask for transparent data about a law school's performance. Specifically when law schools charge (high) fees and students make an investment in studying, they legitimately expect a return upon their investment and reasonably want to know their job market perspectives and their law school's performance in benchmarks and prestige. Thus league tables and accreditation records measuring and showing student performances and progress, employment perspectives, academic standing and other relevant aspects serve a useful function. Also state budget authorities and society as a whole, when largely funding law schools, have ample reason to claim and expect quality in various educational and research domains. Is the allocated budget wisely and adequately spent and does the quality of education and research serve society's needs for quality lawyers, the rule of law and economic prosperity and the relevant contribution of lawyers.

However, I have also argued that increasingly diversity in law schools and in law school programs has increased and many of the (international) league tables assume uniformity. The QS ranking for instance assumes size, international English-speaking programs and international research, published in English language journals. It is in that respect not really an international league table but a league table of schools operating in English, or partially in English, with a focus on internationally operating lawyers and English-speaking international corporations and law firms. It is therefore more a league table of international law schools teaching in English.

For quality purposes and transparent benchmarking and information for stakeholders I do favour, when it comes to education, open and accessible accreditation processes and the availability of transparent data about student progress and labour market perspectives. Accreditation reports are generally drafted by experts who take into account a school's mission and position in the market of law schools; these reports analyse the available data and statistics and can put them into perspective. In the market of MBA's and the different accreditation organizations, stakeholders can orient themselves upon the existence of the accreditation systems and value them as a factor in their choice-making process. For Europe I believe that CHE and Multirank can also provide flexible league tables, tailored to the wishes of stakeholders. I also envisage that like-minded law schools, like-minded in the sense that they pursue similar missions, sit together and establish their relevant accreditation or benchmarking organizations that will do justice to diversity and to quality and transparency.

Chapter 14

LABOUR MARKETS AND REGIONAL LINKS

This chapter focuses on the links with the regional or local setting of law schools and specific segments of the labour market, which are the specific target of the law graduates. The idea is for law schools to be embedded in the region or their environment. Many reasons can be advanced for this link to the immediate surroundings and stakeholders, which I will discuss below.

Generally the idea is that academic institutions and immediate surroundings have a reciprocal impact: the local labour market and regional economic activity benefit from a (large) educational institution; the educational institution might certainly also seek benefits from local government, industry and local businesses and law firms in return. This calls for a policy of law schools to enter the local economic community and local politics and businesses to show what the law school can mean and does mean, in cultural and financial return and as a knowledge center, and how the local community can invest in the law school.

Law schools can invest in the local or regional community with educational practices and legal clinics, or in linking research or law student internships with public authorities, bringing knowledge from academia to the community, and enriching the student with practical expertise and law in action experiences.

Investment by law schools can also be used to show students the responsibility of lawyers for a just society, and how better to practice it than close at home? The link with the geographical stakeholders is linked to the mission of the law school, its particular strengths and other relevant factors. I have no doubt that any law school will benefit when it has strong roots in the vicinity.

1. Input from Legal Practice

Law schools are academic institutions, being part of an overall academic (university) system of education in a given country. But law schools are also (and the extent varies from country to country) professional schools which prepare students for the labour market and for their professional careers. The teaching of law 'presupposes a relationship between the academic institution and the settings of practice, similar to relations between a medical school and the clinic'.[1] Many of the suggestions put forward in this book, and probably many other creative ideas about teaching, skills and the curriculum, have to fit in the domestic legal setting and sometimes have to have, as a practical issue, the approval of the stakeholders. An important stakeholder in many countries for instance is the bar, or in general the legal professions. Or the stakeholder is the legislature, when output criteria and curriculum requirements have been laid down in legislation.

The employability of their students should be a concern of all law schools. That means asking the questions about the jobs for which the students are being educated or trained; about the future developments in jobs and job perspectives; about the skills needed to be in demand in the labour market; and about the knowledge reasonably expected in the labour market from law graduates. Law schools might do a good job in educating and training, but it seems wise that they are in contact with the present and future labour market(s). That makes it important to have a discussion with the stakeholders in the labour markets, thus serving the needs of the future students, the future employers and ensuring a smooth transition between law school and working life.

In many countries there is an on-going debate about the content of legal education and the relationship with the legal professions. Do law schools have to teach 'vocational courses', training the students for the profession? How should good relationships be maintained with all relevant professions, because in the end we want our students to be well prepared for employment? And related to this is a concern articulated by Boon and Webb,[2] who warn against too substantial divisions between legal education and the private sector. Non-responsive law schools could be overtaken by more flexible, market responsive private providers. Another risk lays in the possibility that the legal professions will set up an entry test for the vocational stage. In other words, they write that university legal educators, even taking into account that in the UK (only?) 60% of law graduates go into practice,[3] must consider the legal professions as stakeholder. 'If a case can be made that law degrees, by ceasing to serve the profession's purposes, are no longer sufficiently serving the public interest, they may no longer be accepted as the standard for entry to the profession.'[4] Certainly that outcome does not benefit the value of university legal education, nor the interests of the students, or of legal professions and society as a whole. This implies that law schools have to be able to walk the line between the university aspect of liberal and reflexive legal education and serving the interests of the professions for which the students went to law school. The fact that in this sense legal professions, or maybe even the professions who (substantially) employ law graduates, have a stake in legal education, which however must respect the autonomy of academic institutions.

1 Sullivan *et al.* 2007, p. 9.
2 Boon & Webb 2010, p. 95.
3 Boon & Webb 2010, p. 84.
4 Boon & Webb 2010, p. 95.

Before we continue and discuss the issue how to shape this relationship, within the existing statutory provisions, there is a small side step which explains the law schools' focus on the aspect of autonomy and scholarship in teaching. Increasingly, law schools which are part of university education have been required to meet scholarship criteria: faculty has to publish scholarly articles and research funding has to be competed for, with criteria derived from other sciences and assessed by outsiders (funding agencies). Additionally there is a reduction of regular funding for teaching which has necessitated staff to apply for external funding. In the same vein staff in law schools has been selected on university-wide employee criteria: having a PhD, publishing regularly scholarly pieces in peer reviewed journals, and being able to attract research funding. This trend has certainly driven practice from law schools and made working in a law school a regular career, with specific criteria and consequences.

Research assessments of legal research and their impact on the perceived quality of a school and the ensuing attraction of students, make it necessary for universities, schools and staff to strive for good research profiles, which is also helpful to attract (more) research funding and to do more consultancy and other jobs in the public and private sector. This is part of the game law schools have to play in order to be competitive for the scarce resources, which necessitates competition with other sciences and makes them abide by the rules of science which determine the playing fields of the research funding agencies.

The (legal) professions on the other hand are divided in their perspectives as to what legal education must entail. There are separate legal professions: the public sector versus the private sector. Law schools have tended to accommodate the private sector generally more than the public sector, for instance with legal aid clinics, moot courts and focus on cases and disputes. I once attended a meeting with government officials complaining about this one-sided approach. They asked for study materials and teaching approaches which do justice to the public sector: instead of a moot court a negotiation contest about the drafting of a treaty, or a mock parliament, or an exercise in which students have to draft a specific piece of legislation or have to advise the minister about a sensitive issue. There are large law firms, which are engaged in international transactions and there are main street local lawyers, who do family law and labour and social security law. Law graduates work for big - international - companies and for small local government or small/medium sized enterprises. Some employers hire specialists, some want generalists, some want wise people who can advise on strategy and policy and others want lawyers who do repetitive routine work. Since these demands differ, it is impossible for law schools to accommodate them all to the full; besides in teaching a university legal program, what counts are the skills which are general and academic and which prepare the graduates to enter professional life, in any of these sectors, and which enable them to train themselves and be trained for the very specialist requirements of the job.

This diversity however makes it imperative for law schools, also taking into account the academization of faculty, to establish regular contacts with (legal) professions, in order to be updated on what goes on in (legal) practice in all its varieties. These channels of communication can also be helpful in exchanging views on why curricula are the way they are and why courses are set up in a specific manner.

In some countries (some of the) stakeholders are involved in setting the standards and performing the accreditation of schools and/or programs. In others the standards are set by the legislature (codifying the interests or visions of the stakeholders), which makes the link between stakeholders' preferences and requirements more tenuous. For many models, in which law schools cater for a wide variety of jobs in the labour market and the employability focus is not so much exclusively on the bar, it seems that a close link between curriculum and the preferences of the bar is less evident. It might easily lead to an unbalanced curriculum, in which 'bar' aspects outweigh other skills lawyers (in other settings) specifically need.

In the case of a diverse audience of stakeholders/labour market, many reasons plead in favour of good, close and frequent contacts between law school and employers/labour market. Some relate to the educational process: ensuring that the skills and substance are related to the needs of the labour market and that new labour market developments are channelled back to law schools in an early stage.

Close links also connect students and the labour market and give them an insight into what they are learning for: what kind of job perspectives exist and for which do they want to specifically qualify and where does their preference lie. Further links with the labour market will add to the curriculum in bringing practice into the study of law; in bringing to the law school new cases and problems; or to show to the students how issues are being tackled and solved; and even having the students assist in researching real problems and cases.

Medical schools have their clinics in which students are trained and prepared for their future professional lives; some law schools have clinics as well, but their focus is less representative of future lawyering life than it is for medical students dealing with real patients. Why is that so? There are two reasons which apply in many (and certainly not all) legal systems. The one is that law schools educate lawyers for many other branches other than litigator/lawyer/attorney. Having them therefore prepare for their professional life in a legal clinic setting does not do justice to their future perspectives. It will certainly enhance their skills, but it neglects other skills and provides an incomplete picture of professional future life.

A second reason is that legal clinics do not fully operate as real-life law firms; they cater mostly for specific cases such as labour issues, tenant/landlord issues, social security cases. That is they do not operate as a (big) law firm dealing with commercial contracts, mergers, financial transactions, trade, and high profile criminal law cases. An academic hospital provides a student with a wide variety of illnesses, patients, and cures; for law the equivalent would be a big law firm connected with a law school, where people with minor and major problems have their issues resolved. In that respect law schools have not managed to bring the real, fully-fledged life of lawyers into the curriculum.

This has been counterbalanced by enabling students to do internships in legal settings, and these are valuable solutions, but they differ from medical schools which allow students to participate in practice in many settings and in many disciplines. An internship in a law firm, or participation in a law school run community project or legal clinic, or an internship in an international organization or in the corporate world, is certainly a wonderful experience, but still a limited experience and not an experience which allows a student to practice and observe all the varieties of work law graduates in many countries will be involved in.

The solution to have a framework similar to medical education is in all likelihood not feasible and largely expensive; there is obviously also an important distinction to take into account here. Medical services are in many states public services (national health service), or at least services with national insurances, intensive state intervention and large state budgets involved, and in the opinion of many, with a major state responsibility for quality, scope and reach and equality and accessibility of care for all, rich and poor. For the services of lawyers we have to take into account that law firms are an integral part of the private sector, working for commercial fee-paying clients. Also legal counsels in the corporate world are not performing public services. Therefore, the question here is why state-funded legal education must cater for the needs of these private, profit making sectors, in that their future employees have been fully trained and immersed in practice, during their legal training/education. This important distinction explains the absence of medical school like training settings in law schools. Legal practice has stepped into this 'gap' by providing bar exams, apprenticeships, legal on-the-job training for young incoming law graduates, traineeships and trainee programs in government and in the corporate world. The medical experience for students in medical school in hospitals during clinical work has, as it were, been privatized for law graduates and has become an aspect of on-the-job training during employment. Employers ensure that their new employees receive a proper and adequate training aimed at the needs of the employees and, when this is well done, they improve the qualities of these young lawyers and improve their characteristics on the labour market in general.

Obviously, in various settings employers do hire academics to provide specific trainings for their newly hired employees, and parts of the trainings might be outsourced to institutions (business schools, for instance), but in my experience there is no structural and continued connection between law schools and the on-the-job trainings and training programs by bar associations, employers organizations and separate employers. There might be a lot to gain here when law schools and these stakeholders meet and sit on a more structural and structured basis together to liaise law school experiences and expertise with employers and their training programs and wishes in that respect.

How should that be done? I believe there are many ways. One option is to have at a national level a structural contact and exchange between law schools and employers and employers associations, not only with the bar, but also with large companies and governments. Another way is for one law school to instigate these contacts with what it perceives as its most important employers, hiring, or interested in, its students. These activities and connections can be combined with job fairs and other relevant events.

Many law schools work in a variety of ways in seeking connections between the professional world its students will work in at a later stage and the law school curriculum and the students. Also students themselves are generally very active in seeking those connections by organizing study trips and inviting guests to events they organize as a study association. Law schools will also benefit when they support students' activities in this respect. Support does not only mean making funds available, but it is also support in the sense that the school shows its interest by the attendance of professors, by the dean who is open to suggestions, by professors who assist the students in occasionally making their contacts available etcetera.

Other solid and much used practices are to hire adjunct faculty or professionals for part-time teaching, or to invite professionals to deliver a lecture. These approaches make the link between practice and teaching a very natural one and ensure that courses, though the academic content will be pertinent, also link the substance of the course to real-life examples and to the resolution of actual disputes. These modes of teaching also give the students insight into the diverse aspects of professional life and of the various jobs that are available for them after their graduation. Not only will a course be enriched but also the students will have an opportunity to orient themselves on future employment and their preferences.

Practice in law schools shows a variety of examples of involving practice in a school and its educational programs. Relevant and important are projects in which students engage in day-to-day problems by working in a legal clinic for clients; or in which students do legal projects for specific groups of clients; or do a course which is inspired by actual cases and social problems. For instance by taking a course which centers round a social problem (migration, environmental issues, transboundary crime; international financial markets, international trade etcetera). In this course students can be asked to combine different legal domains (private law, criminal law, international law), to collaborate and to write reports and papers analyzing the issues and proposing solutions. I have come across educational institutions in which projects such as these are a compulsory part of the curriculum and are also geared towards partners in society. These partners are approached and asked to sponsor policy and research questions in which they feel they are interested and have an interest in seeking answers. By sponsoring an academic institution (law school) to assist them in looking for answers and in, so to speak, hiring a university to undertake this as a research project for the benefit of students and society, we train students in doing research, in collaboration, in linking law and society, and in working across legal domains (and probably in many instances) in a multidisciplinary manner. Projects such as these would really fit in a problem-based curriculum of a law school and would also appeal to academic research qualities of the students.

Projects and structures like this might also be embedded in a structural way in a law school. With this I mean through the institution of a Legal Clinic, for example, or through the establishment of a 'Consultancy Branch' in those legal domains for which the law school claims specific expertise in staff and students. Consultancy is a broader project compared to a legal clinic. In the latter we make students work in counselling clients on questions related to rent, employment, family law, social security, tax and similar daily life legal issues. In the former the aim is for another audience: an audience of governments, law firms, companies, private organizations who can ask for legal opinions on issues to be defined by the law school in its consultancy project.

Students work on the legal opinions, supervised by faculty. A law school might have a Criminal Justice consultancy; or one on Migration issues or Competition law; or on Corporate Social Responsibility, or Tort law or Environmental law. A variation on the above projects is what we did in Maastricht for a major building project in the city, the construction of a tunnel for the A2 freeway crossing the city. Part of the project entailed the Construction Consortium paying the law school a lump sum of money. For that lump sum the school has trained students to answer legal questions of all those who feel they might have a legal interest or be affected by the project. Many issues can be imagined: shop owners who fear a decline in sales because of limited access to their stores; home owners who fear damage to their homes; parents who are afraid of dangerous commutes for their children to and from school; real estate owners who are afraid of a decrease of value of their property due to the project etcetera. Students, supervised by faculty, respond to all questions. In cases of serious legal issues and the perceived need for the preservation of rights to hire a lawyer, the client will be informed of the advice to hire a lawyer.

It is necessary to make many arrangements carefully: quality check the advice given by the students; ensure that the students/law school can do their/its work in this project in full independence from the Construction Consortium; and, very important, one has to take care of the issue of responsibility for mistakes and omissions.

Apart from the suggestions and variations described above, I have two further points to make. These relate to the desirability to establish regular and systematic contact with the labour market, with an aim to have open channels of communication and exchange, bearing in mind each other's proper roles and responsibilities, perspectives and ideas about the quality of university legal education.

The first proposal concerns the establishment of an Advisory Board for a law school. The composition of the Advisory Board would be determined taking into account the position of a law school, an agenda to inform stakeholders of the law school about educational aspects and to allow the stakeholders to inform the law school about their perspectives on the access to the labour market and its requirements. The question in that respect is how to determine the relevant stakeholders, without the Advisory Board becoming too large. The composition has also to be related to the mission of the school and its strategy to target specific shares of the labour market. I suggest a representative of the national bar, of the local bar, of the association of judges, of an association of corporate lawyers, and of government lawyers. Furthermore I suggest the inclusion of alumni who work in labour market niches which the law school finds relevant for its teaching portfolio. These alumni have experienced the law school and its educational profile and content and can report on the match between the curriculum and their job experiences.

For law schools with a wide variety of courses and LLB and LLM programs on domestic law, international law, European law and/or other segments of the law, it seems advisable to add smaller curriculum boards, composed of representatives of targeted/selected parts of the labour market and of alumni of that specific program.

Far be it from me to argue that these advisory and curriculum boards must meet frequently or will be given powers of decision making; their purpose must be to maintain contacts and to exchange expectations and experiences, with the law school deciding in the end on whether and how to implement suggestions and comments.

Because of the changes which have occurred in the compositions of academic faculty (own career paths; PhD's; less back and forth exchanges between law schools and legal practice; the scholarization of faculty), the maintaining and deepening of contacts between labour market and schools are relevant.

In that respect there is another factor at play. Students seem to be very much (legal) practice oriented, seeking practice-oriented courses and skills and wanting to make sure that employability is, as it were, guaranteed. To quote Goldsmith and Bamford:

> 'many students enrolled in university law undergraduate degrees express a clear preference for practice-oriented opportunities within the curriculum and during the law school years, while demonstrating a growing impatience with conventional law school curricula and teaching methods'.[5]

Law students are key stakeholders in law schools, which however leads to the legitimate question, to what extent and how should law schools cater for their needs and pressures for an employable program and practice-oriented courses. Law students generally share an interest here with legal practice, that is, with certain segments of the labour market (specifically the traditional legal professions).[6] Faculty is concerned with academic teaching and the connections with research, but in many law schools, exacerbated with the growth of student intake, an increasing number of students consider law school as a mere preparation for legal practice or other jobs in the labour market. Elite schools, that score very high on selection, suffer less from this feature, since they attract the best of the best and their students tend to be welcomed by the large top law firms with international legal practices. Law schools with high intake and therefore with an output which cannot generally

5 Goldsmith & Bamford 2010, p. 157.
6 About this subject: Cownie 2010.

be considered excellent, have a much more diverse student body and must cater for all their needs and worries about employment and their employment possibilities are probably as diverse as the students. This aspect does not ease the concerns of the students but tends to strengthen them (specifically in present day worried Europe). Students seek avenues which they feel prepare them best for the legal jobs and their perception is that this means choosing practice-oriented courses. When one knows one is not a top student, one knows one will not be recruited by a top law firm. An average law student who seeks a career in an average legal job in a law firm, the sentiment is to be as well prepared as possible. For that reason those students want a law study to prepare them for problem solving and practice orientation and less for liberal arts and academic reflection or research skills.

These aspects have led in many places to similar phenomena, as described for Australia by Goldsmith and Bamford:[7] a broadening of the curriculum (theoretical perspectives and contextual frameworks), a growth in skills teaching and clinical legal education. As the authors point out, this was done while the number of students increased, the student-staff ratio's declined and the curriculum was broadened and skills inserted and context required more supervision, feedback and guidance. These developments have done much good, and must be balanced with the liberal arts, university competencies and skills.

However, it could well be that the bifurcation between segments of the legal profession and correspondingly between two categories of law schools,[8] sets a trend towards further diversification between law schools. Or it will become a more visible spit in the sense that a category of schools will successfully focus on academic skills and law and aims to educate top lawyers for top firms and top jobs, whereas other schools educate lawyers for the more local and private client market. In Europe we might see the emergence of European law schools, and maybe we will also witness the emergence of global law schools.

Boon and Whyte[9] have expressed their concerns whether law schools can accommodate future trends for specialization. I do not share their concern. Law firms and other major employers indeed do want specialists, but specialists with a sound and general legal basis, provided for in a general law curriculum. There are also many contacts between major law firms and law schools, so that law schools fully understand the law firms' needs and for these law firms to appreciate the academic flavour in a curriculum. This is even more so the case because precisely that flavour or better characteristic distinguishes the excellent students from the others. My concern relates however more to the pull from other employers (local government, smaller local law firms) that law schools must fully prepare their students for legal practice, with all it takes, in their settings, ready to practice law. In that domain law schools will have to navigate carefully, but I can see here a pull towards a bifurcated system.

7 Goldsmith & Bamford 2010.

8 See Chapter 2.

9 Boon & Whyte 2010, p. 192.

The paradox which is visible is that students tend on average to focus on practical courses, however when having the choice they prefer to go to the older (elite) university institutions, 'despite the unpopularity of their more theoretical, less practical, approach with law students'.[10] Boon and Whyte explain this paradox with the good labour market perspectives for graduates from these institutions.

Another interesting finding is that elite employers (in the UK) prefer conversion course graduates (students with another undergraduate degrees who have subsequently completed a one year law program preparing them for the legal profession).[11] I find this to be an indication for what employers tend to seek in a new legal employee: a graduate with a good academic background and foundation, with the necessary skills and competencies, who subsequently has been taught the necessary legal knowledge. Boon and Whyte call it an anomaly; I would rather call it a confirmation that what counts for legal practice and for legal professions is a solid academic background and skills, added (topped off?) with legal skills and knowledge.

Institutionally, law schools could consider to establish an Overall Advisory Board (for the law school/Dean as such), or to set up different smaller advisory boards (or sub-boards, or panels) for the different programs a school offers. These boards could perform different functions, but the two most important could very well be to connect to stakeholders (such as the legal professions or other segments of the labour market) or to involve alumni and potential donors in the law school. The first function does not only serve the interests of the labour market in that they will be given a say in curriculum and skills, but the purpose must be to have an open exchange, with mutual respect, about the curriculum, the labour market perspectives and developments. This will be (also in relation to other contacts a school may have with the legal professions) an important channel through which a law school can be informed about labour market developments. An Advisory Board could also be given a role in the quality assessment and assurance procedures. In order to ensure that a Board is not solely a representation of the legal professions, it could also consist of regional/local stakeholders (industry, government) and of alumni who work in legal education in another institution. This composition will ensure that a law school will benefit from external input. A school can test its new courses and methods of delivery, or its focus, on sympathizing outsiders. When one feels that this structure might lead to a new pattern of fixed structures and the same ideas, the best solution is to have term limits for the members of these boards. That will ensure that over the course of time one will have an increasing number of people with an involvement in the school and that ideas will be fresh and possibly innovative.

10 Boon & Whyte 2001, p. 213.

11 See, for instance, <www.bpp.com/graduate-diploma-in-law.aspx>; the BPP Law School offering its one year Graduate Diploma in Law (no prior knowledge of the law is needed, according to the website); see also for this Graduate Diploma: <www.college-of-law.co.uk/Want-to-work-in-law/Non-law-graduates/>.

2. Connections to Labour Markets and Regions

We educate students so that they will become responsible lawyers, in whatever capacity they might come to work. Despite the fact that I have argued that we must educate lawyers in an academic fashion, in the end law schools must educate competent, skilful and responsible lawyers, who have access to a relevant labour market and who are employable. In that respect for many jobs the academic skills and the other lawyering competences as well as the knowledge obtained must be up to date, relevant and effective. Employability is not the only criterion to build a curriculum and it is certainly not the least important, but it is included in a good and proper academic legal education with all aspects I have described in earlier chapters.

Employability is and must be a factor: in rankings it is often visible as one of the parameters for assessing the quality of a program or a school. The QS ranking (mentioned in Chapter 13) also measures employment and employers' satisfaction. Students, for that reason, also find employment aspects relevant, and not only when they are (high) fee paying, and therefore want a return on their investments. Accreditation agencies and assessment committees also relate to data about access to the labour market and employers' feedback about the qualities of the graduates. Governments, when funding law schools, have an interest in students' study progress, and want to know whether the money is well spent and contributes to a good level of education and the improvement of society with skilful lawyers.

In other places in this book I have related to other international rankings, for instance the World Bank ranking about the ease of doing business in specific countries. Some factors in these rankings imply the quality of the legal system and therefore the quality of the law, legal certainty, the court system and lawyers, and such aspects as the enforceability of contracts and the accessibility of the tax system and of government services. In these domains lawyers are employed and contribute to the quality of the legal system as a whole and the rule of law, and the services in and through legal services. Good lawyers, and in general a well educated population, are certainly (economic) assets for a country, as well as contributors to civil society and to a well-functioning rule of law and democracy.

The labour market and employers' satisfaction are not the only parameters to measure the quality of legal education but they are certainly relevant. And, for that matter, it is of the utmost importance for law schools to connect to the labour market(s), in many ways: in the curriculum; with possibilities of internships; through extra-curricular (student organized activities; with guest lectures and faculty with professional experience; through moot courts and other settings mimicking professional practice; offering professional life-long learning courses, lectures or programs, bringing professional life into the law school; and through organizing input from practice into the law school. Some schools organize career services, offering students the possibility to receive training about interviews, feedback about their CV's and application letters, and to be assisted in making good choices in their curriculum and employment search (what are their strengths and weaknesses and preferences and personal skills).

One of the ways is to involve the labour market in the curriculum, that is, in teaching and giving feedback in skills and through participation in moot courts. In Maastricht we have extensive experience with involving the Maastricht district court judges in the moot court training and they enjoy doing so. These judges have real-life experience and can create a real courtroom setting and get the students' attention and make them realize the seriousness of the business at hand. It is however always a combination of factors: faculty plus professionals, in order to ensure didactical standards, fit with the curriculum design, and coherent standards.

Another option is to hire or involve legal professionals for guest lectures, special tutorials, or even specific courses within their expertise. These activities ask for coordination and for embedding them in the curriculum and the didactical set up. Also, the professionals must be prepared, and have the possibility, to engage themselves for a certain period of time at specific hours for teaching their course or giving their lectures. These aspects require good coordination and willingness on both sides, and they also require that the legal professional has the competences to be a good teacher.

In my experiences the best possible venues to involve practitioners in teaching courses is in an advanced stage of the curriculum and within a setting with full-time faculty. This setting will enable the practitioner to be coached in how things are being done and it will ensure a backup in case of emergencies and sudden unavailability.

Students appreciate (good) legal professionals in teaching advanced courses and it works both ways. The outsider practitioner teaching a course will gain insight into a law school and in students' abilities, (s)he also will teach a class of interested students who are advanced in their studies and might be interesting new hires for practice. The students will hear first-hand how legal practice operates, which stakes are involved and what different jobs really imply and do require. One could consider this option as an informal career service and career information.

As in many things, the above must not be overdone: though it might be attractive for financial or capacity reasons to resort to outsiders on an extensive scale. Overdoing it has obvious disadvantages and will tilt the scales of the balance.

There might be too few tenured staff to ensure a setting within which the practitioner can work; another risk is that the advanced courses will lack an academic focus and will on the contrary become too practice oriented. And finally the coherence of the faculty in making up an academic community and organizing an academic coherent curriculum could be endangered.

How about internships as part of the curriculum? Internships facilitate a variety of goals: they can show to the students examples of professional life and thereby ease their choices about future careers; they can contribute to skills and knowledge in a specific domain; they can function as tools for future employers to get to know possible future employers; and internships can be a feedback instrument for the faculty about the quality of the students; and in general, a system of internships, is, or can be, a communication tool between law school and legal practice, involving legal practice in the education of students.

An obvious issue with internships is whether they can be included as part of the curriculum, or rather must be an extracurricular activity by the students (which may or may not be facilitated by the law school with an internship office). Must a law school make scarce curriculum space available for internships which undoubtedly contribute to a student's education but also and very much so enhance the student's CV's and the employer's connection to law schools and to future employees (the students!). Related to this is the scarcity of space in a law curriculum, with all requirements I have laid out in earlier chapters of this book.

There are many factors to consider here. In some countries students have relatively long academic vacations, which are meant for and can be used for internships or clerkships. In those settings the law school already has taken into account the desirability of this connection and has enabled the students and the legal practice.

I have underlined in this book the specific setting of law schools: as schools training skills and doing so for the legal professions (and other relevant jobs), and as academic institutions. Both aspects must certainly be catered for. I believe it is the strength of good legal education to combine both features. Without wanting to equate medical education and legal education, there is a comparison to be made. Internships form a very elementary and limited form of clinical stage (which in many settings medical students must do in all/most medical disciplines). In those cases, however, the hospital (and the medical doctor/specialist who is involved in supervising the internee) have a specialized relationship with the medical school; expertise is regulated; rules about supervision and about activities by the students are agreed upon; and the supervisors have a role to play and are frequently guided and trained in that role. Law schools have, to my knowledge, not advanced to that stage, which they should, I believe, when an internship is a part of the curriculum and leads to the award of credits.

There might be two alternatives (or additions) to an internship as part of the curriculum. The first is to develop courses and settings organizing real-life problems. Here we enter a domain with many, many possibilities: consultancy, law in context practices, practical assignments and others. What they will have in common is that reference is made to real-life cases or problems. They could relate to legal disputes or policy problems of a government agency, or a major corporate issue. These issues could be (partially) made up, or handed in by a firm or client, seeking advice. Law schools host a lot of expertise and skills and with and through the students also have an abundance of original creativity, energy and out-of-the-box thinking. In order to mimic real labour market situations a law school might set up a consultancy within the domains of the specific expertise available in the law school and provide advice to clients for competitive fees. We have come to know legal aid clinics in law schools but since increasingly in many jurisdictions law students also seek employment in various consultancy and lobby firms, law schools could improve students' preparation for the labour market by offering those kinds of labour experiences to their students. Harvard Business School[12] has thoroughly altered the program so as to allow students to immerse themselves in practical problems and real-life issues. I suggest that experiments like this one might also apply for law and assist in educating lawyers for later practice.

The second is to organize a legal clinic, mimicking professional practice and inspired by the medical education concept. The question here is whether practical legal training can be modelled on medical schools. Maxeiner has pointed out a major difference.[13] He argues that public money pays for health care but that is not the case with legal work. Clinical medical education funds itself. But when one sets up clinical legal education, funding is complex and most likely to take resources from the curriculum.

His second reservation[14] is that doing service to clients in a legal clinic is different from most of later legal practice (whereas in hospitals it is the same work). Legal clinics in law schools deal with specific aspects of the law and specific clients (welfare law, social law, labour law, housing law, family law), but generally not with competition law, mergers and acquisitions, corporate law, international contracts etcetera). Legal clinics run by law schools could train the students to improve on their skills of interviewing clients and drafting legal documents and filing court cases, but they do not cater for many labour market perspectives of many students after law school.

These issues are difficult to remedy: one might consider a law school setting up its own law firm, operating on a commercial basis, with regular clients, however, with the proviso that students are involved in handling cases. This method could generate income and thereby make the legal clinic experience less costly for the law school. On the other hand, running a law firm is not really a law school's business and it is questionable whether this would lead to a thriving cost-effective business.

Another option is to establish close links with a selection of law firms and other legal practices, under which students would receive careful guidance and perform specific tasks and assignments. This option might guarantee a better incorporation of the internship in the legal curriculum, ensuring an effective use of time and exercise of many skills.

For students, awareness of the labour markets and career possibilities is an avenue to explore. This means that law schools must provide them with information about entrepreneurship and what it takes to set up shop and run one's own business. In the vicinity of universities one can witness locations for spin-off's and campus-related smaller industries. Embedding law students in these businesses could be an interesting endeavour, and could link legal expertise with entrepreneurism. I have also wondered whether law schools could develop small legal

12 <http://www.hbs.edu/mba/hbsadvantage/>.

13 Maxeiner 2008.

14 Maxeiner 2008, p. 46.

businesses, facilitating students to start small businesses as consultants in expert domains, such as public procurement, competition, private international law, free establishment, financial transactions etcetera. Or possibly law schools could connect with the other small businesses a university generates offering assistance about corporate law or intellectual property.

Considering the increasing complexity of legal issues and the flexibility and competition of experts and expertise, law schools could seek avenues in this domain to facilitate preparation by students for these prospects.

An issue which I have not addressed is the impact of a law school on its locality/city/region/country and how this localization impacts upon a school. There is to my knowledge no general research as to the benefits of a law school to the local area, but it must definitely be true that a law school has an economic impact; has a social and cultural impact and is beneficial to the area. Whatever the local circumstances are, this aspect is and must be a factor to take into account.

Higher education and research are important engines in local economies. The presence of universities does impact local employment; attracts other jobs and (research) activities and heavily influences the composition of a city's population.[15] For law schools I am not aware of any specific impact study. Impact is certainly present in the domain of primary and secondary employment but also in community activities such as legal clinics or other relevant community services. A law school also provides life-long learning (continued) education activities for the legal professionals (lawyers, judges, and others) and can provide law graduates who start or take up employment in the area or region in which the law school is located. In that respect some law schools find themselves in 'legal places' (capitals, financial capitals/districts, and corporate headquarters) and can set up links with these legal sectors, connecting research, professional training, educational programs and the profession and employability of the students.

I believe that law schools must (and they do) benefit from their locality and must take the locality into account. We see with many law schools how they benefit from the presence of courts, banks, governments and corporations and law firms in setting a policy for guest lectures, sponsorships and other connections. Some cities also have their separate attraction for students: for example, Washington DC, New York, Hong Kong, Amsterdam, and Paris. Law schools not located in such cities with attractive and well-known features in and of themselves, and not connected to a vibrant legal community in its direct vicinity, must therefore build their own proper strong points and must build them in the mission and strategy of the school and the connections to the location, whatever the location is. For a harbour town: make connections to trade, shipping, transport and commerce. For a city with an international organization on food or police: set up links with regard to food safety

15 For The Netherlands this has been researched and reported in *Kennis als economische motor* (Onderzoek naar het ruimtelijk-economisch effect van hoger onderwijs), TNO-rapport TNO-034-DTM-2009-02905; Delft 2009.

or police powers. It is recommendable for law schools to specialize in domains also which reflect the strengths or features or industries and organizations in the direct area. Whatever the case may be, it is stimulating to reflect on connections not only with the global world but also with the immediate surroundings.

Another connection is within the university and its strong points and strategies. A university with a strong and well-respected business school might tempt the law school to seek collaboration in business and law programs or an educational profile on (international) commerce, trade and corporate governance. With the presence of a strong political science school or department the focus may be had on international politics, parliamentarism and multi-level governance could be the focus; the presence of environmental studies could link to environmental law. This is not to mean that a law school will have to carve out a course based only upon other faculties and schools but that links and multidisciplinary connections will certainly be valuable in building strengths and in showing to the students that multidisciplinarity and collaboration are helpful and essential.

Chapter 15

ORGANIZATION AND LEADERSHIP OF A SCHOOL/FACULTY

This chapter does not deal with the substance of legal education, or the modes of delivery, but focuses upon leadership and organization. Major differences exist in the world between organization structure, size, and wealth of law schools. Law schools must adapt to the legal rules and organizational structure, as well as the demands posed upon deans in different settings. When a law school is highly dependent on external funding and high tuition fees, this calls for a different strategy than in the context of law schools which are primarily funded by the state, without the possibility to substantially raising money through fees.

However, despite the many differences, there is also a great deal of commonalities. One can think of the development of a law school's strategy and mission and of an organizational structure which enables the school to implement the mission it has carved out for itself. Furthermore an organization is relevant which promotes good legal education and facilitates the dean and the professors and the students in performing optimally. An organization must be tailored to the needs and strategy of a law school.

Leadership is also highly relevant here: a dean (or a head of department or faculty) is the figure head of the school. Like a head of state, the dean represents what the school wants to achieve and stands for, uniting an academic community in order to achieve the best results; and praising successes and defending staff and students against undue interferences, as well as stimulating the academic community to achieve the best results. A dean must also be actively involved in and responsible for the prosperity of the law school in the interests of the staff and the students. Whoever is in charge of a law school, whatever the powers of the head or dean are, however a dean is appointed or elected, (s)he must promote the interests of the school and therefore push for improvement, necessary choices and the best performances possible as well as for a continuous reflection on the future of the law school, legal education and legal research.

1. Leadership

Leadership of law schools differs considerably over the world. Most schools operate on a collegial model: faculty decides on the major questions of policy, research and education, leaving it to a dean to execute and implement those policies. The opposite model is the model in which the university board appoints a dean with strong budgetary and policymaking powers. The dean really leads the school. Naturally, many in-between and mixed models do exist.

Leadership of an academic institution, such as a law school, brings along with it many challenges. Neither a university nor a law school is a cookie factory, where orders can be given and targets imposed and a strategy is imposed to be implemented. A law school is an academic institution, with highly-skilled professionals, who are experts in their field and who are articulate and outspoken.

A law school is in my analogy not unlike a sports team and the dean is the trainer/coach. There is/must always be an ambition to achieve better, to educate students better and write more, better and more influential scholarly articles. A law school is also a team. The school's performance is a collaborative effort. One might have good offensive players, but if the defence is weak, or the goalie has many off-days, this will eventually influence the performance and the rankings. Faculty members also have different strengths in teaching, research, attracting external funding, supervising PhD's, management and innovation. It is a rare oddity to have a school composed of faculty members who excel in everything, and the question is whether that would indeed lead to an excellent team.

Most schools will have to seek the best fit for the job: a team composition which meets the law school's mission and strategy and targets.

I have argued before that a law school needs a coherent (and ambitious, but doable) strategy and a mission which it sets out to achieve in terms of education and research. I have argued that the strategy must focus to align the resources, research and teaching. For teaching one must agree upon a set pedagogy, admission of students, labour market focus, curriculum design and content, skills trainings and definition of graduates. This is extremely important, because it defines the school and it prioritizes the school's and faculty's efforts and it enables focused HRM policies. It also assists in the evaluation of what one sets out to do: evaluation is coupled to goals and perspectives. A curriculum has its proper objectives and only through the definition of these can one formulate evaluation policies and HRM structures and organize consultations with stakeholders in the labour market.

The above, as well as the continuous implementation of the strategy and the constant reflection on the effectiveness of the policies and the introduction of new tactics and adaptation to new needs and challenges from abroad, requires leadership in a law school. It also requires an excellent management information system, quality assurance system and a circle of implementation, which assist leadership, the heads of school or the deans, to lead and to execute the strategy. It specifically requires the tools and instruments to enforce changes and to overrule (perceived) autonomy of staff ('academic freedom'). Leadership needs to have the levers to execute a given policy and to implement evaluations and the recommendations resulting from them. This implies that legal positions of faculty and university/faculty structures and decision-making procedures allow for the enforcement of a law school's strategy, mission and the implementation thereof.

Leading a law school is not (only) about enforcing policies; certainly not. The best strategy and the best leadership are when the faculty carries out and implements the common goals and does what it takes to move the school forward.

For strategy setting and implementation, and for policy making and execution, strong leadership is essential: a university or school leadership which can make the choices and enforce the relevant decisions.

A school of law is a professional organization with competent and intelligent staff. However, when a school decides on strengthening its profile in a national or regional or international setting, one ought to give the accompanying powers and tools to a leader that can work towards this goal.

Implementation of an ambitious strategy requires many choices and many decisions as to priorities and selection of students, staff, research and educational programs. It might lead to the termination of some research focus areas and the strengthening or starting of other research domains and similarly with respect to bachelor, master and professional programs and these decisions will affect the faculty.

To create a setting of leadership and clear decision-making structures is not often very easy. Academics will invoke their autonomy and the concept of academic freedom. The idea is then that faculty ought to be in charge of the hiring process, decisions about promotion and tenure, and challenges with regard to research domains and programs and the curriculum design.

Specifically, major decisions ought not to impact upon academic freedom of teaching and writing. In some countries this is even further complicated by the fact that (some) professors receive separate funding, or receive their funding for the chair independent from the funding of the school. Furthermore, the legal position of professors can be such that a law school leadership has very little, if at all, power to impose quality targets or other assignments and cannot supervise, other than by way of conversations and the powers of persuasion, the professors with tenure.

Let me turn this around. I will not deny that schools or universities, constructed on the basis of these or similar structures, might be top schools. However, I submit that such status is primarily, or at least substantially, created with huge funds enabling the best to be attracted to the school. If, however, a smaller school wishes to climb up in the rankings or to improve in status and build better research visibility and quality and to design and teach better educational programs, which are attractive for the student and labour market, then it is necessary to build a better organizational structure. And this has to be done without stifling academic creativity and quality output of the professionals. Again, allow me to make a sport's analogy here. In Europe some football clubs, which are wealthy or have a wealthy owner, can buy players and try to buy excellent teams. Other clubs, which have less funds available, must set up elaborated strategies in recruiting young players and give them the best programs possible. That implies that such a club fine tunes its training programs and sets player profiles for its young players who are then raised to become top players. Most law schools are in the position of poor(er) football clubs and can strive for better performances by educating young staff, by creating focus in teaching and research and collaboratively working on a joint mission with a strong focus. These law schools perform best by setting a specific profile, concentrating their efforts, and educating young and talented scholars and educators.

Here lies of course a problem: the growing bureaucracy and the increase of procedures and software programs and assessments and targets and supervision and quality control, have changed academia. For many law schools in the world, budgets have decreased and student numbers have gone up. The context in which law schools operate has changed. There are more and more different expectations from students, labour markets and (funding) governments. Law schools operate in more playing fields, with increasing globalization and student and staff exchanges. This calls for general skills and academic skills and it asks for the sheer necessity that law schools make choices in their course offering, in the research portfolio, in the preparation of the students for (segments of) the labour market and in seeking external funding. And on top of that we have witnessed the substance of what we teach grow exponentially. This implies that law schools must make choices; and making a choice in favour of one strategy and mission brings along with it that other strategies will not be pursued. This also means that some lines of research will not be continued; and that some specializations will be discontinued in favour of other (new) expertise; or that centers of excellence are set up and with them, accompanying master programs. These choices require leadership and organization. And these are, unless all faculty perceives the immediate need for reasons of almost bankruptcy or bad evaluations, in many cases hard choices. I have worked to set up a clear focus in my law school in Maastricht. Bucerius law school is another such example of a school with a precise strategy and focus and so is McGill law school.

The best timing for strategic choices to be made and implemented is, however, not in times of crisis, but in prosperity and success, when one can see the clouds coming in. Law schools must foresee and be prepared that success will not last forever, not even in specific successful domains. When one wishes to be at the forefront, innovation requires that the question is asked continuously whether new avenues of teaching and new programs and research will bring the school further and will contribute to the education of lawyers for the future! The drive for innovation must be that schools do not rest but seek new opportunities.

Good leadership in a law school ensures that the innovation drive and (future) quality of the educational programs is a permanent item on the agenda of a school. It also implies that innovation is permanently facilitated: members of faculty are enabled to develop new courses, new modes of delivery, new E-learning techniques and challenging new programs. This also requires the abolishment of other courses, an avenue many law schools have difficulty in pursuing. One could also allow and stimulate, for instance through an innovation budget or through a seed-money budget, changes and improvements in teaching and research which will keep academic teaching alive and makes innovation part of the job. Money is then also seen to be spent on quality improvements in education and that is a signal, when it coincides with the strategic plan of a school, which will not be misunderstood and leads to major work in that respect, unleashing all creative forces.

2. Organization

Organization follows and facilitates strategy. It follows that the organization must make the implementation of the strategy possible. It facilitates in the sense that a good organization makes it possible to develop a good and stable strategy.

Organization is needed for everything I have described: aspects such as curriculum design, integrated skills, academic flavour and attitude, staff/faculty composition, quality control and evaluations, management data and benchmarks, admission and selection of students. These are the tools needed to implement the strategy.

For leadership to perform the duties I described in the previous paragraph it is relevant to have an organization which can perform the following tasks:

1. Manage the student body (admission, selection, graduation of students; exam organization; scheduling; information to the students; counselling; student management information).
2. Recruitment, promotion and termination of faculty (HRM and HRM management information).
3. Control: manage the budget; grant administration and third-party contracts; monthly/quarterly budget reports.
4. Research and academic support (secretarial functions; conferences and research meetings; research management information, research funding).
5. Graduate School duties: PhD recruitment and guidance of progress; honours classes; course work.
6. Career and internship. Counselling about the labour market; mediating in internships.
7. Student exchanges and international collaboration.
8. Didactical unit.
9. Skills unit.
10. ICT support.

For these administrative and support offices or functions it is essential that a school is provided with the proper and accessible software to enable it to enter and access the relevant information and to be able to work with it and to create the relevant management information. Also faculty must have the opportunity to rely upon software to facilitate their work. Examples here are not only the software but also the trainings. In my school we have developed software to deal with the registration of teaching load and holidays for instance; students have to hand in their bachelor and master essays through a special program, which records all drafts submitted and the grade given and it automatically checks for plagiarism. The electronic learning environment must run smoothly and so must all information available to students and staff.

The book *Educating Lawyers* calls for 'institutional intentionality':[1] this refers to having a mission as a school – aligning students' learning and course effectiveness. It is a call to be explicit about their goals and actively plan strategies to achieve them. From experiences in engineering and medical schools the authors conclude that

> '(t)hese other professions seem to recognize that achieving a high degree of alignment among the interests of the school's internal and external constituencies and using the process to articulate clearly the institution's goals and priorities contributes significantly to educational quality. This may involve deciding, for example, whether the school aims to produce legal generalists (mostly practitioners or perhaps judges) or scholars and legal specialists'.[2]

This message underlines one of the conclusions in this book, that strategy, mission, focus, alignment of practices and mission, pedagogy, content and skills, organization and commonality work towards quality in education. Since the world has become international and diverse, and legal education is as diverse as the world is, we have to make explicit our assumptions, and be prepared to discuss them. We have to be explicit in the goals we pursue and how we pursue them. This requires a proper organization, leadership and a coherent and capable faculty, willing to discuss educational strategies and curriculum and to find a consensus on them, in alignment with the markets, resources, stakeholders and expertise.

Modern-day management theories about organizations, and not only professional organizations, such as universities and law schools, consider that innovations and improvements do not primarily come from top-down, but on the contrary come from bottom-up. Those working in teaching, or those working in support, have the best knowledge about improving things and innovating new programs and courses and support efficiency. This does require that faculty and other staff is challenged and engaged in constantly working to make things better and devising new courses and programs which make the law school more competitive and better adapted to modern day circumstances.

This presupposes that faculty and staff feel challenged by the (domestic, global and regional) competition, by the rankings and by the need to acquire a better position in the rankings and the benchmarks. In industry this challenge is part of the reason of being of an enterprise: competing on the market; improving its products; find new markets for its products; anticipate on future markets; making production cheaper and more efficient. This also applies to services as well as to tangible products. So, why does it not apply to law schools and the (quality of) legal education they provide?

1 Sullivan *et al.* 2007, p. 180 *et seq.*
2 Sullivan *et al.* 2007, p. 182.

In Europe most of the universities and law schools receive their funding from the governments. This feature has hindered law schools from innovation: the only trigger has been an internal motivation (the academic attitude always to improve) or pressure from the labour market, for instance the bar association calling for adaptations in curricula and courses. Being funded by the government, and therefore not being externally triggered to explore markets and seek better standings in rankings and getting larger shares of the students markets (and maybe even larger shares of full fee paying students), has made many schools complacent. In research and research funding we have seen a decline in government funding and a growth in external funding (EU and domestic), which has made academic staff increasingly more (pro-)active. But I am inclined to say that this trend did not occur in the domain of teaching. This does not imply that some schools and/or universities have not been very active in that respect, but I believe that where this happened it happened through a strong university/faculty strategy. An example of this could be for the law school to set aside budget for educational innovation projects, or the development of new programs, or the exploration of new markets for student recruitment.

To rely solely on government funding carries along some risks. The most important one is the gradual and creeping decline in government funding for university education, including for law schools. Ritzen finds that

> '(t)he dismal story of Europe is one of a serious expansion of university education in the 1960s, 1970s and 1980s accompanied by a more or less constant (real) budget, thus leading to more or less a halving of per student expenditures over the period 1975-2005'.[3]

It was also problematic that universities 'were not allowed to compensate this decrease with tuition fees while other private funds were not available'. Tuition fees are still low in many European countries (or even absent or extremely low), with the most notable exceptions the UK and Sweden. This situation has hindered universities and law schools (probably law schools even more because of the domestic legal cultures and virtually absent international competition) from innovating and improving education. Stimuli, if any, came from assessments and rankings (such as the German CHE ranking), if and so far as they existed and had an impact on student numbers and student intake. For many years law schools in European countries did not have to worry about student numbers; at least not about them being too low! So, why bother?

This is going to change for those law schools that seek a place in the global or European market for students and research. They need to design the necessary quality programs and build the links with the labour markets and ensure employability. For them it is imperative to innovate with regard to the programs and the facilities and services for the students. A change will also occur when demographics

3 Ritzen 2010, p. 155; on p. 136 he shows a figure indicating the steep decline of per student funding in the Netherlands over the last decades.

will make themselves felt, in that there will be less students from the regular student intake, or when students will note that it does matter for future careers and labour market perspectives what and where they studied! In these circumstances all law schools will undertake action in order to have their proper share of the market.

Another need to change and innovate is through and after education assessments (by the bar, or by the domestic accreditation agency) or through intentional university and law school policy. Many countries have a form of assessment of universities/law schools on a regular basis. Sometimes they lead to a ranking; sometimes they take place on an individual basis. What they do have in common is that it is checked whether all schools meet the set minimum standards. For that purpose they are useful exercises, however they take the national system and the average national levels for granted and are not a real stimulus for further innovations and improvements. Obviously, standards have to be set for all schools to conform with, but it is doubtful whether these domestic exercises lead to innovation and to a push to improve on the international ladder. That requires much more: foremost, to have international assessment committees, to enable the mix of international ideas and suggestions and the implementation of international standards and experiences. Specifically we hope for these committees to have an international composition, to have, as their members, educators/lawyers who are asked to reflect seriously on quality and international competitive standards.

Universities and law schools themselves can also do a lot to create incentives to innovate and improve. Obviously this could be done by making it an important subject as such and part of faculty discussions, HRM policies and similar activities, but also one could initiate a budget for innovative educational policies, or for new programs and curriculum changes. Doing this at the university level has as a great advantage that schools and departments can and will learn from each other and that multidisciplinary initiatives will be a likely outcome as well (business and law; forensic sciences; law and economics; and health law). The university's mission and strategy, and a law school's position in that respect, certainly help in giving a direction and ensuring that research and teaching and the school's policies and scarce resources all work in the same way and strengthen each other. Budgets for these purposes do not need to be large smaller sums for seed money or for rewarding creative initiatives and prizes can also do the trick.

These comments take two major issues and preconditions for granted. The first is the presence of a law school's mission and generally-shared strategy and an overall willingness that this is a (the) way forward. Secondly, staff and faculty must have the skills, the attitudes and abilities and willingness to innovate and reflect on education and law school strategies in that respect. This implies that the recruitment of staff and the regular evaluation of faculty must take account of these aspects. Quality of teaching and research are obvious items on the evaluation agenda of faculty and serve as criteria for recruitment. However, the capability and willingness to reflect on teaching and on strategy and programs and pedagogy might be worth being added. For these reasons the next paragraph will be devoted to HRM policies and academic staff expertise and qualifications.

3. Faculty: Academic Staff, Expertise and Qualifications

Faculty must reflect the curriculum and the curriculum must be ready for the future generation of lawyers. It must match the profile of the law school and the demands of academic education and the labour market (which sometimes means a reconciliation of contradictory demands). Whatever it is one wishes to strive for in the curriculum must be present among the teaching staff. Focusing upon academic values in education means that staff in their research and teaching must possess these values and practice them in teaching and research. Focusing on comparative law cannot do without comparative legal expertise in and research by the academic staff; the incorporation of skills in courses must necessarily mean that faculty are able to incorporate those skills, can teach them, can assess them and give proper feedback.

Also, for a law school, which has set out to employ a coherent teaching philosophy, a didactical concept according to which the curriculum is organized, it is important that this pedagogy is visible in the curriculum and is followed by all faculty. It is important in that respect that not only faculty is trained in teaching but also that faculty is properly trained in teaching according to the specific pedagogy of the law school.

In this respect it is also of importance that faculty is competent in integrating e-teaching and learning; is capable of ICT developments such as blackboard, power point and other software; and also can relate to legal practice in the sense of being aware what employment is taken up by the students after graduation and which developments take place there in order to be able to include future-oriented aspects in the teaching of skills and substantive law.

Many of my proposals in this book are not cost neutral: they will ask for investments in time and budget. Training faculty and organizing faculty awareness is important but time consuming. Spending time and energy on teaching and reflecting on teaching and on grading papers and giving feedback to students also take time and are therefore budgetary investments. There are two comments I like to make in this respect. First of all, for law schools there is an on-going tension between research and teaching. Cutbacks on budget strain the relation between teaching and research and requiring more energy for teaching only adds to that strain. There are no miracles here, but there is an underestimated corollary of teaching for research, and that is to make teaching advanced courses benefit research. Designing new courses on challenging subjects and contextual issues, and teaching them to and with eager students, will advance research output. Utilize teaching for work in research areas and do so with the students. That will stimulate the students; educate them in discovering new areas and in doing research. For instance, arrange that the students write papers on different subjects and make presentations in a student conference. This will create enthusiasm among the students who feel that they are serious partners in research and really participate in a research adventure. Faculty will also find inspiration and assistance in their research projects. This is another reason that I promote junctions in research priorities and projects and teaching programs, and even more so in the advanced courses.

In McGill, to which I have referred before, the design of the transsystemic law program also explicitly led to the need to have new educational books and materials for the students. Working on the curriculum, and developing and offering the courses, publications were scheduled as well as scholarly work about their teaching project.[4] Also in my home law school in Maastricht, research projects and teaching influence each other. When new courses are designed and new approaches in integrating comparative law are developed, this also leads to the development of scholarly work.[5]

A second comment to make here is that graduate/advanced/PhD students could be involved in teaching, as well as regular students. The first categories of students could be involved in teaching classes and organizing feedback for students as part of a training program for them to receive training for teaching purposes.[6] Participation in teaching, and being trained for that goal, will enhance the qualities of these students and add substantially to their knowledge, skills and capabilities.

Regular students can also be involved in teaching and in feedback and discussion exercises and other skills aspects. This is in line with what the authors of Educating Lawyers[7] call the experience of a case conference: imagine the setting of a problem or of a client (in a medical setting a patient with symptoms) and students have to analyze and come up with a diagnosis, tests to be performed, treatments and procedures. This is similar to law firms in which new cases which have come in might be discussed among a group of lawyers. The other students in the same conference comment on the method of action, make additional suggestions, ask for clarification, and finally the meeting agrees upon strategy, questions and problems, research and what to do next. This might be a setting in which students give feedback to each other; in a similar way, in moot court settings, instead of inviting faculty to be the judges, invite students to rotate and be active as moot judges as well. Invite them to comment/give feedback on the achievements of the two parties. Another option is to split large groups of students into smaller sections (possibly to be supervised by an assistant) and have them work collaboratively on a joint project. That will also train them, not only in collaboration, but also in feedback about each other's efforts and input.

4 For instance, Glenn 2010.

5 For instance, Ius Commune Case Book project; Klip 2012; Kiiver & Kornet 2010; Heringa & Kiiver 2012.

6 See also Nussbaum 2010, p. 125: she discusses the need for small classes, or at least sections of classes 'where students discuss ideas with one another, get copious feedback ....and have lots of time to discuss their work with instructors'. In that respect she advances that 'graduate students are teaching assistants, (who) frequently teach their own tutorials or small classes, and are supervised by faculty, since one all-important part of a job file is a "teaching portfolio", including professorial recommendations and student course evaluations'.

7 Sullivan *et al.* 2007.

These comments do not detract from possible major budgetary issues or severe teaching/research conflicts. I hope to have made clear that creative solutions do exist, which come down to strategic thinking about education and research and about strengthening the links between them instead of focusing on the conflicts.

To come back to the issue of quality of faculty and teaching on the law school level, it is relevant for law schools to be in discussion and develop benchmarks with other schools, globally, regionally and domestically. Within a law school it is important to have continuous discussions and exchanges of good or best practices and also within a university, among law schools in a country,[8] continent/international organization (such as the European Union),[9] and even globally.[10] Forming networks, which also centre around or focus upon teaching and education practices, is relevant for the improvement of teaching and also for a more intensive attention for teaching: what do we teach, how do we teach it, exchange of practices, learning from (practices in) other disciplines, learning about innovations. Also, exchange of practices, research and findings about and of relevance to legal education, in legal journals can all be organized.[11]

Let me give some examples of how to do what I have referred to above and how to make teaching an integral part of HRM-policies.[12]

1. A coherent basic training program for all academic staff about didactics, teaching, learning by students, exams and assessment and feedback, related to the law school specific didactic philosophy. For such a program, specifically concerning basic elements of teaching and learning, a national coordination and mutual recognition system might be advisable, allowing faculty to have their program acknowledged by other schools.
2. Participation by faculty in specific workshops about relevant issues such as more in-depth knowledge and exchange of views on examinations, lectures, e-learning etcetera.
3. Ensuring faculty-wide discussions about the curricula and their coherence and the experiences of staff and students and student evaluations and the skills obtained. This would also enable professors who teach in one specific program to evaluate and discuss the program as such regularly: to what extent do the courses relate to each other and is the program still up to date, and meeting the goals and requirements.

8 For example in the context of the American Association of Law Schools (AALS).

9 European Law Faculties Association (ELFA).

10 International Association of Law Schools (IALS).

11 In that respect the AALS publishes quarterly the Journal of Legal Education; the Association of Law Teachers (an English Association) publishes three times a year The Law Teacher, The International Journal of Legal Education. Under the responsibility and on the website of ELFA (<http://elfa-afde.eu/EJLEISSUES.aspx>) is also the *European Journal of Legal Education* (EJLE) which had its latest issue in 2009.

12 In the following I also relied upon Schreurs & De Grave 2010.

4. Involving senior faculty with a lot of experience in teaching in the guidance of junior staff and in becoming teachers in faculty teacher-training programs.
5. Participate in national, regional, global networks and associations about legal education, by attending, presenting papers and learning from others.
6. Cooperate with domestic and/or like-minded schools (for instance in the context of Socrates networks or networks in which international partners collaborate with joint or dual programs) for the exchange of views about education and teaching and for joint courses and/or visiting teaching jobs.
7. Experiment with common or joint examination exercises, making exams and answers available to external colleagues to discuss examination techniques and create awareness of standards of courses and examination.
8. Publish teaching materials/make them available on the web or by reworking them into textbooks; this is also a tool to be transparent on teaching content and modes of delivery and it contributes to improving the teaching of law and related skills.

Teaching in short must be on a law schools' agenda and in the mind of all faculty.

This is more so the case since more and more ICT developments will be incorporated in curricula, such as virtual learning environments and e-learning tools, as I have discussed earlier. It means that staff will have to invest in expertise in these tools and their implementation in the curriculum.[13]

This is the 'soft' side of the issue; the 'hard' side is that teaching quality and performance, as well as research performance, must be part of HRM-policies. For research performance law schools can set and have set criteria, such as having a PhD, or publishing x-number of scholarly articles in peer reviewed journals, and/or speaking at renowned conferences. For teaching, also in order to secure a balance between teaching and research, it is definitely necessary to make the quality of teaching part of HRM-policies and individual career tracks and to set parameters to assess performance and teaching quality. In that respect HRM-policies pertinent to the quality of teaching must ultimately be part of quality assurance. Teaching performance (related to the gathering of data and the evaluations) ought to be part of annual evaluations between deans (or heads of department) and faculty. Policies must be set about career paths and their links to performance in domains such as research, funding, management and also teaching. To make tools for individual assessment, teaching performance criteria have to be formulated. Which criteria will these be partially depends on the profile and mission of a law school, but the following criteria I suggest could be useful and could be adapted:

1. an average minimum score on the course evaluations;
2. exam results;
3. effective use of the didactical teaching methods;
4. inclusion and implementation of the relevant skills;

[13] See also: Schreurs & de Grave 2010.

5. effective use of the electronic learning environment and the use of ICT tools;
6. implementation of the evaluations' recommendations;
7. participation in law school evaluations and discussions about teaching and the overall curriculum;
8. life-long learning of teaching skills and competences;
9. textbooks and other teaching materials.

Some of these can be very well quantified in objective data (1, 2); 3, 4 and 5 can also be deduced from the collection of data and evaluations; 6 ought to be visible in the course book and follow from earlier course evaluations and conclusions drawn from them. Number 8 will follow from a law school's policy on educational training of its staff and of its continued participation in updating educational expertise and knowledge; 7 seems to be the most subjective, measuring a staff member's input in a law school's reflection on its didactical and curriculum courses of action. However, this criterion might be blunter than the others; putting this item on an evaluation list opens up the floor for a discussion about this staff member's input.

I have hesitated whether to add as a 9th criterion that faculty publish on education and/or do write educational textbooks. I am inclined to believe that faculty members do have an educational obligation to write and author educational materials such as textbooks, casebooks, education/course formats, skills trainings and the like. In many schools these activities would count as part of research and research output. However to qualify this output, I count these activities certainly as relevant and part of the duty of faculty, also in terms of education and teaching.

In Chapter 13 I discussed international rankings and concluded that law schools might want to pursue an active policy in some domains if they choose to climb in the rankings. I mentioned a couple of methods to implement this in a strategy and pointed to tools of Human Resources, and making it a part of day-to-day HRM-policies to engage the school with the labour market, to score better in citation indexes, and to be visible (in teaching and research) in the English-speaking world. The five aspects I mentioned in that chapter should be made to play a role in recruitment policies, in the promotion or termination of faculty and in the targets set for individual professors, legal institutes and departments. If and when we consider rankings and/or benchmarks to co-determine our strategic ambitions, we will have to integrate what they measure into our policies, missions, strategies and HRM-policies and tools.

In an earlier chapter in this book I referred to the McGill experience of setting up a new transsystemic legal curriculum. In that respect reference is made to the need to have a school with faculty expertise in the newly devised curriculum and way of teaching; this expertise must be built by linking research to what is taught, by setting up training programs, by promoting co-teaching, and by hiring new faculty who fit the law school's profile and mission. Also it seems imperative to organize the curriculum in such a manner that the 'what and the how' fit together. And finally, teaching materials have to be designed, (re)written and tested, and student evaluation and assessment must be an issue to be addressed. These issues[14] can be addressed and overcome; not only is the atmosphere of collegiality and collaboration amongst the professors important, and the availability of resources and funds, but also the link between teaching and research.[15] This link has been underlined also in other places in this book, and is indeed an indispensable feature of successful and high quality teaching.

An important focus of the quality of teaching, of education and therefore also of legal education, is the quality of the teachers. For secondary education the OECD PISA Index supports this reasoning. This ranking shows that countries can manage to get excellent results without spending too much money, and, vice versa, that spending money as such is no guarantee for better results. In The Economist Andreas Schleicher of the OECD is quoted saying

> 'that only 9% of the variations in achievement can be explained by how much is spent; the rest is down to how it is spent. High achieving countries have large classes taught by great teachers. Poor performers employ less effective teachers for smaller classes, recruiting extra staff from further down the ability range'.[16]

In universities this, because of the (international) competition between schools and programs, does relate to money! More money can buy better professors and thereby guarantee better standing in (research and) teaching!

However, the lesson to be learned is that the quality of teaching staff does much to deliver a good program and improve on learning outcomes and the quality of the graduates. Therefore, the focus on teaching skills in hiring policies is relevant. Also the training of faculty to become better teachers becomes essential, and so is a faculty policy to stimulate teaching and the making of study materials and to focus on improving teaching qualities and methods of delivery and innovation in teaching. Coherent efforts in this domain do pay off and can make a difference. Not all of our professors and teachers have the natural talent and gift to be a brilliant lecturer, who lectures while the students sit in awe and admiration. Not all of our professors and teachers are world-renowned scholars, who maybe are not the most brilliant speakers, but do get the message across of their great knowledge and inspiration comes from that.

Training faculty in teaching and teaching techniques, as well as in skills training and examination, will assist us in improving the general level. A well-structured and well-taught curriculum, does credit to the law school.

14 As described by Jukier 2006.

15 Jukier 2006, p. 185-186.

16 The Economist, 'The best of the rest, Academic Excellence: British schoolchildren are falling behind those elsewhere', 11 December 2010, p. 40.

4. Miscellaneous and Conclusions

In one of the previous chapters we discussed the academic fit, and the desirability to have counsellors and mentors to guide the students, not only in the (beginning of the) first year, helping the students to overcome the transition from secondary school/college to law school but guidance is also needed for assistance to students in choosing career paths, electives, internships, clerking and international exchanges. I believe we all accept that study results are better when students feel at ease in a program and in a law school and that it is more effective to solve problems students are confronted with in an early stage than later (or too late). Guidance is needed for different purposes and at different stages. In the beginning of law school it is the transition from secondary school to university which necessitates guidance for quite a few. Later the focus will shift to making choices in courses and specializations and (master) programs with already a perspective on the labour market and the options available there. In many schools a variety of options are on offer, creating for students an abundance of choices in which they might easily get lost. Then at the end of the study the focus is on the labour market and on a further specialized master poses itself: seeking internships; writing application letters; having job interviews; getting access to the diverse labour market.

In the meantime there may be financial issues, sickness, family problems troubling a student; all causing a student to find it difficult to concentrate on the study and focus on exams. What should be done when, due to sickness, for example, a student has built up a backlog of work and exams? What is the best way to deal with this and what is the best way to ensure progress, without overburdening the student?

For all the above reasons universities and law schools employ study counsellors or mentors or academic advisors and provide guidance to students with information meetings about study abroad programs, exchange, job fairs, career services training, electives and master programs, internships and other relevant issues.

PART E

CONCLUSIONS AND EUROPEAN PROSPECTS

Chapter 16

CONCLUSION

Diversity, future orientated, internationalization, skills, multidisciplinary and quality are key words for legal education. I certainly do not intend to argue that all law schools and all lawyers must be identical. Not all law firms and not all lawyers will operate on a European or global scale. Not all students or law graduates are or will be lawyer statesmen or top lawyers or lawyer-diplomats. I have tried to argue consistently that diversity is a better perspective for law schools and suits the need of students, societies and the labour markets better. However, the feature of comparative law to enhance the quality of legal education is, in my opinion, undisputed, as is the necessity to infuse the curriculum with academic skills and more than legal (black letter law) knowledge. However, the intensity or the scale and level might certainly differ. I do see the need for a diversified legal education, even within specific countries. Some schools aim for the very best and offer top level education for global lawyers who will indeed operate on a global scale. Others educate lawyers to become public defenders or work in local legal aid clinics. Those jobs require different skills and different capabilities and competences. The labour market will certainly require extreme diversity and students will follow a variety of paths to end up becoming lawyers.

Education will also diversify under the influence, not only of the labour market (or labour markets) but also because of the international exchanges and international competition, and the international influences or inspiration. Parts of legal education will be transferred to or taken over by the professions (apprenticeships, traineeships, professional training) for one because of the tendency of many governments to make ends meet and therefore to cut expenses for education. The US and the UK have taken the lead, but the privatization of parts of (legal) education (for instance of the second cycle, the master phase) is not inconceivable in Europe.

The extent of the need for advanced legal training, or the extent of the need for training grass roots basic lawyers, will also differ from country to country and will vary with respect to economic development. We certainly need different kinds of lawyers.

It is inevitable that we are in a process moving towards the establishment of very different kinds of law programs and of law schools. From the previous chapters I deduce the following characteristics of future law schools:

- Top transnational/international law schools that educate lawyers who will be sought after globally and across borders; these schools will compete globally, will (have to) be selective in intake, and will teach international/regional programs on a high academic level.[1]
- Regional/domestic schools: they will cater for the top domestic/regionally-oriented law markets; they will also (have to) compete with other schools from other countries and they will train lawyers in, for example, European expertise. These schools, in order to maintain quality and meet the high requirements of the curriculum, will also be selective in the intake.
- It might well be that these first two categories of law schools will be difficult to distinguish since they have in common a trans-boundary international outlook, and therefore intake of students. How it will work out will to a large extent depend on the development of international legal rules and legal systems and on the demands of the labour markets.
- The third category will consist of the schools that aim at a predominantly local audience and also cater for the domestic/local legal labour market. Their mission will be (although not un-academic) more professional and aimed at lawyering skills for more routine cases and specific domains of the law (welfare law, housing law, criminal law, consumer law, and family law).
- I can certainly also see the emergence of highly specialized/focused/selective small-scale law schools/programs, with a very specific profile and mission, for instance for legal aid work or focused on government lawyers (public service), or on European law or on international law. Schools will specialize maybe not so much in the undergraduate phase but in the masters they offer (with a link to specialized research).
- Another focus might also be in general whether or not there is a strong link with research:[2] research oriented law schools versus schools whose primary aim is to train adequate lawyers.
- In many countries we will also have the very large and broad law schools with a wide (and maybe even unselective) intake. These schools could offer selective tracks or specializations, even trying to build double profiles: an international program for a specific group of students and a domestic program.

I am not sure how the variations will play out precisely, but I am certain that the landscape of law schools will be reshuffled, since international competition has made its debut known. We can already see that some schools do better in the

1 Van Zandt 2004 also envisages a similar diversity and the emergence of global law degrees offered by strong universities around the world. 'Students will choose law schools based on the quality of the degree and the education behind it [...]. There will be borderless competition among law schools. Likewise, employers will seek out the best graduates with these degrees. [...] Of course, demand for more local or national degrees also will continue in order to provide lawyers for local regulatory and litigation practice as well as to serve purely local clients.'

2 About Legal Research, and the legal researcher: Smits 2012.

rankings, in international research and funding and in international networks. Student streams and research money will influence the strategy and the profile of law schools and therefore the diversified landscape of legal education.

Abandoning the notion of uniformity of legal education is of the essence. This uniformity has not existed between countries or continents. It is certainly feasible that 'uniform' or similar law schools will develop all over the globe, which are eager to compete globally and will want to provide truly global legal education.

Domestically, the notion must be abandoned that all law schools are identical and uniform and that all law programs must be seen to cater for all law students, even without an intake selection. Such 'equality' will detrimentally affect the quality of programs and graduates. It is, in domestic, regional and global competition, inevitable that law schools diversify their programs, or that law schools diversify and offer programs for different students and different labour markets: top programs for top (innovative) lawyers and average programs for average students for legal jobs of a more repetitive nature. The availability of resources, from students' fees/government funding and from research money, will be different and will diversify law schools and legal education even further.

For law schools, whatever course they will want to take, it is of the utmost importance to reflect upon their mission and strategy and the execution thereof, as well as on their resources and place in the global and domestic markets, in terms of input (students) and output (graduates' positions on the labour markets and the needs of those labour markets and the role a school wants to play in society), but also taking into account the expertise of faculty. Having defined their strategy and mission, the first and foremost task is to adapt the curriculum to the intake, and the needs and the output and the future roles of the graduates on the labour market.

A connection has also to be made with the expertise and qualities of the faculty. Strengths and weaknesses have to be identified and the school has to strategize in that respect about hiring policies and staff qualifications. Going back to the analogy of a soccer club, which has set its goals to a specific achievement level, it defines the quality of the coaches and trainers, the players and the accommodation, and maps the goals of achievement and the road towards these goals and how to attract better players, for which positions, with which requirements, expertise and experiences. I have included accommodation here since that is relevant for soccer clubs to attract a larger audience and thereby generate more income but it is certainly also of interest and importance to law schools, with regard to their specific ambitions. For a moot court, adequate sized and equipped lecture halls, library, tutorial rooms, ICT facilities and work space for students and staff etcetera must meet the ambitions set in the strategy of the school. Also, as in the case with soccer clubs, an analysis has to be made with regard to the support staff - study advisers, career advisers, organization of teaching schedules and assistance with internships - these functions must also be ensured in order to be in line with the school's strategy, mission and goals.

With regard to the curriculum, I have proposed to build a curriculum (again within the parameters of possibilities and the law school's ambition) which is more than just (black letter) law but contains academic and multidisciplinary and real-life problem-solving skills. In that respect I have proposed projects summarized as 'Law in Context', in which, and there are certainly many variations, students deal with real-life issues and social problems. Students must analyze the issues, which are in many cases related to complex legal problems and tackle them with policy papers, or research, or a presentation. The perspective is to use their analytical and academic skills to work in as realistic as possible circumstances and possibly also enabling the students to work in collaborative groups.

A second feature which I have elaborated upon is the aspiration to include in the law curriculum and give attention to (a selection of) other disciplines. In order to make the students realize that the focus on other disciplines is an integrated necessity for lawyers, the curriculum as such must make clear that the non-law aspects are indeed essential and have a high added value. The knowledge of other disciplines and the teaching of economics, psychology, sociology, logic or political science, etcetera, could take place in separate modules, but they also need to be implemented in law courses by showing the students why and how this multidisciplinary knowledge reflects on the law and is relevant for dealing with disputes and conflicts. This means that in constitutional law, political science ought to be incorporated; in tort law, law and economics and psychology; in criminal law, criminology and psychology; in European law, macro-economics; in international law, international relations; and in legal writing and oral skills, reference to law and logic.

In this respect I also recommend integrating the application and exercise of skills (also) continuously in every course. This is not to say that all skills must be resorted to in each and every course, but that teachers also devote attention and give feedback to skills and do not simply refer them to skills classes; and that different skills may be allotted to different courses, allowing for an even distribution of skills and a balanced build up of the necessary skills.

These aspects require attention in the design of the curriculum and the courses, as well as requires the required expertise and the willingness to include (certain aspects of) skills and a multidisciplinary outlook among faculty in their courses and modules.

Finally I urge law schools to utilize comparative law in the curriculum and the courses taught. In the most advanced form this could lead to a truly international/transnational curriculum/law school, but in a more modest format it will help in expanding the students' horizons and in broadening their (research) skills and creative reflection about the (quality of the) law and the different ways and perspectives to make and assess laws, judgments and legal solutions to social problems and disputes.

We have to train our students in many more skills and disciplines than we used to do, in order to prepare them for the seven challenges I laid out in the Introduction;

and we have to do so in an academic manner as in university education, training students to be critical, imaginative, out-of-the-box and skilled to work the trade.

1. Globalization will help us to use the world and the countries in it as our many laboratories; international collaboration will sharpen the legal minds and assist in defining better legal solutions.
   Comparative law gives us access to these laboratories in the world and the 'legal experiments' which are being conducted everywhere and all the time; and comparative law helps us to reflect more and better about our own domestic legal system.
2. Establishing international classrooms[3] will improve the critical and reflective attitude of future lawyers; confronting (legal) cultures in a classroom will further and deepen discussion and understanding. Classes and teaching ought to be international and diverse as I have indicated, but it also needs to rely upon interactive technology, and the international classroom might be facilitated through video lecturing, connecting two or more continents and to allow for international co-teaching. Helpful in this respect to train students as global citizens and lawyers are features such as international student exchanges and exchanges of professors and courses, visiting professorships and co-development and co-teaching of courses.
3. Comparative law as an integral part of the curriculum improves the content of the curriculum, as well as allowing it to function as a didactical tool, instilling a critical, evaluative attitude among the students.
4. A multidisciplinary content of the curriculum is further needed: (social) sciences, statistics, forensics, business, and economics must find a way into the curriculum and must be a part of an academic legal training.
5. ICT skills will, as I have argued, be a minimum requirement for lawyers: being able to work with modern-day communication technology and Internet platforms, is essential based upon my assumption that legal work will partly shift to Internet applications and virtual offices.
6. Entrepreneurship will be an indispensable tool for future graduates: how to run a virtual or real office? How to be self-employed? How to connect to other lawyers in a network organization, or simply a network?
7. As the example in the Introduction shows (arguing that compliance will be one of the new domains for lawyers), lawyers must be pro-active and imaginative, relevant to the particular business or enterprise: which obstacles might be perceived and are related to the product, business, or service rendered?

[3] Van Zandt 2004 identifies five internationalization approaches: International Faculty, International Courses, Exchange opportunities, Summer Abroad Programs, and, relevant here: International Student Infusion, effective when the foreign students can be effectively integrated in the host law school's curriculum and culture.

8. Training students to work in Internet dispute resolution cases, as well as training them to be able to do mass routine work, as this will be the fate for many law graduates.
9. And, not to forget, the skills that come with it all and which I have described in this book: negotiation, communication, reading, writing, pleading, arguing, researching and problem solving and anticipating.

The aspects I have described need to make up part of law schools' curricula (or of the education setting in a country, for example in preparatory colleges or in further professional training if such exists), but there is more to desire. As I have argued in this book, law is not just about legal documents and statutes and court decisions, but also, and in my opinion increasingly so, law in context. That is, lawyers are part of teams who are called upon to work on complex issues, in which legal aspects play a part, but interact with other disciplines and other actors. To prepare students for this feature of future employment, they must be trained and be given the opportunity to prepare for such teamwork in identifying, discussing and contributing to the resolution of complex issues. As an example I have suggested to design as part of the curriculum a course in which this is being reflected.

Supra I have already mentioned comparative law, and also international law, as very relevant aspects in many, if not most or all, domains of the law, necessitating lawyers with cross-boundary skills and knowledge and expertise. But most definitely we need lawyers with many skills: skills to cope with the quick changes in the law and in society (and also life-long learning skills). They need to know about other sciences and need to have due regard for the functioning of the law and of legal systems, through empirical sciences or law and economics, or as criminal lawyers they need to understand forensic sciences, such as psychology, or they need to grasp game theory if one is working in the domain of setting up or participating in schemes of emission trading.

Curricula of law schools have intensified; schools in general and law schools have not escaped this trend and are asked to fulfil a variety of tasks when teaching the students (councillors, career officers, internship offices). This comes in addition to the fact that there is now more law than ever on the domestic level and more domains of the law which seek a place in a law school's curriculum (environmental law, financial law, consumer law, health law, etcetera). But there is also more multi-level interaction of legal systems. Law operates in a societal context, but law is also a multi-level context of international, regional (European) and domestic regulators. Law making is therefore more diverse, and so are the actors involved and the inspiration and input in the law-making process. The scope and impact of international rules are immensely expanding. We cannot make our students experts in everything, including the comparative legal perspective. We cannot expand the curriculum and make it even longer. But what we can do and must do is to teach the basics of a legal system, or of legal systems, and make them understand the multi-layered legal orders. We can ask from students to show that they know how to specialize in a specific area of the law and this is a greatly valued skill! We can instil an attitude of life-long learning in our students and a deep responsibility for their knowledge. We can train them in comparative and multi-(inter)disciplinary approaches and we can train them in acquiring all the lawyering skills.

At the end of the study of law we can rely upon them to be mature, critical, morally balanced, responsible lawyers and also lawyers who know after graduation what they do not know and are not capable of doing, and how they can cope with that with a great deal of life-long learning and study, with reflection and creativity, and with flexibility to be employed in changing settings and jobs, and in which they can tackle the new challenges in society for the next 40-50 years or so.

For law schools the message is to insert in the curriculum of their programs of study as many aspects as possible which build upon the changes and developments of the law and the projected demands of society, national, regional and global. In that respect I expect many changes. Considering that many schools have not yet fully integrated the intricacies of globalization, comparative law and skills aspects I have mentioned, there is still a lot of work ahead.

Are law schools evolving into schools geared towards business and transactions and increasingly law and economics approaches? On a regular basis the World Bank publishes 'Doing Business', a ranking on the ease of doing business. It assesses categories such as how long it takes to register a company; the costs involved; the complexity of registering property; obtaining a construction permit; enforcing a contract through the courts; tax issues; and winding up an insolvent firm. It is efficient and crucial to have these benchmarks and for governments to avoid unnecessary red tape, and also to show good practices for changes in the law and to learn from each other. However, these tables also carry an obvious risk, namely that we might tend to forget about other aspects: the World Bank table, for example, does not take into account Corporate Social Responsibility aspects, or environmental aspects.[4] According to The Economist cutting red tape makes countries richer. However, does it also make those countries fairer, cleaner, and with better labour conditions? Law and law reforms ought to be considered also from those perspectives and law schools have to be the ones to teach those intricate issues.

Singapore and Hong Kong lead the World Bank ranking; under the Freedom House scoring list they are the two countries which are considered to be partially free. Is there a link between their respective top positions and being less free under the Freedom House criteria?

Law is an instrument of fairness but also of achieving other goals: effectiveness, efficiency, prosperity. We want the law to be conducive to the rule of law and to economic growth and prosperity. Instrumentalist thinking made us believe for many years that the law was a powerful tool which ought to be able to achieve societal changes and eradicate all wrongs. Modesty has returned in that we have

4 See also The Economist, 'Pointless Regulations. It's a jungle out there', 22 October 2011, p. 73-74.

witnessed the shortcomings of full-scale government interference in society through law. The market economy has returned with the assumption that the law then only needs to prevent excesses and provide for basic arrangements and with it came the notion that the law must withstand cost-benefit analysis.

In recent years we witness a return to (another) trust in legal intervention and an intervention by independent authorities (be it not courts) to supervise and control that all private and public actors abide by the law. This is a movement away from politics and away from courts to another category of experts. Politics gives away part of its powers to those independent experts, which may become a variant of the third branch. We see this happen in agencies in the financial sector, in the banking sector, in competition agencies and agencies which supervise the telecom market or the energy market. We see it occur on the European level, with the call for a stronger control and supervision of national governments in their budgetary policies and whether they live up to the commitment of reducing national debts and budget deficits. Politics gives away their 'supremacy' in political decisions by asking others to control them. Is this the end of politics as we know it, towards a system of law in which we increasingly define issues in technical terms and then ask independent outsiders to supervise whether they are truly implemented?

These trends signify a simplification of decision making and of criteria: simplifying parameters and making decisions into issues for experts. Where does that leave democracy? The paradox is that, at the same time, we dislike politicians when they are being seen not to take into account significant expert consensus on issues.

In law schools, as academic institutions, it is the proper place to teach these and other developments in a coherent manner. That requires a lot of effort from faculty and students, since they will have to research trends and discuss connections between various domains of the law. However, I am convinced that this will make better and more learned lawyers.

In other domains of the law other issues present themselves for academic teaching: corporate governance and the role of share- and stakeholders; the definition of profit and growth and how to take into account environmental damage and other corporate social responsibility issues'; the system of Tort Law and its perspective on damages; for criminal law, psychology research of the brain and its impact on legal definitions of guilt and on relevant forensic disciplines; and the many issues that can only be resolved globally: financial markets, international trade, competition and transactions, international crime and environmental issues. Law schools must have a role to play here instead of solely training technicians who know how to technically do things with rules. Law schools must educate the students to reflect on the quality of law, the interaction of law with society and with other sciences, and on best solutions and ways forward. Naturally, that requires knowledge of legal issues and of the law; but it also requires a trained academic brain, which can detect the essence of problems, which can connect to other disciplines, which has access to comparative law to seek solutions, and which is trained to seek those solutions from different angles (costs, benefits, economic impact, social justice and fairness, stability and durability, comprehensibility, legitimacy, and the fit in the legal system).

What I notice in recent years is that in many countries many law schools have grown substantially. That might have been the consequence of legal rules (open intake), or of law school or university decisions (to become the biggest) or for financial reasons (more students means more money). However, I do not believe that law schools can fully offer a large-scale truly-academic education in law when intake is unlimited and without a selection, or when finances are weak and the situation is not such that a decent student-staff ratio can be offered. Apart from student-staff ratio, and interactive teaching, many of the aspects I have proposed are not basically very costly. A quality moot court can be done and set up without a specifically-designed moot court room. Counselling skills, academic skills, legal writing, legal clinics, do not have to be very costly in terms of facilities. In terms of student-staff ratio, I suggest that peer teaching, peer coaching and peer assessment could be introduced on a larger scale, involving students in solving problems, making presentations, and commenting on each other's performances are techniques which will make their educational process better.

A far bigger problem to cope with is the size of a law school. A small school might have (when funded on the basis of number of students) an issue in making enough money to have a substantial faculty with skills and competences in many domains. Large schools, schools with an intake of over 1,000 students a year, are confronted with another problem (other problems) - assuming that the finances grow with the number of students and are not used by the university for other purposes. Size and the absence of a qualitative intake selection make many of the issues I have raised in this book extremely complicated to realize for the full number of students. There is a question of full quality faculty being hired in large quantities; there is the issue of creating an academic community; there is the issue of differences within the student body.

We will try to solve this with special honours classes for the excellent students or special programs for a few, but it also means that standards will be adapted to the average student. I do believe on the contrary that legal education will benefit from (at least) a two-track system: a track offering top-notch academic legal training with a focus on intellectual legal skills and a second track with a focus on legal skills and knowledge. The former schools or tracks (because the two tracks might be offered in the same law school) will be selective and demanding and fully academic and it will educate for academic functions in law and in society. It will also be connected to research and require that faculty is fully immersed in research. The second track will train for hands-on jobs in law.

I do believe that we have to diversify our law schools to ensure that students have an opportunity for equal access, and then gradually diversify according to abilities, skills, effort and competences. The labour market is diverse, so why not the law curriculum?

In many liberal arts colleges and programs, students have an opportunity to select their tracks; this is not an unlimited freedom, but there is a scope to adapt the curriculum to one's needs, capabilities and interests, guaranteeing, however, the necessity of a broad academic education. I hope that law schools can learn from these experiences. I suggest also that law schools define different missions, pedagogy and teaching goals, because doing so will generate a discussion within schools, among faculty, about the mission, the curriculum and the pedagogy, with reference to the intake and the output.

Of crucial importance for law schools in many countries will be the issue of resources. In many European countries, in which legal education is funded by the state, student numbers have gone up and funding has not been raised to the same extent. Law schools have been hindered from raising their own revenues (fees!) because of state-set tuition and other impediments. Budgetary constraints, coupled with open access to law schools, will be important challenges for the future for many schools, combined with the complicated labour market situation for young graduates in quite a few countries. Add to that picture, national regulation which impedes leadership and effective strategic decision making in universities and law schools, and specifically law schools, in those countries where these factors do occur and coincide, will be in a difficult position. They will have problems in competing globally and regionally, and they will find it hard to educate the lawyers with all modern qualifications required by the labour markets.

This situation not only harms the quality of legal education, but it also harms the competitive state of affairs of the country concerned, in terms of legal services and the quality of the legal system, which subsequently leads to a decline of attractiveness for businesses.

This situation of law schools (and higher education in general) being affected by the declining state funding and ceilings on their fee structures is visible in Belgium, France, Germany, Greece, Italy and Spain for instance. In the UK block state funding has also been reduced, but higher education has been allowed to raise their fees up to 9,000 English pounds (for EU students) and market fees for non-EU ('overseas') students. In Sweden, as of 2011, the possibility was also created for law schools (and universities for that matter) to require substantial fees (up to 9,000 euro), with a corresponding decrease in government funding. The UK and Swedish approach will make their schools and programs competitive and allow the law schools to relate resources to output and the quality of the programs. It gives them an opportunity to invest and to seek income for legal education in order to keep up the quality and meet modern-day demands with increasing diversity and competition. That is certainly a better situation than for those law schools in countries where funding is government funding which is decreasing and where schools have no real discretion to compensate lower funding with higher fees and other income, which leaves those schools in a difficult position in having to compete with quality programs and programs which anticipate the changes and demands from the labour market(s).

In the Netherlands funding has also been decreased substantially but, at the same time, university boards and deans have been given many executive powers, and fees are, though relatively low, still above the European average (1,700 euro for

EU students) and market oriented for non EU students. Dutch universities have also been allowed to offer non-state funded programs with market based fees.

I do believe that a combination of factors is needed in these respects to ensure innovation, and quality and competiveness of education: resources, competitive fee structures, student selection, and leadership with the accompanying authority to set and implement strategies and move law schools forward. For many of these aspects in many countries law schools rely upon state authorities to set the right conditions for a flourishing and competitive legal education. However, it is certainly proper and useful for law schools to engage the discussion with the appropriate authorities and to do so collectively. In that respect, I also refer to Chapter 13 paragraph 4 where I have proposed that national and international associations of law schools and national and international associations or meetings of deans meet and establish benchmarks, standards and criteria for (good and competitive) legal education.

There is also another option related to diversification and increasing the quality of education and that is to have all law students follow an undergraduate (liberal arts) academic training before they enter law school. This (American and South Korean) option assumes that academic intellectual skills and connections to many sciences will be taught at that stage.[5] This might make it easier to teach law (and presuming academic skills and reflection) in a post-graduate setting.

However, here we have to be careful not to hand over the graduate legal training fully to practice (the bar in most cases), and also to allow for academic legal issues and interdisciplinarity and law in context to be taught here at this stage. A large part of the American discussion about the quality of legal education is concerned with the grip the bar has on law schools' curricula. There are many discussions about the proper balance between learning the law and being prepared for the bar exam and the other intellectual skills.

Discussions within law schools, in domestic settings and on regional and global scale, are relevant because they will impact what we do. How we teach, what we teach and what the level of our teaching has to be, and also how we compete for a place in the market are relevant issues. This discussion is extremely relevant related to innovation, improvement in legal education, and it will come about with faculty, schools and students, working on new courses, new modes of delivery and on the relevant structural aspects. In these changes we can and should benefit from each other and the changes can occur through exchanges of curricula, courses, innovations and ideas. Improvements can be made through collaboration and adaptation.

Legal education across the globe differs substantially, although (also in Europe when discussing the recognition of degrees) we tend to discuss legal education as

5 For many arguments in favour of a liberal arts education prior to professional schools: Nussbaum 2010. However, this is assuming that the college does not suffer from the defects described by Arum & Roksa 2011. Also critical, Hacker & Dreifus 2010.

an item with the same issues and discussions in all countries. This is certainly not the case. When we consider the perspective on legal education in the US and compare this with European (after Bologna) university legal education, the many differences are apparent. These differences explain why the US debate is so much focused on the argument that legal education moves away from legal practice and focuses too much on scholarship. Anthony Kronman argued in that respect that the value of practical wisdom was in danger.[6] This discussion can be understood from the idea that law schools predominantly train for the bar and for the bar exams. This background is much less (not?) prevalent in civil law Europe. Legal education has been part of university training for many centuries; lawyers have many types of jobs and certainly not only jobs as traditional legal professionals. In the US this professional focus is visible since law schools are positioned after college education, as a professional school (in the same vein as business and medical schools).

In Europe the academic flavour of legal education has been accepted fully and is part of the length of the curriculum and due to the absence of a preceding liberal arts training. The link with scholarly work has to a greater extent been accepted, making up for the need for universities to distinguish themselves from professional schools, as long as students have also received proper basic legal and skills training. The legal professions have accepted that they also have a role to play in that some skills and further training is offered to beginning young lawyers as part of their apprenticeship or entrance exams.

Under the Bologna process,[7] no exceptions were made for legal studies, they were considered to be full academic programs meriting the three cycles (bachelor, master and PhD), while leaving some room for the states to determine the length of studies in the master and PhD phase. This starting point allows the law schools to introduce academic aspects in the curriculum. In many European states the regular (ba+ma) phase, which generally leads to access to the legal professions, is five years.

I have focused in this book upon the need for law schools to charter their own courses as much as possible. For research, choices have to be made and for specializations in teaching, there is the same need for choices. This also is the case for the labour markets and the competition a law school will seek for its students and itself.

Strategies in this respect require leadership and a law school which operates as a unity. They also imply that resources, tools, collaborations, HRM-policies, links with alumni and the labour markets, pedagogy, all work in the same direction.

A law school strategy requires more to know the competition and the student and labour markets and to be aware of the benchmarks and rankings which co-determine success.

6 Kronman 1994, p. 168.

7 About legal education in Europe after the Bologna process: Baldus, Finkenauer & Rüfner 2007.

Strategy in the domain of teaching requires expertise with regard to the effectiveness of legal education and about the best modes of teaching. In that respect, as I have commented upon before, law schools do not have a great tradition in doing research or making research findings and good/best practices available to other schools. A suggestion in this regard might be that domestically, regionally and globally, law schools exchange information and make information and legal education-related research available. This could be done by setting up a website enabling schools and researchers to make available and consult research and practices that have been conducted and good practices that have been developed. This website could also facilitate mutual assistance in developing courses and trainings.

The preceding paragraphs and chapters basically mean to take legal education in our capacity as deans, professors and teachers very seriously indeed. It also definitely asks for collaboration, exchange of ideas, and reflection on the times that are changing and require new identities of law schools, new programs, new modes of delivery, adaptation to the new generations of students and to technology and global perspectives. In the US and the UK, legal education moved from legal practice to universities; in Europe legal education has undergone immense influences through exchanges, the development of European law and the emergence of more and more 'common' rules. Globally we witness the development of an English-speaking legal labour market and the emergence of many new law schools, specifically in China. These developments change the rules of the game and pose new challenges to societies, law students and law schools. Lawyers are known for sticking to the rules and for always being behind social developments, and some conservatism is indeed part of the breed; however, lawyer statesmen and lawyer diplomats have also contributed to the changes in the world. Legal education will take up the challenges and make sure that students will be well equipped to serve domestic and global societies.

Chapter 17

POSTSCRIPT: TOWARDS A EUROPEAN LEGAL EDUCATION?[1]

For my first year students, and for prospective students, I once set up a quiz: which areas are covered or regulated by law? Or maybe even better, which domains are NOT regulated by human made laws? The outcomes of this exercise were invariably that students started to discover very early on how much law there actually is. A variable of this quiz is: how much European law there actually is, or which legal domains have NOT been affected by European rules. And, to be precise, with European law I tend to refer to hardcore European law (regulations, directives, decisions, court cases) as well as to the domains of softer European impact: through comparative law and meetings of experts, civil servants and others. A prime example in that respect is the European contract law, Draft Code as published by the European Commission in May 2011, or the development or discovery of common (constitutional) principles, and the reliance by domestic courts, the Luxembourg Courts and the Strasbourg Court of Human Rights, upon common principles and common practices.

I am not (yet) implying that what we might call European law in this broad sense is similar to what in some domestic legal systems has developed over the past two centuries as major codifications of private law, administrative law, criminal law, labour law etcetera. However, ignoring the unmistakable trend of the expansion of European law, including the harmonization through comparative law and exchanges and consultations, would be an error. The question then arises how law schools in Europe deal with this trend and try to include it in their legal curricula and also what would be the best way forward for these schools? Furthermore, and related to this, ought there be a concerted European effort, in consultation between the European Commission with stakeholders such as the European Bar Association, to further or establish or promote a future-oriented truly European legal education?

1 This final chapter is the amended and updated version of my contribution in the volume Educating European Lawyers (2011) and of an editorial in the *Maastricht Journal of European and Comparative Law* (MJ 18-3 (2011)), p. 221-224, entitled 'European Legal Education or Legal Education in Europe'. With reviews of Androulla Vassilou, Stefan Grundmann, Niccolo Rinaldi, Marcel Brus, Jacqueline Kinghan, Krystyna Pawlowicz and Christine Godt in MJ 18-3 (2011), p. 421-430.

For many decades now, legal education is a purely domestic affair: students are trained in the laws and doctrines of their national legal system. What that entails is settled by the legislature and/or by the national bar associations. The language of instruction is the national language(s). The development of European law (and international law) has led to the insertion of courses on European law (institutional/ substantive) and international law. Erasmus/Socrates exchanges of students and staff and Erasmus Mundus programs have stimulated law schools to set up (more) courses that appeared to be attractive for those exchange students and collaborative networks. This led to an expansion of courses on (aspects of) European law and international law but also comparative law. And in those countries where the national language was not such that they could expect many exchange students who were fluent in that language, schools started to offer those courses in English.

For many jobs, employers started to appreciate an international exchange experience, and the accompanying knowledge of a foreign country/other legal system, as well as the expertise in another (legal) language. Journals in English about European law, comparative law (such as this one) sprang to life. In many domains of legal practice (the bar, in government offices, in corporate and banking law) the playing field and the expertise needed has become increasingly international. Government officials regularly travel to Brussels for meetings and discussions; corporate mergers need a competition law check; and the financial and commercial world are increasingly European and global. This trend is particularly noticeable in smaller jurisdictions, such as the Netherlands, but the trend is also affecting other countries and jurisdictions.

It is my conviction that this will have to lead to another legal education, maybe not to a fully-fledged reform of all European law schools but at least to the establishment of Law Schools that cater specifically for the needs for European and transnational and international lawyers.

A major stumbling block here is the national jurisdiction for law schools, in some instances shared with (or delegated to) domestic bar associations. The EU has no competence for legal education as such. The present state of affairs and the ensuing de facto limited freedom of movement and establishment of lawyers are true barriers to a development of a European legal education. In the day-to-day practice of lawyers in law firms and corporations, as well as for government officials, Commission officials and also for academia, the present situation is not well suited as the best way forward.

What should be done and what should not be done?

My proposals are based upon a couple of presumptions. The first is that the European trend towards an increasingly larger impact for European law and European harmonized output will continue and that cooperation will increase formally and informally.

The second is that we note a tendency that legal harmonization also implies that those who participate in the growth of European law have set up their discourse in English. Maybe not the 'English English', and possibly Euro English, but a common legal language which is also well suited or made to suit the EU terminology and concepts (comitology, transparency etcetera).[2]

Thirdly, the labour market will continue to seek law graduates with an extensive European, international and comparative law background and with an international/European outlook and training.

Fourthly, European law and (European) comparative law have expanded and developed to such an extent that they can support a Bologna-proof bachelor-master curriculum in law. This probably needs some explanation, specifically for those jurisdictions that are accustomed to training and submerging their students in the large codifications and the doctrinal intricacies of the various areas of law. However, without ignoring the merits of their and these legal trainings, I am very much convinced that European law, international law and comparative law have certainly grown to such an extent that they warrant a European legal training.

I am fully aware that this perspective is also very much related to my views as to legal education and skills and academic legal training. My perspective is that studying law in a university, as an academic study, ought to be precisely that: an academic study, as well as a preparation for the professional training for the bar or the judiciary, which has to follow (and in many instances does follow). What does that mean? It implies that law students must undergo a vigorous training in critical and analytical training and that they must learn how to evaluate legal rules and court judgments and to assess the quality of legal rules. One of the tools in that respect is that students are being taught comparative law – comparing legal systems, rules and legal solutions. Comparative law assists us to establish our own laboratory and utilize it, and the various countries that we then have at our disposal. It enhances our creativity and can help us to reflect on the quality of legal systems and legislative and court solutions to similar problems. In order to help us and the students to order the abundance of legislative options we also need to train students in acquiring the tools to assess the quality and (dis)advantages of legal rules and solutions. Which one is cost-effective; which one is fair and why; which one does meet our objectives quickly and smoothly; which one does best fit in a given legal culture and why, etcetera? I favour therefore very much the existence of courses on (law and) economics; sociology (of law), (law and) psychology. Knowledge of disciplines other than law will also help lawyers during their professional life as judges, lawyers or government officials.

Naturally we also have to teach law to students. We must certainly not forget to give in-depth training in a variety of legal fields (private law, public law, criminal law etcetera) and to teach them how legal minds work, how to solve complicated legal puzzles, and how to cope with complicated legal concepts and doctrines. But this ought not to mean that we necessarily must train them and must teach them in all there is to know of law in a given legal context. Laws tend to change and laws tend to change quicker and quicker, and what we above all must train and teach is

2 Van Zandt 2004.

how to cope with changing circumstances and rules and how to learn life-long and how to be able to immerse oneself in new fields and legal issues.

On top of that, and as part of the skilful lawyer, we have to train students the skills of the trade: listen, analyze, dissect, argue and respond, present a paper, write a paper, plead, chair a meeting, linguistic skills, negotiate, interview a client or a witness.

When we set up the first years of law school in this manner, by resorting to comparative law, European and international law, we can subsequently allow students to do a specialization and to find out in which country do they want to practice and study the 'black letter' law. My plea is therefore for a LLB program of three years in legal studies/law, with the possibility to switch to a specific legal system subsequently for one or two years.

Where would the above lead us? I propose a pluriform European model.

1. Some law schools continue to train and teach domestic law and do so for the domestic legal market.
2. Other schools transform into European Law Schools: they teach law in a LLB program as I have summarily described.
3. In order to facilitate this transformation, European and government support, as well as recognitions from the stakeholders, such as bar associations, are necessary. I submit that a selected group of interested quality schools convenes and works towards the European Law School model. However, for it to be viable, it is absolutely necessary that graduates can continue their studies, when and if they so wish, with a domestic law master entitling them to practice law locally.
4. However, it would also be a great asset to find ways to accommodate those students who do a European/international/comparative law bachelor and want to become European law specialists by continuing with a European/international/comparative law master. For those students we will need a European recognition, which will also fall under the headings of free movement and establishment of lawyers, with recognition to practice law (albeit if so desired after having taking a domestic bar exam, the equivalent of bar exams such as the New York bar exam, which is feasible after a couple of months of hard and intensive study).

Many of the assets of this model I have already tried to indicate. It might be added that the group of schools joining this initiative would attract an international diverse student body, which will add to the features and attractiveness. It would also prepare the students for their international professional work and it goes without saying that student and teaching staff mobility has to be among the leading features.

Undeniably my proposals stem from a long experience in teaching, with comparative law and in the Maastricht University based European Law School program. Mid-2011 a book was published by Intersentia publishers entitled *Educating European Lawyers* (edited by Bram Akkermans and myself). It purports to discuss this program and options of training truly European lawyers. We have presented our perspectives and visions to the world and hope to generate a discussion. There is one thing I am very sure of, reforming European legal training is absolutely necessary to ensure a body of European lawyers to keep up with the intricacies and complexities of European and international law. Academia has to respond to that need, specifically when doing so promotes and ensures a top quality academic and intellectually stimulating education. Instead of legal education in Europe we can work towards European legal education.

Presently there is no such thing as a uniform European Legal Education, not within the context of the European Union (27 (soon 28) Member States), let alone in the context of the Council of Europe (47 Member States). Between the 27 (in 2013: 28) EU Member States great disparities exist in the length of the curriculum, the intake of students, the labour market for the students (access to the bar, for example), who sets the curricula and whether there are any bar (or state exams) after graduation, the access to professional legal training afterwards, the content of the curricula and the courses, the languages of instruction, the requirements for teachers and professors, the teacher-staff ratios, the qualities of the buildings and facilities, etcetera. Also, there is, apart from the European University Institute in Florence (only offering PhD training) and the European Colleges in Belgium (Bruges) and Poland (Natalin), only offering LLM programs, no European legal education or no general discussion,[3] let alone a common understanding of a European Law Curriculum, as there is no common European labour market for lawyers.

I submit here that legal education through this lack of a common training is lagging behind the legal and political developments of the EU and of EU Law.

A major problem is that the EU has no competence over (legal) education and there is no joint understanding of a European labour market. Also European law and domestic law are interrelated. However, the issue I raise here, is whether it is not time to seek such a common European legal education in parallel to the many developments in European law that have taken place. I suggest to work towards a number of schools in Europe providing European legal training which will train the students for European-wide careers and which will be recognized by the different competent bodies in the Member States as lawyers in their own right. Possibly such recognition could be awarded after having done a very basic bar exam similar to domestic law, or, going even further, by setting up a European Bar Exam or mutual recognition of national bar exams. This could be very straight-forward indeed since they are already lawyers, a basic exam (comparable to the bar exams in the US) might suffice.

3 Also in the same vein Maduro 2010.

Before I develop this argument further, let me first briefly do some stock taking and describe in a basic manner the main developments upon which my proposals rest.

Recent developments in legal education in Europe

The idea that the Bologna Declaration and the ensuing process of harmonizing of higher legal education have led to a uniform model of higher education is a myth. One of the reasons for this is that the Bologna document is based upon a voluntary approach and another is that the several participating states have seen fit to implement Bologna according to their own higher education history and finances. Famously, Bologna introduced the three-tier system: bachelor, master, Ph.D. That concept sounded simple enough, however, some states started with a four-year bachelor's degree;[4] most with a three–year model;[5] many set up a two-year master,[6] others only a one-year master,[7] or a mixed model: both two-year and one-year masters.[8] Some states were quick in reforming higher legal education in the Bologna format,[9] others (most notably, for example, Germany) have been very slow so that only incidentally German universities (or law schools) have set up a Bologna model of bachelors and masters.[10]

The fact that this is so, and that even within the European Union no uniformity or complete equivalence has been created, is caused, or explained, by the fact that the EU has not been given the rule-making power in this domain. There is simply no authority (competence) for the EU to regulate education. The best way to have a European impact upon higher legal education is by making funds available for desirable projects, such as research, student and staff mobility, and student exchanges (Erasmus/Socrates,[11] Marie Curie, Erasmus Mundus,[12] Jean Monnet).[13] But since the Member States carefully guard and protect their sovereignty in the domain of education, the Bologna process, while a joint endeavour, is still a voluntary process.

In law, the situation is even further complicated by the fact that the domestic regulation of the legal profession is very much a domestic issue, partially regulated by the domestic bars and, at least, very much linked to national aspects, traditions,

4 E.g. France and Austria.
5 E.g. Belgium.
6 E.g. Belgium.
7 E.g. the Netherlands.
8 E.g. France/the Netherlands.
9 E.g. The Netherlands and Belgium.
10 E.g. Bucerius Law School in Hamburg.
11 See generally European Commission, Education and Training, <http://ec.europa.eu/education/lifelong-learning-programme/doc80_en.htm>.
12 See generally Erasmus Mundus - Scholarships and Academic Cooperation, <http://ec.europa.eu/education/external-relation-programmes/doc72_en.htm>.
13 See generally The Jean Monnet Program: understanding European Integration, <http://ec.europa.eu/education/lifelong-learning-programme/doc88_en.htm> [hereinafter *Jean Monnet Program*].

and (legal) culture. The process to become a practicing lawyer, or judge, or prosecutor, is very much in the hands and at the discretion of legislatures and/or the legal profession. The role of legal education varies and so does the labour market, the intake of students, the length of studies, the content of the studies, the accreditation processes, etcetera.

Without doubt these developments, setting up a coherent model, facilitating exchanges of staff and students, developing a common credit system known as ECTS, all helped in preparing the scene for more changes and common developments. In transnational sciences such as engineering, medicine or chemistry it is a lot easier to develop joint curricula and allow for the simple recognition of degrees, but law has for the last centuries been linked with national sovereignty and domestic legal systems. In the 19th century codes were adopted and the development of the law in many European countries was nationalized and became an increasingly domestic matter. Domestic legal culture mattered; the domestic bars and judiciaries developed their own admission criteria; lawmakers created their own educational systems and models and the study of law had to fit in the requirements of the bars and the legislatures. Therefore, what we have witnessed in the 19th and the most part of the 20th century was an increasing nationalization of the study of law. It has been a recent development, under the influence of the EU, that European law has increasingly impacted upon national sovereignty and (therefore) also on the domestic law. Increasingly law is becoming European and also global. Parts of the sovereign law-making powers became European; not only in the domains of the internal market in Europe and all its related aspects, but also in areas such as torts, contracts, property, administrative law, criminal law: areas of the law long considered to be purely and exclusively national!

What also happened was that scholars (and I will come back to that in more detail later) started to work on the Europeanization of the law, and they needed a common language, since law and language are inherently interrelated, and gradually it seems to me that the English language has occupied this role. This trend was unmistakably furthered by the growth of the EU and the increasing trend there towards English as a most prominent language: English as the lingua franca.

Related to this, larger law firms opened shop in Brussels, seeking international alliances, and increasingly operated in English and also wanted to hire new lawyers with international (European) backgrounds: students who had studied abroad, were fluent in English (next to their native language) and had knowledge of European law but also of more than one (their own) legal system, students who could work in a European setting and could work in European law *strictu sensu* but also within and between different legal systems and with lawyers from different legal backgrounds.

This was not only the case in commercial legal practice but also within governments: the increase in EU policies and law making made it necessary to have civil servants who spoke their languages, had foreign experiences and could work with different legal cultures and legal systems.

But whatever these trends were and have been taking place, I am under the impression that legal education as a whole did not catch up quickly and, when it did, domestic bar associations were and are very reluctant in adapting and making the necessary changes. The feeling is that what has been the proper way for raising lawyers, in a one-size-fits-all model, must still be good in these times of Europeanization.

Luckily the situation that the study of law is predominantly a domestic issue and is therefore governed by domestic rules and traditions only is very much in flux. Although the above appears to indicate a deadlock in the sense that legal education seems to be fixed and domestically oriented, there is still a lot of movement below the surface. Bologna and Socrates have triggered a lot of gradual changes and all kinds of reforms, having an impact upon both European legal education and European law faculties.[14] Also, other EU rules and principles have been leading toward progress in this area.[15]

In the first place, the EU has set certain rules regarding the freedom of services and free movement of workers within the EU relating to qualifications and recognition of diplomas that also affect the profession of lawyers ('attorneys-at-law').[16] Basically, the EU rules allow a person who is qualified to practice as a lawyer in one state to also practice in another state.[17] Lawyers can also acquire the lawyer title of their host Member State, either after practicing the law of that state for three years or by passing an aptitude test.[18] Much still needs to become clearer in this respect, through decisions by the European Court of Justice and possibly through new EU directives, but the trend is clearly towards an increasing movement of lawyers and their services.

Secondly, many areas and domains of domestic law are increasingly influenced or determined by EU regulations or directives.[19] This means, for example,

14 Developments such as student and staff exchanges have led to the development of joint programs; courses that could be followed by exchange students and collaboration between law faculties. Courses for exchange students often related to courses in the domain of European, international and comparative law, thereby adding new courses to existing curricula.

15 An example is the increasing impact of EU rules and principles in areas like consumer law, social law, freedom of movement, migration, establishment, freedom of services, contract law, tort law, and proportionality, as it relates to institutional and constitutional law.

16 See generally European Commission - The Single EU Market: Professional qualifications, <http://ec.europa.eu/internal_market/qualifications/index_en.htm>. Judges' professional qualifications are not regulated therein, because most Member States still require that the judge be a national of their country, before acceding to the vocation.

17 See Council Directive 98/5, Facilitate Practice of the Profession of Lawyer on a Permanent Basis in a Member State Other Than that in Which the Qualification was Obtained, 1998 *O.J.* (L 77) 36 (EC).

18 *Ibidem* Art. 14.

19 One only has to consult the Official Journal and the case law of the Court of Justice and the new EU treaties as amended by the Lisbon Treaty to see the expansion of the policy areas of the EU and how EU rules and regulations impact criminal law, environmental law, immigration, contracts, non-discrimination, social security, state aid, competition, public procurement etc.

that important aspects of company law appear to be domestic law and part of domestic legislation and codes, but that they are basically translations and implementations of EU directives. Many aspects of what used to be purely domestic law are now, in effect, European law, as such and in disguise. Primary examples are company law, competition law, public procurement law, consumer law. This harmonization implies that students, when properly educated, all over Europe will be taught the same substantive law. This also applies to European law proper. This is not to say that all European legal curricula properly cover European law and its broad implications. In fact, many universities still mainly focus upon domestic law while in my view neglecting European law and its impact. However, here the situation is gradually and steadily improving (one of the stimuli in this respect has been the Jean Monnet program, funding chairs and courses in European subjects).[20] Another nice illustration of what is going on here is the (quality of the) participation in the annual European Law Moot Court Competition, showing the growth in European law in curricula all over Europe as well as its depth. However, I still have the impression that much can and should be improved. A glance over many law curricula in Europe still makes me doubt whether enough is being done. This impression is underlined by noting the knowledge of European law among new master students in my own faculty of law in Maastricht. We teach an advanced course in European law and note that many students who came from all over Europe have significant difficulties in catching up because of limited knowledge of European institutional law and substantive law.

As a consequence of the previous aspect of increasing the importance and impact upon domestic law of EU law, and also as a separate independent development, legal academics started to research (also for the benefit of drafting new European legislation) common rules and principles and their transformation in domestic legal concepts. As part of its endeavour to promote trade and business within the EU and between the Member States, the European Commission has even mapped out a course of seeking to codify these principles into European principles.[21] Many academics now work in different projects and collaborative initiatives drafting common principles of tort law, contract law and property law. In Maastricht, we have translated these efforts in making grand case books on common European principles of tort, contract, property, civil procedure, judicial review, non-discrimination, each underpinning as a research project the codification exercises and enhancing our knowledge for teaching purposes.[22] These developments do not take place as purely autonomous efforts, irrelevant for legal practice. They are merely the consequences of European legal developments; the expansion of a concept such as freedom of movement for workers, goods and services, implying that it is easier to contract across borders when one knows that there are similarities (for example, in

20 See *supra*, Jean Monnet Programme.

21 See European Private Law (CoPECL), <http://www.copecl.org/>.

22 See METRO - Ius Commune Casebooks, <http://www.unimaas.nl/default.asp?template=werkveld.htm&id=OO11IA6XU2XFTA11S02P&taal=en> (last visited 4 September 2010).

the domain of consumer law which has been very much regulated by the EU); or the development of an own EU concept of tort (the *Francovich* case law and its aftermath),[23] developed by the ECJ; or the relationship between the notion of freedom of (financial) services and cross-border mortgages which might have an impact upon property law. In general, the EU has seen tremendous political and legal development: its powers have been expanded with a series of treaties (Single European Act 1986; Treaty of Maastricht, 1992; and subsequent treaties of Amsterdam; Nice; and now, since December 1st, 2009, the entry into force of the Lisbon Treaty). Even more recently the economic crisis has indeed spurred thinking about further integration and the possible establishment of a political union, banking union, financial union, economic union and the like. Also the European Commission has been given a greater role in supervising domestic budgets since 2011, and we have witnessed in 2012 the development of the ESM Treaty and the Fiscal Compact. In less than a quarter of a century, the EU has emerged as a strong polity with, for many members, a common currency, and a whole new list of powers for the EU's institutions, and with one certainty, that the developments have not come to a standstill.

These powers, explicit or implicit, have seriously impacted upon domestic law and have also led to reflecting upon domestic law and to a larger attention for comparative law. Harmonization of laws of Member States also means that one has to know how they are and what can be done and what are common traditions and principles which could be relied upon in European law making or in the case law of the European Court of Justice. Studying European law proper is therefore benefited by the knowledge of domestic legal systems. Working in a domestic legal system for instance in preparing a domestic law implementing an EU directive, or for negotiations in Brussels it might be necessary to be immersed in comparative law and the search for commonalities and differences.

My point here is that unmistakably European law has advanced to such an extent that it certainly warrants its legal education proper: training in European law, comparative law, the interaction between domestic law and European law, would lead to a new European wide legal education.

The question could be asked whether there is sufficient 'substantive' European law (in the broadest sense) to be able to construct a law curriculum with enough system and doctrine to warrant and fill a legal curriculum. It is my conviction that there is: as well as with European law proper as with comparative law courses; the latter lend themselves for academic training in law, even better so than purely domestic law courses. Let me briefly explain why, though the response relates to the reason of being an academic university teaching of law as distinguished from professional training for the bar and the judiciary. For the latter, it is indeed important to know and understand the law as it stands with the pertinent case law. For the former it is indispensable to train legal minds: students who can reflect and ponder solutions for social and legal problems; to understand the basics of contract law and the variations, and also for other domains of the law; students who can reflect on

23 See *Francovich and Others*, Joined Cases C-6/90 and C-9/90, [1991] ECR I-5357.

the quality of the law and look and find creative new solutions. For these purposes, comparative law courses lend themselves excellently; they teach truly academic training and make it subsequently easier to study one specific system for legal practice.

A major method to do this in comparative law is to start from general legal questions and doctrines, such as the making of a contract, the termination, requirements for tort, separation of powers, etcetera, and subsequently construct, on the basis of abstract analysis as well as through comparative analysis, which abstract solutions might exist and which ones do exist in practice. These approaches give a student infinite insight and academic training in legal thinking and analysis. It might therefore lead to a truly academic legal training.

Law School Curricula in Europe

All the above developments have found their places in many curricula in European law schools; however, I submit that still, in too many law schools and European universities, developments have been too slow in fully making room for the EU's expansion. For this very, very slow integration, there are, in my perception and based on conversations with law professors in a variety of institutions, many factors, including:

1. the interests (and in some countries, powers) of incumbent professors: many do not like to create room for EU-related subjects;
2. the sometimes overwhelming influence of the domestic bar associations;
3. the conservative nature of lawyers;
4. the scarcity of good people with knowledge of EU law and the competition with law firms (who generally pay higher salaries than universities);
5. the political climate;
6. the absence of power for law school deans or university presidents to make reforms;[24] and
7. the difficulty (yet necessity) to integrate EU law in existing curricula (to integrate aspects of EU law in for example a course on contracts) due to the absence of good materials and a lack of knowledge on the part of professors.

Finally, I would like to draw attention here to the immense impact upon the future generation of lawyers and upon the development of new courses, of the new lingua franca (English, or maybe better Euro-English); of collaboration between European law schools and the emergence of new European law journals, through not only the previous developments but also by the Erasmus/Socrates exchanges, facilitated by

[24] Due to the modus operandi of universities in some states and the relative lack of power of deans.

the European Commission, as well as a pan-European credit system (ECTS: 60 ECTS per academic year).[25]

European law schools have developed new courses in English, developed courses adapted to exchange students, or designed courses based upon the development of EU law and research findings. However, as I argued before,[26] these developments have been more advanced in some places than in others. Some countries have been slow in adopting English-taught courses for reasons of domestic language policy or because foreign students came also for a study in their domestic language (Germany, Spain, Italy, France). Others quickly adapted to the need to have English-taught courses in order to cater to foreign exchange students (Sweden, the Netherlands). Belgium also moved along these lines but was hindered by domestic legislation prohibiting law schools from offer more than a few English-taught courses. Obviously the United Kingdom (UK) did not have to change, as all courses offered were already taught in English; moreover, even the courses offered basically remained unchanged, addressing domestic law.

In the beginning, the courses that were taught in English in Dutch law schools were the obvious courses: international law, various courses on European law, and comparative law.[27] Gradually, under the influence of the increasing impact of European law within and upon domestic legal orders, we started to design courses that focused upon areas of law, integrating comparative law and European law.[28] These courses build upon academic research with respect to common principles of European law, in combination with comparative law, seeking for the 'common law' of Europe.

Law school curricula in Europe are characteristically primarily focused upon domestic law and, necessarily and consequently, taught in the domestic language(s) of the country with electives that might have been developed in English for exchange students on comparative law or international and European law. In only a few countries, apart from the English-speaking countries such as the UK and Ireland, English-taught LL.M programs have been developed (Scandinavia, the Netherlands, Belgium). Toulouse University in France is now also in the process of setting up an English-taught, one-year masters program on international, European, and comparative law; in Germany, a private Hamburg-based law school runs an English-taught program; and Mannheim University is also constructing an English-taught LL.M program. In Switzerland, the new Luzern University Law School also offers a great variety of English-taught courses. However, despite these and possi-

25 See European Commission – Education and Training, European Credit Transfer and Accumulation System (ECTS), <http://ec.europa.eu/education/lifelong-learning-policy/doc48_en.htm> (last visited 4 September 2010).

26 See *supra* in this Chapter.

27 See generally Maastricht University, European Law School English Track, <http://www.maastrichtuniversity.nl/web/Faculties/FL/TargetGroup/ProspectiveStudents/BachelorsProgrammes/Programmes/EuropeanLawSchoolEnglishLanguageTrack1.htm> [hereinafter *European Law School English Track*].

28 *Ibidem*.

bly some more initiatives, the predominant feature is that law is taught in the domestic language, with some added courses on European law and occasionally a number of courses in English for exchange students.

Labour Market and Intake; Tuition and Funding and Research

Before moving on to describing and discussing further law school curricula and efforts to change and adapt them to modern-day European needs and the needs of a partly globalizing labour market for lawyers, a few words need to be said about student intake and output. The intake of students into universities and law faculties is very different from country to country. In Scandinavia, access to university is very selective: only the best students will be admitted. In the UK, there seems to be a shortage of places and the top schools have the first pick. In Belgium, France, Italy and Germany there is open access: all students who qualify (successfully graduate from secondary school) must be admitted. This is also the case in the Netherlands, but legislation allows law faculties to expel students (after one year) who do not meet the standards set by the school.

Funding is most commonly provided by the state: public funding seems to be the rule, with most countries allowing for no fees or only very low fees (a few hundred euro's). In the Netherlands, the fee is around 1,800 euro per year and in the UK, fees are even (much) higher.[29] Public funding means that there is less and limited access for private funding (of education); for research the situation is different and more competitive. But in that domain, European research funding is increasingly of great importance, also for legal research, which surely heavily impacts upon the directions of legal research and the (comparative, European, international) substance.

Law faculties in most European countries train lawyers, but not necessarily solely or predominantly for law firms or the judiciary. Many graduated lawyers do not take the bar but use their legal education as an academic training and pursue other labour market avenues, such as legal departments in companies; civil servants in governments and the European Commission; policy advisors and policy makers; legal experts in agencies; consultancy firms; NGOs; lobby organizations, etcetera.

As I have mentioned before, research in Europe among legal academics started to develop in the areas of comparative law, common European principles, Europeanization of domestic law, and related aspects. Many projects flourished, one of them in the Maastricht law faculty which set up a major collaborative research school, with Leuven, Utrecht and Amsterdam: the Research School 'Ius Com-

29 State of affairs 2007/8: Austria: (prices in euro): 363 per semester; Belgium 500-800 per annum; Bulgaria 50-200 per annum; Cyprus: 0; Czech republic: 0; Denmark: 0; Estonia: 420-1,200 per semester; Finland: 0; Germany: 0 in some states; between 100 and 500 per semester in others; Greece: university fees; Hungary: 16-48 per month; Ireland: 0; Italy: minimum 750 per annum; Latvia: 700-5,811 per annum; Lithuania: 0- 3,475 per annum; Luxemburg: 100 per semester; Malta: 0; The Netherlands: 1,600 per annum; Norway: 0; Poland: 0; Portugal: 500 per annum; Romania: 350-650 per annum; Slovak Republic: 0; Slovenia: 0; Spain: 550-900 per annum; Sweden: up to 9,000 euro; UK: up to 9,000 per annum. See *ibidem*.

mune'.[30] Journals were set up on European constitutional law, European private law, and European and comparative law (such as the *Maastricht Journal on European and Comparative Law* (MJ)).[31] Maastricht started the mentioned case books project, under the supervision of Professor Walter Van Gerven.[32] Maastricht also started a Ius Commune book series.[33]

Maastricht European Law School: Its Start in 1992

In the context of European developments, we perceived in Maastricht that it was necessary to reflect upon the future of legal education in Europe and upon European legal education. Our perspective was that there was a gradual growth of European law and of European common law, leading up to the future need to educate European trained lawyers. Lawyers with a good training in European institutional law and substantive law, who have a good command of Legal English (as a second legal language), and who were trained in the common principles of European legal systems so that they could operate across boundaries and were able to communicate with foreign colleagues about drafting new European rules and decisions and contracts would be indispensible. For that purpose, in 1992 we started a commercial post-graduate LL.M. program, entitled *Magister Iuris Communis* (Master of European and Comparative Law).[34] In this program we offered, for domestically trained lawyers, a curriculum with courses on European law proper as well as on European and comparative tort, contracts, property law; administrative law, company and business law etcetera.[35]

In 1995, we used the knowledge and experiences gained with this master program to offer a European Law School program (at that time, pre-Bologna), a four-year program with courses on Dutch law in the first two years and English-taught courses in the latter two years, focusing on the subjects mentioned and

30 See Ius Commune Research School Homepage, <http://www.iuscommune.eu/startpagina.aspx?language=english>.

31 See Maastricht University, *Maastricht Journal of European and Comparative Law*, <http://www.unimaas.nl/default.asp?template=werkveld.htm&id=IHA3VONPFP25175R1IJP&taal=en>.

32 See Maastricht University, Ius Commune Casebooks for the Common Law of Europe, <http://www.unimaas.nl/default.asp?template=werkveld.htm&id=OO11IA6XU2XFTA11S02P&taal=en>.

33 See Maastricht University, *Ius Commune Europaeum Book Series*, <http://www.unimaas.nl/default.asp?template=werkveld.htm&id=M772225M74X20LMX367H&taal=en>.

34 See University, Master's Programs, <http://www.maastrichtuniversity.nl/web/Main/ProspectiveStudents/MastersProgrammes.htm>. This MIC program has been reformed now into a master on International and European Economic Law, since the Maastricht European Law School LL.M includes the courses previously taught in MIC. See *ibidem*.

35 These are casebooks analysing case law in different EU Member States looking for common principles and solutions.

expanded with courses on criminal law, trade law etcetera.[36] This program has been a great success but suffered from two great disadvantages:

1. it was difficult to attract foreign students (because of the first two years in Dutch); and our idea was to seek a way to have an international classroom in which comparative law can flourish and which is truly European;
2. the need to train lawyers under Dutch law in order to educate them for a European labour market; i.e. the absence of a Europe-wide system of legal education and of Europe-wide standards of access to the legal profession, or at least the absence of some commonality in this respect.

In this respect Filippo Ranieri has also argued that the Bologna process, as well as the development of European scholarship and legal concepts and common rules, might create the chance to develop a truly European curriculum, with an international student body.[37] He continued by arguing that not the domestic peculiarities must be the primary issue, but the common European wide principles and basic structures. Not so much the present day details of domestic law, but the methodical foundations of the courses and legal domains. He also continued by arguing in favour of teaching students from several countries a 'Gründlagenstudium europäischer Prägung und Ausrichtung anzubieten, verbunden mit einem eigenständigen Universitätsdiplom. (...) Der Weg zu neuen europäischen "Law schools wäre damit eröffnet".'[38]

Ranieri also indicated how to establish the best teaching method. He refers in that respect to the problem or case method, and proposes these as teaching concepts for his European law school curriculum. However, he also remarks that the cases to be read, and from which to distil common concepts and principles, must be studied in the original language and not in their English translations. Although I certainly appreciate the arguments for doing that, and for preferably studying and understanding cases and rules in the relevant legal culture and legal language, the consequences of his proposal are problematic. It will inhibit many students from being able to read and discuss cases from a relevant number of European countries. For that reason, combined with the availability of large projects on common principles of private law, and the development and availability of many European cases and rules, which are present in English, I submit that for practical reasons we can make do with textbooks, case books and other materials, and with teaching in English in our newly modelled European law schools. This is also, in line with Ranieri's arguments, to have a truly international student body.

In 2006, Maastricht University dared to take the next step: offering a fully-fledged program on law, taught in English, from day one, with a focus on European

36 See Maastricht University, Bachelor's Programs, <http://www.maastrichtuniversity.nl/web/Faculties/FL/TargetGroup/ProspectiveStudents/BachelorsProgrammes/Programmes.htm>.

37 Ranieri 2006, p. 87.

38 Ranieri 2006, p. 88-89.

law, comparative law and international law. This step was obvious: considering the many developments in the domain of European Union law and the growing expertise in European and comparative law, we decided to reform the European Law School curriculum once more and to add a track (taught in English from day one) which basically is a three-year bachelor in International, European and comparative law. For those who opt for access to the legal profession we offer them a third year in Dutch in which we train them in Dutch law (which gives them two years to learn Dutch by the way).[39] If a student does not have the desire to enter the bar, (s)he will simply finish the LLB with English-taught courses.[40]

The full curriculum is relatively simple and straightforward, and not very revolutionary if not for the focus upon international, European and comparative law, in which courses such as Introduction to Law, Legal English, Skills, Moot court training, comparative contract, comparative tort, comparative property, comparative government, European legal history, International and European law, European Law Foundations, European Substantive Law, comparative criminal law and criminal procedure, European company law are taught. In the subsequent master program, students take further courses on these areas in addition to courses on competition law, civil procedure, European criminal law, etcetera.

Clearly, we still feel hindered by the second disadvantage mentioned before; we still have to offer possibilities for students to take the bar if this is what they want. They can still opt for Dutch law courses (but must learn Dutch), or they can go for the one-year English CPE (Common Professional Education, training students with a non-English law bachelor and preparing them for the Bar Vocational Course).

However, despite these bar access problems, we see many benefits in our program and we also believe that, with the assistance of large law firms who operate at a truly European level, gradually the barriers will dwindle and disappear. I certainly see the benefits of our program, and that is why our graduates are very much wanted, for a variety of reasons:

1. the students attracted are very motivated students;
2. they have been trained in different languages (native language and (legal) English);
3. their international and European legal training meets a real need in the market for lawyers; and
4. their comparative approach and knowledge have trained them better than others for European labour market demands.

39 See European Law School English Track, *supra* note 27.

40 See Maastricht University, Bachelor's Degree - Program Structure, <http://www.maastrichtuniversity.nl/web/Faculties/FL/TargetGroup/ProspectiveStudents/BachelorsProgrammes/Programmes/DutchLaw/ProgrammeInformation/ProgrammeStructure.htm>.

The exercise of setting up this curriculum very much went hand-in-hand with research and the development of novel, tailor-made teaching materials. I already referred to the case book project and also Philipp Kiiver and Nicole Kornet published a book on the comparative, international and European legal provisions needed in our courses.[41]

It is premature to provide solid data with respect to the labour market perspectives of our European Law School graduates. The students in the classic European Law School were very much welcomed on the labour market and, compared to other law programs in the Netherlands, they entered international jobs on a large scale. Also, we found that a large proportion (larger than in other Dutch law school programs) found jobs in large law firms (25%).[42] Recent figures relating to access to the bar even showed higher percentages for Maastricht graduates: in 2009, 154 of Maastricht law graduates entered the bar (out of the 309 Maastricht master degrees awarded in the same year and out of the 999 total number of applicants to the Dutch bar in 2009).[43] For them, as well as for other law school graduates, the labour market was positive.[44]

The perspectives for the European Law School students cannot be predicted; law firms still hire new graduates, but certain areas (mergers and acquisitions) seem to suffer. On the other hand, qualitatively good students still find jobs and are still very much in demand, especially if they have done something different or extra such as internships, study abroad, language courses and the like. On domestic levels, there is also an increasing demand for these new lawyers; governments seek lawyers and other civil servants with excellent knowledge of European law, the interface between European law and domestic law, and legal English. The interaction between Brussels and domestic governments is so intensive that governments are desperate for expertise.[45] Recently, the European Council of the EU also called upon the national governments to improve legal training and expertise. One of the reasons for this was a general consensus that domestic lawyers and domestic

41 See generally Kiiver & Kornet 2010.

42 ROA (see *infra* note 44) research done for the Faculty of Law in 2004.

43 Since Maastricht is the smallest law school in the Netherlands with in total 9 law schools, this means that a large share of Maastricht graduates enter the bar (Jaarverslag Orde van Advocaten 2009 - Annual Report of the Dutch Bar, p. 52); in 2009 almost 50% of the Maastricht graduates entered the bar: 154 out of 309: which is an exceptionally high number (Annual Report/Jaarverslag 2009 Maastricht University, p. 10).

44 Loopbanen na Maastricht University: metingen 2008 en 2009, Research Centre for Education and the Labour market/ROA, 2010, ISBN 978-90-5321-485-5. I only found information in Dutch for this book.

45 I have no specific data on this but conclude from interaction with recruiters and government officials that they specifically seek students with knowledge of both English and European law.

judiciaries lack the necessary expertise and knowledge in the relevant domains of European law and its intricacies and entanglement with domestic law.[46]

Conclusion and Agenda

Many interesting developments take place in Europe and in European legal education. I have not even touched upon benchmarks or features of what might constitute a good law curriculum.[47] Nor have I discussed how to teach (Socratic method, case method, problem-based learning and others), or how to instil an academic attitude in students, or how to distinguish between academic training and professional training, or how to teach and integrate skills, or how to peer review curricula within countries and trans boundary. Nor have I touched upon what constitutes good teaching materials, case books and other materials and whether and how to include other sciences, (economics, psychology, forensics, philosophy, criminology etc.) in a legal curriculum. Some of these issues are discussed by contributors to the volume *Educating European Lawyers* and all are items that I will certainly commit myself to in other writings. I have purported to describe briefly legal developments in Europe, their consequences as I see them for legal education and how we can prepare the stage for tackling these issues and build a European legal education and do so European wide.

At this stage, I submit that in Europe there is certainly room to move forward with regard to discussing European legal training. Europe needs lawyers who are fully trained in academia in languages, European law, comparative law and the interaction between domestic legal systems and European law. A challenging new approach in this respect is the Maastricht European Law School project.

Maduro identified in a recent paper a similar trend for legal education in Europe in the context of a plurality of jurisdictions and legal sources. He argues that the law to be taught is different and so is the profile of the lawyers demanded by the market. European law schools will increasingly be competing in a European market, which requires in his opinion a complete restructuring of legal education and even law schools. He concludes by stating that

> 'a truly European and international legal education can only take place in a truly European and international context (which) requires a diverse and multinational community of learning with a diverse and international faculty and student body'.[48]

46 See Council Resolution 2008/C 299/01, Resolution of the Council and of the Representatives of the Governments of the Member States meeting within the Council on the training of judges, prosecutors and judicial staff in the European Union, 2008 *O.J.* (C 299) 1.

47 See Centre for Higher Education Development, Ranking, <http://www.che-ranking.de/cms/?getObject=613&getLang=en> (last visited 5 September 2010). There is not yet a European-wide benchmark for European higher education; the best (and increasingly covering more universities) is CHE; it is not yet available for non-German speaking law schools. See *ibidem*.

48 Maduro 2010.

Still, we have to find a solution to ensure that these new lawyers will be accepted as fully-fledged lawyers and be recognized for what they are: European lawyers.

Let's therefore turn our attention to what might be the road ahead and the actions to be undertaken. I submit the following model for European legal education.

1. The first conclusion is to recognize a two-tier approach: in some selected schools focus is to be had on 'European' legal training (which I will explain shortly); in most schools the law is taught as it is now for the domestic bar and legal professions with a curriculum which is primarily nationally oriented with the proper attention on (the impact of) European and international law.
2. For the 'European Law Schools' the mission will be different:
   2.1. access for students will be selective and limited;
   2.2. these schools will need an internationally diverse student body;
   2.3. they will need an internationally diverse faculty;
   2.4. they will teach European (and international) law and comparative law for two to three years as a general basic legal academic training, in English;
   2.5. they will join efforts and resources in a joint consortium aimed at discussing and improving courses and curricula; engage in staff and student exchange; this consortium will also develop into an accreditation and quality assurance organization;
   2.6 the consortium will be the partner for the European Commission and will have to be sponsored and funded, as an important means and tool to improve legal education and work towards the goal of increasing the knowledge of European law and its effective application and implementation.
3. The legislatures of the Member States and its bar associations will work towards a recognition of the degrees obtained in the European law schools by setting up bar exams allowing the students to have access to legal professions.
4. On the European level the consortium will work with the Commission and a representation of the bar associations and other stakeholders to allow for a common European Bar exam for European Law School graduates, to allow them access to European legal jobs as well as the bar in domestic jurisdictions, and recognition of the European bar exam.
5. The European Law Schools will strive to establish professional trainings for domestic judges and lawyers and assist in training them in the domain of European law in the broad meaning of the term (including comparative law).
6. The consortium will make available a platform for discussions about European legal education and the setting of the agenda for a future-oriented European legal education of high quality, combining academic training and professional skills.

BIBLIOGRAPHY

Annema & Ooijevaar 2011
Annema, A. & Ooijevaar, J., 'De invloed van eindexamenresultaat op success in het hoger onderwijs (The influence of final exams grades on success in higher education)', *Tijdschrift voor Hoger Onderwijs*, 2011 (29)2, p. 65-81.

Arum & Roksa 2011
Arum, R. & Roksa, J., *Academically Adrift. Limited Learning on College Campuses*, Chicago: University of Chicago Press 2011.

Ault & Glendon 1975
Ault, H.J. & Glendon, M.A., 'The Importance of Comparative Law in Legal Education: United States Goals and Methods of Legal Comparisons', *Journal of Legal Education*, 1975 (27), p. 599-608.

Backer 2008
Backer, L.C., 'Internationalizing the American Law School Curriculum (in Light of the Carnegie Foundation's Report)', in: J. Klabbers & M. Sellers (eds.), *The Internationalization of Law and Legal Education* (Ius Gentium: Comparative Perspectives on Law and Justice, 2), New York: Springer 2008, p. 49-112.

Baldus, Finkenauer & Rüfner 2007
Baldus, C., Finkenauer, T. & Rüfner, T. (eds), *Juristenausbildung in Europa zwischen Tradition un Reform*, Tübingen: Mohr Siebeck 2007.

Beekhoven, De Jong & Van Hout 2002
Beekhoven, S., De Jong, U & Van Hout, H., 'Explaining Academic Progress via Combining Concepts of integration Theory and rational Choice Theory', *Research in Higher Education*, 2002 (43)5, October 2002, p. 577-600.

Benneworth 2010
Benneworth, P., *A University Benchmarking Handbook: Benchmarking in European Higher Education*, Bath/London: The European Centre for Strategic Management of Universities, the Centre for Higher Education Development, the International Centre for Higher Education Management/the Institute of Education, University of London 2010

van Berkel *et al.* 2010
Berkel, H. van, Scherpbier, A., Hillen, H. & Van der Vleuten, C. (eds.), *Lessons from Problem-based Learning*, Oxford: Oxford University Press 2010.

Bolman & Gallos 2011
Bolman, L.G. & Gallos, J.V., *Reframing Academic Leadership*, San Francisco, CA: Wiley, Jossey-Bass 2011.

Boon & Webb 2010
Boon, A. & Webb, J., 'The Legal Professions as Stakeholders', in: F. Cownnie (ed.), *Stakeholders in the Law School*, Oxford: Hart Publishing 2010, p. 65-95.

Boon & Whyte 2010
Boon, A. & Whyte, A., 'Students as Stakeholders in the Legal Academy', in: F. Cownie (ed.), *Stakeholders in the Law School*, Oxford: Hart Publishing 2010, p. 185-224.

Bowen 2011
Bowen, W.G., *Lessons Learned; Reflectons of a University President*, Princeton: Princeton University Press 2011.

Camara 2005
Camara, W.J., 'Broadening Predictors of College Success', in: W.J. Camara & E.W. Kimmel (eds.), *Choosing Students. Higher Education Admissions Tools for the 21st Century*, London: Routledge 2005, p. 81-106.

Camara & Kimmel 2005
Camara, W.J. & Kimmel, E.W. (eds.), *Choosing Students. Higher Education Admissions Tools for the 21st Century*, London: Routledge 2005.

Chesterman 2008
Chesterman, S., 'The Globalisation of Legal Education', *Singapore Journal of Legal Studies*, 2008, p. 58-67.

Chesterman 2009
Chesterman, S., 'Three Conceptions: The Evolution of Legal Education: Internationalizing, Transnationalizing, Globalization, *German Law Journal,* 2009 (10)7, p. 877-888

Christensen 2010
Christensen, L.M., 'The Power of Skills Training: A Study of Lawyering Skills Grades as the Strongest Predictor of Law School Success (Or in Other Words, It's Time for Legal Education to Get Serious About Skills Training If we Care About How Our Students Learn)', *St. John's Law Review,* 2010 (83)3, p. 795-826 (<http://ssrn.com/abstract=1235531>).

Christensen & Eyring 2011
Christensen, C.M. & Eyring, H.J., *The Innovative University. Changing The DNA of Higher Education from the Inside Out,* San Francisco: Jossey-Bass 2011.

Cownie 2010
Cownie, F. (ed.), *Stakeholders in the Law School,* Oxford: Hart Publishing 2010.

Dedek & De Mestral 2009
Dedek, H. & De Mestral, 'Born to be Wild: The "Trans-Systemic" Programme at McGill and the De-Nationalization of Legal Education', *German Law Journal,* 2009 (10)7, p. 889-912.

Dochy 1999
Dochy, F., *Instructietechnologie en innovatie van probleemoplossen: over constructiegericht academisch onderwijs,* Utrecht: Lemma 1999.

Donkers *et al.* 2010
Donkers, J., Verstegen, D., De Leng, B. & De jong, N., 'E-learning in Problem-based Learning', in: H. van Berkel, A. Scherpbier, H. Hillen & C. van der Vleuten Ieds.), *Lessons from Problem-based Learning,* Oxford: Oxford University Press 2010, Chapter 13, p. 117-128.

Economides 2001
Economides, K., Legal Education, *International Encyclopedia of the Social & Behavioral Sciences,* 2001, p. 8629-8634.

The Economist
- 'Not enough lawyers (Barriers to entry in the legal profession; Lawyers keep their numbers carefully pruned, pushing up costs)', 3 September 2011, p. 38-39.
- 'An alternative vote (Teaching methods; Applying science to the teaching of science)', 14 May 2011, p. 84.
- 'Bargain briefs (Alternative law firms; Technology offers 50 ways to leave your lawyer)', 13 August 2011, p. 52.
- 'Flipping the classroom (Hopes that the Internet can improve teaching may at least be bearing fruit; Electronic education)', 17 September 2011, p. 42-43.
- 'Pointless Regulations. It's a jungle out there', 22 October 2011, p. 73-74.
- 'The best of the rest, Academic Excellence: British schoolchildren are falling behind those elsewhere', 11 December 2010, p. 40.
- 'Legal Services, Psst, wanna buy a law firm?', 28 January 2012, p. 55.
- Schumpeter, 'A Guardian and a guide; Chief legal officers have more power than ever before', The Economist 7 April 2012, p. 62.

van Erp 2011
Erp, J. van, 'Teaching Law in Europe: from an Intra-systemic, via a Trans-systemic to a Supra-systemic Approach', in: A.W. Heringa & B. Akkermans (eds.), *Educating European Lawyers* (Ius Commune Europaeum, 98), Antwerp: Intersentia 2011, p. 79-99.

Farnsworth 2007
Farnsworth, W., *The Legal Analyst. A Toolkit for Thinking about the Law*, Chicago: University of Chicago Press 2007.

Fauvarque-Cosson 2007
Fauvarque-Cosson, B., *The Rise of Comparative Law: a Challenge for Legal Education in Europe*, Groningen: Europa Law Publishing 2007.

Finkelstein & Levin 2001
Finkelstein, M.O. & Levin, B., *Statistics for Lawyers*, 2nd ed., New York etc.: Springer 2001.

Frankel 2001
Frankel, T., *What Makes a Great Law School?*, Boston Univ. School of Law Working Paper No. 2001-13 (<http://www.bu.edu/law/faculty/papers> and <http://papers.ssrn.com/abstract=288435>).

Friedman & Mandelbaum 2011
Friedman, L. & Mandelbaum, M., *That used to be Us; how American fell behind in the World it invented and how We can come Back*, New York: Picador 2011.

Glenn 2010
Glenn, P., *Legal Traditions of the World, Sustainable Diversity in Law*, 4th edition, New York: Oxford University Press 2010.

Grant, Jagtenberg & Nijkerk 1988
Grant, J.P., Jagtenberg, R. & Nijkerk, K.J. (eds.), *Legal Education: 2000*, Aldershot: Avebury 1988.

Goldsmith and David Bamford 2010
Goldsmith, A. & Bamford, D., 'The Value of Practice in Legal Education', in: F. Cownie (ed.), *Stakeholders in the Law School*, Oxford: Hart Publishing 2010, p. 157-184.

Grossman 2008
Grossman, C., 'Building the World Community Through Legal Education', in: J. Klabbers & M. Sellers (eds.), *The Internationalization of Law and Legal Education* (Ius Gentium: Comparative Perspectives on Law and Justice, 2), New York: Springer 2008, p. 21-36.

de Gruijter, Yildiz & 't Hart 2006
Gruijter, D.N.M. de, Yildiz, M. & 't Hart, J., *VWO-examenresultaten en succes in de propedeuse Rechten* (Seconday school exam results and success in the First year of Law), ICLON Leiden, rapport No. 165, March 2006.

Haarala-Muhonen 2010
Haarala-Muhonen, A., *First Year Law students' Challenges in Studying* (in Finnish with English summary, (Oikeustieteen ensimmaisen vuoden opiskelijoiden haasteet opiskelussa)), Helsinki: University of Helsinki 2010.

Hacker & Dreifus 2010
Hacker, A. & Dreifus, C., *Higher Education. How Colleges are wasting our Money and failing our Kids – And what We can do About It*, New York: St. Martin's Griffin 2010.

Hage 2011
Hage, J., 'Comparative Law and Legal Science', in: A.W. Heringa & B. Akkermans (eds.), *Educating European Lawyers* (Ius Commune Europaeum, 98), Antwerp: Intersentia 2011, p. 65-77.

Heringa 2011a
Heringa, A.W., 'Towards a Truly European Legal Education. An Agenda for the Future', in: A.W. Heringa & B. Akkermans (eds.), *Educating European Lawyers* (Ius Commune Europaeum, 98), Antwerp: Intersentia 2011, p. 3-18.

Heringa 2011b
Heringa, A.W., 'Legal Education in Europe or European Legal Education', *Maastricht Journal of European and Comparative Law*, 2011 (18)3, p. 221-224.

Heringa & Akkermans 2011
Heringa, A.W. & Akkermans, B. (eds.), *Educating European Lawyers* (Ius Commune Europaeum, 98), Antwerp: Intersentia 2011.

Heringa & Kiiver 2012
Heringa, A.W. & Kiiver, P., *Constitutions Compared* (Ius Commune Europaeum, 104), 3rd edition., Antwerp: Intersentia 2012.

Hiscock & Van Caenegem 2010
Hiscock, M. & Van Caenegem, W. (eds.), *The Internationalisation of Law, Legislating, Decision-Making, Practice and Education*, Cheltenham: Edward Elgar 2010.

Hondius 1999
Hondius, E.H., *Juridisch onderwijs in vergelijkend perspectief* (Preadvies voor de Nederlandse Vereniging voor Rechtsvergelijking, 56), Deventer: Kluwer 1999.

Hyatt 2007
Hyatt W., 'A Lawyer's Lament: Law Schools and the Profession of Law', *Vanderbilt Law Review*, 2007 60(2), p. 385-400.

Jukier 2006
Jukier, R., 'Transnationalizing the Legal Curriculum: How to teach what We live', *Journal of Legal Education*, 2006 56(2), p. 172-189.

Klabbers 2007
Klabbers, J., 'Legal Education in the Balance: Accommodation Flexibilit', *Journal of Legal Education*, 2007 (56)2, p. 196-200.

Klabbers 2008
Klabbers, J., 'Reflections on Globalization and University Life', in: J. Klabbers & M. Sellers (eds.), *The Internationalization of Law and Legal Education* (Ius Gentium: Comparative Perspectives on Law and Justice, 2), New York: Springer 2008, p. 7-19.

Klabbers & Sellers 2008
Klabbers, J. & Sellers, M. (eds.), *The Internationalization of Law and Legal Education* (Ius Gentium: Comparative Perspectives on Law and Justice, 2), New York: Springer 2008.

Kiiver & Kornet 2010
Kiiver, P. & Kornet, N. (eds.), *The Maastricht Collection: Selected National, European and International Provisions from Public and Private Law*, 2nd edition, Groningen: Europa Law Publishing 2010.

Klip 2012
Klip, A., *European Criminal Law*, 2nd edition, Antwerp: Intersentia 2012.

Koo 2007
Koo G., *New Skils, New Learning: Legal Education and the Promise of Technology*, Research Publication No. 2007-4, March 2007, The Berkman Center for Internet & Society at Harvard Law School: <http://cyber.law.harvard.edu/publications> and <http://papers.ssrn.com/abstract_id=XXXXXX>.

Kornet 2012
Kornet, N., 'English-Medium Legal Education in Continental Europe: Maastricht University's European Law School: Experiences and Challenges, in: X. Arzoz (ed.), *Bilingual Higher Education in the Legal Context*, Leiden: Martinus Nijhoff 2012, p. 313-339.

Kronman 1994
Kronman A.T., *The Lost Lawyer. Failing Ideals of the Legal Profession*, Cambridge: Belknap Press of Harvard University Press 1994.

Leiter 2006
Brian, L., 'How to rank Law Schools', *Indiana Law Journal*, 2006 (81)47, p. 47-52.

Lo 2010
Lo, V.I., 'The Internationalization of Legal Education: a Road Increasingly Travelled, in: M. Hiscock & W. Van Caenegem (eds.), *The Internationalisation of Law, Legislating, Decision-Making, Practice and Education*, Cheltenham: Edward Elgar 2010, p. 117-131.

Lokin 2005
Lokin, J.H.A., 'Academische vorming, een romantische illusie?', in: J.G. Brouwer (ed.), *Wat maakt een goed jurist?*, Den Haag: Boom Juridische uitgevers 2005, p. 98-103.

Mackinnon 2006
Mackinnon, J., 'Problem Based Learning and New Zealand Legal Education', *Web Journal of Current Legal Issues* (<http://webjcli.ncl.ac.uk/2006/issue3/mackinnon3.html>.

Maduro 2010
Maduro, M.P., *Legal Education and the Europeanization and Globalisation of Law*, Contraditorio, Policy Paper 2010/01, February 2010, <www.contraditorio.pt>.

Madsen 2011a
Madsen, M.R., 'Legal Diplomacy: Law, Politics and the Genesis of Postwar European Human Rights', in S.L. Hoffmann (ed.), *Human Rights in the Twentieth Century: A Critical History*, Cambridge: Cambridge University Press 2011, p. 62-81.

Madsen 2011b
Madsen, M. R., 'The Protracted Institutionalisation of the Strasbourg Court: From Legal Diplomacy to Integrationist Jurisprudence', in: J. Christoffersen & M.R. Madsen (eds.), *The European Court of Human Rights between Law and Politics*, Oxford: Oxford University Press 2011, p. 43-60.

Matasar 2004
Matasar, R.A., 'The Rise and Fall of American Legal Education', *New York Law School Law Review*, 2004 (49), p. 465-504.

Maxeiner 2008
Maxeiner, J.R., 'Integrating Practical Training and Professional Legal Education', in: J. Klabbers & M. Sellers (eds.), *The Internationalization of Law and Legal Education* (Ius Gentium: Comparative Perspectives on Law and Justice, 2), New York: Springer 2008, p. 37-48.

McCrimmon 2010
McCrimmon, L., 'Reform, regulation and risk: the internationalization of legislation and legal policy, in: M. Hiscock & W. Van Caenegem (eds.), *The Internationalization of Law, Legislating, Decision-Making, Practice and Education*, Cheltenham: Edward Elgar 2010, p. 55-70.

Minow 2010
Minow, M., *Legal Education: Past, Present and Future*, 5 April 2010, <http://www.law.harvard.edu/news/spotlight/classroom/related/legal-education-past-present-and-future1.pdf>.

Moens 2000
Moens, G.A., *Problem-based Learning: Combining Enthusiasm and Exellence*, <http://www.tedi.uq.edu.au/Conferences/teach_conference00/papers/moens.html>.

Moens 2007
Moens, G.A., 'The Mysteries of Problem-based Learning: Combining Enthusiasm and Excellence', *University of Toledo Law Review*, 2007 (38), p. 623-632.

Morgan 2006
Morgan, T.D., *Educating Lawyers for the Future Legal Profession*, 2006, <http://ssrn.com/abstract=881846>.

Morgan 2009
Morgan, T.D., *The Last Days of the American Lawyer*, 27 January 2010, <http://ssrn.com/abstract=1543301>.

Naolski, Kirschner & Merriënboer 2006
Naolski, R.J., Kirschner, P.A. & Merriënboer, J.J.G., 'Process Support in Learning Tasks for Acquiring Complex Cognitive Skills in the Domain of Law', *Learning and Instruction*, 2006 (16), p. 266-278.

Newton 2010
Newton, B.E., 'Preaching what They don't Practice: why Law Faculties' Preoocupation with Impractical Scholarship and Devaluation of Practical Competencies Obstruct Reform in the Legal Academy', *South Carolina Law Review*, 2010 (62), p. 105-156.

Nievelstein 2009
Nievelstein, F.E.R.M., *Learning Law, Expertise Differences and the Effect of Instructional Support* (ICO dissertation series), Heerlen, Open Universiteit 2009.

Nussbaum 2010
Nussbaum, M.C., *Not for Profit, why Democracy needs the Humanities*, Princeton: Princeton University Press 2010.

van Oostrom-Streep 2010
Oostrom-Streep, N.C. van, *Tussen Scylla en Charybdis: op zoek naar koers en Waarde in het juridisch onderwijs*, Antwerpen/Apeldoorn: Maklu 2010.

Pashley, Thornton & Duffy 2005
Pashley, P.J., Thornton, A.E., Duffy, J.R., 'Access and Diversity in Law School Admissions', in: W.J. Camara & E.W. Kimmel (eds.), *Choosing Students. Higher Education Admissions Tools for the 21st Century*, London: Routledge 2005, p. 231-249.

Ranieri 2006
Ranieri, F., *Juristen für Europa, Voraussetzungen und Hindernisse für ein "europäisches" juristisches Ausbildungsmodel* (Münsteraner Studien zur Rechtsvergleichung/ Muenster Studies in Comparative Law, Band 122), Münster: LIT 2006.

Rauhvargers 2011
Rauhvargers, A., *Global University Rankings and their impact*, EUA Report on Rankings 2011 (<www.eua.be>).

Reisman 1996
Reisman, W.M., 'Designing Law Curricula for a Transnational Industrial and Science-based Civilization', *Journal of Legal Education*, 1996 (46)3, p. 322-328.

Ribstein 2011
Ribstein L.E., Practicing Theory: Legal Education for the Twenty-First Century, *Iowa Law Review*, 2011 (96), p. 1649-1676; <http://papers.ssrn.com/sol3/papers.cfm?abstract_id=1776043>.

Ritzen 2010
Ritzen, J., *A Chance for European Universities*, Amsterdam: Amsterdam University Press 2010.

Schreurs & de Grave 2010
Schreurs, M.-L. and de Grave, W., 'Faculty Development', in: H. van Berkel, A. Scherpbier, H. Hillen & C. van der Vleuten, Lessons from Problem-based Learning, Oxford: Oxford University Press 2010, Chapter 18, p. 167-175.

Schwartz 2001
Schwartz, M.H., 'Teaching Law by Design: How Learnng Theory and Instructional Design can Inform and Reform Law Teaching', *San Diego Law Review*, 2001 (38), p. 347-462

Shapiro 2005
Shapiro, H.T., *A Larger Sense of Purpose, Higher Education and Society*, Princeton: Princeton University Press 2005.

Smits 2011
Smits, J.M., 'European Legal Education, or: How to prepare Students for Global Citizenship?', in: A.W. Heringa & B. Akkermans (eds.), *Educating European Lawyers* (Ius Commune Europaeum, 98), Antwerp: Intersentia 2011, p. 43-64.

Smits 2012
Smits, J.M., *The Mind and Methods of the Legal Academic*, Cheltenham: Edward Elgar 2012.

Sonsteng 2008
Sonsteng, J.O., *A Legal Education Renaissance: a Practical Approach for the Twenty-First Century*, 2008, <http://ssrn.com/abstract=1084098>.

Sousa 2011
Sousa, D.A., *How the Brain Learns*, 4th edition, California: Corwin 2011.

Strauss 2006
Strauss, P.L., 'Transsystemia – Are we approaching a New Langdellian Moment? Is McGill leading the Way?', *Journal of Legal Education*, 2006 (56), p. 161-171.

Stuckey *et al.* 2007
Stuckey, R. *et al.*, *Best Practices for Legal Education*, St. Paul, Minnesota: Clinical Legal Education Association 2007 (<http://cleaweb.org 2007>).

Sullivan *et al.* 2007
Sullivan, W.M., Colby, A., Welch Wegner, J., Bond, L. & Shulman, L.S., *Educating Lawyers, Preparation for the Profession of Law*, San Francisco: Jossey-Bass 2007.

Sursock 2011
Sursock, A., *Examining Quality Culture Part II: Processes and Tools – Participation, Ownership and Bureaucracy*, Brussels: European University Association Publications 2011 (<www.eua.be>).

Susskind 2008
Susskind, R., *The End of Lawyers? Rethinking the Nature of Legal Services*, Oxford: Oxford University Press 2008.

Twining 1997
Twining, W., *Law in Context*, Oxford: Clarendon Press 1997.

van Vught & Ziegele 2011
Vugt, F. van & Ziegele, F. (eds.), *U-Multirank; Design and Testing the Feasibility of a multidimensional Global University Ranking*, Final Report, June 2011, Consortium for Higher Education and Research Performance Assessment/CHERPA-Network (<http://ec.europa.eu/education/higher-education/doc/multirank_en.pdf>).

Washburn 2010
Washburn, K.K., *Elena Kagan and the Miracle at Harvard*, July 2010, <http://ssrn.com/abstract=1631496>.

Welch Wegner 2010
Welch Wegner, J., *More complicated than we think: a Response to Rethinking Legal Education in Hard Times: the Recession, Practical Legal Education, and the New Job Market*, <http://ssrn.com/abstract=1533788>.

Wolniak & Engberg 2010
Wolniak, G.C. & Engberg, M.E., 'Academic Achievement in the First Year of College: Evidence of the Pervasive Effects of the High School Context', *Research in Higher Education*, 2010 (51), p. 451-467

Wolski 2002
Wolski, B., 'Why, How, and What to Practice: Integrating Skills Teaching and Learning in the Undergraduate Law Curriculum', *Journal of Legal Education*, 2002 (52), p. 287-302.

Van Zandt 2004
Van Zandt, D.E., *Globalization Srategies for Legal Education,* <http://ssrn.com/abstract=1529706>.

IUS COMMUNE EUROPAEUM

A peer-reviewed book series in which the common foundations of the legal systems of the Member States of the European Union are the central focus.

The *Ius Commune Europaeum* series includes horizontal comparative legal studies as well as studies on the effect of treaties within the national legal systems. All the classic fields of law are covered. The books are published in various European languages under the auspices of METRO, the Institute for Transnational Legal Research at the Maastricht University.

Recently published:

Volume 101: *The Power of Punitive Damages. Is Europe Missing Out?*, L. MEURKENS and E. NORDIN (eds.)
Volume 102: *The Changing Role of the European Council in the Institutional Framework of the European Union*, F. EGGERMONT
Volume 103: *Linked Contracts*, I. SAMOY and M.B.M. LOOS (eds.)
Volume 104: *Constitutions Compared* (3rd ed.), A.W. HERINGA and PH. KIIVER
Volume 105: *Alternative Ways to Ius Commune*, A.L.M. KEIRSE and M.B.M. LOOS (eds.)
Volume 106: *Property Law Perspectives*, B. AKKERMANS and E. RAMAEKERS (eds.)
Volume 107: *Constitutional Conversations*, C. VAN DE HEYNING and M. DE VISSER (eds.)
Volume 108: *Enforcing Health and Safety Regulation*, L. TILINDYTĖ
Volume 109: *Administrative Law of the European Union, its Member States and the United States. A Comparative Analysis*, R. SEERDEN (ed.)
Volume 110: *Market Integration through 'Network Governance': The Role of European Agencies and Networks of Regulators*, M. ZINZANI
Volume 111: *Truth and Efficiency in Civil Litigation. Fundamental Aspects of Fact-finding and Evidence-taking in a Comparative Context*, C.H. VAN RHEE and A. UZELAC (eds.)
Volume 112: *Law and Security in Europe: Reconsidering the Security Constitution*, M. FICHERA and J. KREMER (eds.)
Volume 113: *Inside Policy Custody: An Empirical Account of Suspect's Rights in Four Jurisdictions*, T. SPRONKEN, E. CAPE and J. HODGSON (eds.)
Volume 114: *Motive Matters! An Exploration of the Notion 'Deliberate Breach of Contract' and its Consequences for the Application of Remedies*, M. VAN KOGELENBERG
Volume 115: *Legal Education*, A.W. HERINGA

www.ingramcontent.com/pod-product-compliance
Ingram Content Group UK Ltd.
Pitfield, Milton Keynes, MK11 3LW, UK
UKHW051927100926
8556IPUK00022B/1412

9 781780 68166